Healing Spiritually

Renewing your life
through the power
of God's law

The Christian Science Publishing Society
Boston, Massachusetts, U.S.A.

ISBN: 0–87510–290–5

Library of Congress Catalog Card Number: 95–071156

Publisher's Cataloging in Publication
(Prepared by Quality Books Inc.)

Healing spiritually : renewing your life through the power of God's law.
p. cm.
Preassigned LCCN: 95-71156
ISBN 0-87510-290-5
1. Spiritual healing. 2. Prayer. 3. Christian Science—Doctrines.

BT732.5H43 1996 234'.13
QBI96–40223

Printed in the United States of America

CONTENTS

Section I

Finding a path to spiritual healing

Section II

Healing and guidance in every stage of life

Section III

Gaining control over the unexpected

Section IV

Christian healing throughout life

HEALING
Spiritually

To the Reader

Spiritual healing is for everyone. Everywhere. Every day. In *Healing Spiritually*, people from many different backgrounds and cultures—men, women, children—tell how they were healed through prayer. They speak from the heart, and in their own words. At times dire calamity threatened. Sometimes they longed to be free of enslaving addictions. Or perhaps they just wanted peace in their lives. Sometimes they were told they were going to die. All turned to God and were helped and healed. How did this happen?

Only recently in the world's history did mankind discover the laws governing aerodynamics, and understand them sufficiently to develop airplanes. Now, aircraft crisscross the skies and men have walked on the moon. Yet, the laws of aviation were always present—even before they were discovered.

In the same way, the laws of spiritual healing have always been present. Occasionally, inspired individuals glimpsed and applied these laws—as did the prophets in the Old Testament of the Bible.

Two thousand years ago Jesus healed spiritually and taught his disciples to do the same. He said (according to the King James Version), "He that believeth on me, the works that I do shall he do also." *The New Testament in Modern English* (J. B. Phillips) translates that promise this way: "I assure you that the man who believes in me will do the same things that I have done" (John 14:12). Peter, Paul, and other apostles in the New Testament caught this vision and successfully practiced Christian healing.

However, it was not until the second half of the last century—in 1866—that the laws governing spiritual healing were discovered and explained, making Christian healing available to everyone. Mary Baker Eddy, a woman from New England, made this discovery and called it—appropriately—Christian Science. Of this healing she writes: "The physical healing of Christian Science results now, as in Jesus' time, from the operation of divine Principle, before which sin and disease lose their reality in human consciousness and disappear as naturally and as necessarily as darkness gives place to light and sin to reformation" (*Science and Health,* p. xi). She set out the rules of spiritual healing in her book *Science and Health with Key to the Scriptures.* Since she wrote it, that book has been translated into 16 languages, and more than nine million copies have been sold. From the time of its first publication, in 1875, people were healed by reading *Science and Health,* just as they are healed today.

Jesus based his healing work on prayer to "Our Father which art in heaven" (Matthew 6:9). This is still the foundation of Christian spiritual healing—God and His unchanging, universal law of good. Spiritual healing is the application of this wholly good law of a wholly good God, deleting sickness, disease, and sin from human experience just as turning on a light dispels darkness. The result is tangible, a transforming change for the better—physically, mentally, morally.

Healing Spiritually is built around testimonies of healing. They illustrate some different ways of "Finding a path to spiritual healing" (Section I), and then show the practicality of "Healing and guidance in every stage of life" (Section II). Next, these experiences show the reliability of God's law in "Gaining control over the unexpected" aspects of human life (Section III). Finally, several testimonies reveal the continuity of good that naturally comes from "Christian healing throughout life" (Section IV). At the end of the book is a list of publications referred to in the text. An explanation of terms mentioned is listed under "Helpful information."

All of the healings in this volume were selected from the many thousands of accounts published since 1966 in the *Christian Science Sentinel* and *The Christian Science Journal,* periodicals which include a collection of verified healings in every weekly and monthly issue. (On file with each published healing are three letters from individuals who either witnessed the healing or who know the person who was healed. In many instances there is also medical confirmation of the condition and the healing.) The healings included in this book were reverified prior to publication. *Healing Spiritually* is a sequel to an earlier book *A Century of Christian Science Healing,* which highlighted the healing record of Christian Science from the time of its discovery in 1866 through 1966.

In today's world, "spirituality" is a subject which evokes considerable interest among a seeking public. But spirituality seldom has been considered as based on law. The descriptions of Christian healing in this book confirm that anyone who believes in and trusts God completely, can rely on His law alone for health, happiness—and healing.

The Christian Science Publishing Society

Section I

Finding a path to spiritual healing

Prayer is as individual as people are individual. Some of the various paths to spiritual healing are illustrated in the experiences of the writers in this section. Complete reliance on God, individual spiritual discovery, allowing prayer to change thought, and persistence in prayer—the goal is the same—to know God better. And the result is healing.

1

God heals anything!

When people turn without reservation to God for help, they find that "with God all things are possible"—and are healed and protected. The experiences of the men, women, and children in this chapter show the unlimited range of God's power and care, especially in times of danger, personal crisis, and when severe illness threatens.

This healing taught me that God is the healer.

On a cold winter day in 1972, I fell while riding a horse and landed on my back on frozen cornstalks. I was taken to a hospital, where X-rays revealed that not only was my back broken in three places, but I also had an arthritic condition that was causing my spine to disintegrate slowly. The doctor said that by my lying flat for six to eight weeks, the broken back would heal, but there was absolutely nothing that could be done about the degenerative arthritis. He also said my physical activities must be greatly restricted; there could be no more horseback riding, or for that matter anything that might jar my back. This came as quite a shock, as I had three young children and led a very active life.

Because of the discouraging medical diagnosis, I telephoned the only Christian Scientist I knew to ask what she would do. (I knew very little about Christian Scientists, except that they "didn't go to doctors.") The next day she brought me *Science and Health with Key to the Scriptures* by Mary Baker Eddy and a current copy of the *Christian Science Sentinel,* a weekly magazine about healing spiritually. She said not to worry if I didn't understand all I read, but just to keep reading.

I read the book constantly; I couldn't put it down! Although I'd had little religious training as a child, I'd always wondered about God and about man's purpose in life. I was elated to be finding answers to my many questions.

During the second week the severe pain greatly decreased. I began getting up and resuming my household tasks. By the end of the third week I felt fine. My husband and I decided to go ahead with a scheduled vacation, and I played tennis each day.

When we returned home and my doctor learned what I had done, he insisted I be X-rayed again and meet with the hospital's chief surgeon to see what damage I had done. This was at the beginning of the fifth week. The chief surgeon held up the two sets of X-rays to the light to compare them, and said in awe, "No one would believe these X-rays were of the same person; there is no trace of injury." I explained that the healing had occurred while reading *Science and Health.*

This healing taught me that God is the healer; healing is not dependent upon a person, either oneself or another. I hadn't discussed Christian Science with anyone or even known about Christian Science practitioners, who help people through prayer. In the Preface of *Science and Health* the author explains, "The physical healing of Christian Science results now, as in Jesus' time, from the operation of divine Principle, before which sin and disease lose their reality in human consciousness and disappear as naturally and as necessarily as darkness gives place to light and sin to reformation" (p. xi).

I have continued to lead an active life, including much horseback riding, and have never had any further problem with my back.

MARY S. OSBORN
Glenmoore, Pennsylvania
Christian Science Sentinel September 20, 1993

My God had been a god of paradoxes and contradictions.

Originally written in French

Early in 1977 my wife was having severe problems with her blood pressure and was very frequently ill. A doctor, who was a friend of ours, examined her and concluded that she would die before long. Then he asked me to take her home, which I did. At that point I had lost faith in medicine and tribal witchcraft; and I had never really had any in God. Her death appeared imminent.

Later that afternoon, on my wife's nightstand, I found two copies of the monthly *Herald of Christian Science* (French edition). After two hours of reading all the articles in one copy of the *Herald,* I had discovered the true God. He was not like the God I had been told about, a God who kills; who makes mistakes; who requires mercy but who Himself always gets revenge; who created hell and heaven; and who is not impartial and certainly is not good. (I had believed that He wanted to kill my wife!) In a word, my God had been a god of paradoxes and contradictions.

But reading this *Herald,* I discovered the real God, the only creator, the only cause, the only possessor and provider of all good to man, who is His image; the one, totally spiritual originator, absolute in love, grace, and mercy; perfect, good, immortal.

Enriched by my "discovery," I rushed into the room where my wife and our children were and said, "I am becoming a Christian. . . ." This statement opened my wife's eyes.

She smiled and said to me, "That's great! May God hear you." All our children were astonished, as much because of my change of heart as because of what their mother had said.

I ordered a copy of the book mentioned in the magazine—*Science and Health.* Within two days of receiving the book (and beginning to read it), my wife was up and going about in a normal way. Before long the blood pressure trouble was completely healed, along with other illnesses that had affected her stomach, liver, kidneys, and heart.

At one time I drank a lot, only high-quality champagne. My friends "helped" me in this lifestyle by doing all they could to procure drink and Havana cigars for me. I began studying the Bible and *Science and Health* and praying in an effort to be healed of alcoholism and the addiction to tobacco. Two months later I was repulsed by tobacco and by just the smell of alcohol. I had been healed suddenly and completely of these plagues.

In gratitude for these first blessings, I set out to practice what little of Truth I understood. . . .

I rejoice in the victories my wife and I have won and in the spiritual progress we have made.

ELÉAZAR M'BOCK II

My husband's testimony, including the accounts of his healing of atheism, my physical healing, and our progress in applying the laws of God to daily life, is true.

I had been sick since the age of ten but was completely healed.

CÉCILE M'BOCK II
Yaoundé, Cameroon
The Christian Science Journal June 1985

We were both heavily addicted to alcohol.

As one who had been reared in a church-going, God-fearing, Bible-reading family, I had good exposure to the Scriptures, but only from a literal and material standpoint. My questions about God and my relationship to Him went mostly unanswered. . . .

During the years of an emotional wilderness experience, at a time when I would not even have a Bible in my house, I had become a successful businesswoman who was married to a successful businessman. But we were both heavily addicted to alcohol. We attended a self-help group for alcoholics. However, we still had not found the peace and freedom for which we longed, although we appreciated the group's efforts to aid us.

I enjoyed playing golf daily, partly because it kept me out of the house and partly because it helped to dull the obsession for drink. (Soon after my marriage, I had stopped working.) But there came a time when the temptation to take a drink became so obsessive that I did not sleep for two days and nights. On the morning of the third day I was so harassed and weary of struggling not to drink that I thought, "I will either be dead or drunk before this day is over."

The thought of suicide then became so strong that I checked my husband's gun to see if I knew how to use it. I begged God (I knew no other way to pray) to give me the courage to take my life or to show me what He wanted me to do, and to please make the answer so plain that I could not mistake it. I even was willing to give up my husband. (My early religious training had made me feel guilty for remarrying after a divorce. This deep guilt had contributed to the drinking and left me feeling greatly burdened.) At that point, with the gun in my hand and with complete acquiescence, I prayed, "Thy will be done" (Matthew 6:10), words that I remembered from my early acquaintance with the Bible.

I knelt by a table where the telephone was. Suddenly the telephone rang at my elbow. A woman with whom I frequently played golf was calling to see if I would join her for a game. (She knew of the drinking problem.) She urged me to come on out to the club and said that if I didn't want to play I could walk around the course with her. At first I declined, but the mesmeric impulsion to fire the gun had been broken, and I agreed to go.

On the first tee I asked my friend to share with me her concept of God. She had always seemed so poised, loving, gracious, and peaceful. I longed for an attitude like hers. So during six holes of golf I poured out my distress, remorse, and desire to be free of the addiction to alcohol. As we prepared to tee off on the seventh hole, I told her I would be going into the clubhouse when we finished that hole to have a drink.

I continued to pour out my remorse to her, and she gently indicated that the troubles were not part of my real identity. I thought that she was just saying that because I was her friend and she did not want to believe those things of me. When I repeated that I was going in to have a drink, she asked me, "Do you really want to be drunk?" It was a most provocative question, and I answered, "No, I just want oblivion." Immediately she said that what I really wanted was peace of mind and that she could tell me how I might obtain that and be free from wanting to drink. She said that I did not have to live with remorse for the rest of my life. This sounded incredible to me, and I asked, "How?"

She suggested that we sit on a nearby bench, and she began the conversation by saying that she was a Christian Scientist. I pulled away from her, mentally and physically, as I thought she was going to preach to me. She lovingly asked that I hear her out, and added that she would never mention Christian Science to me again unless I first mentioned it to her. Remembering my earlier prayer, "Thy will be done," I listened.

She quoted the first chapter of Genesis, which gives the spiritual account of creation, and she assured me that I, too, was made in the image of God. She explained to me that since "God saw every thing that he had made, and, behold, it was very good" (1:31), what God hadn't made could have no power.

As she emphasized the spiritual import of the Scriptures, I began to see a ray of hope for me. I had no awareness of how long we sat talking, but a feeling of peace settled over me, and the desire for alcohol left me, along with the deep remorse and guilt. Sometime later we finished our round of golf. The sense of peace remained with me, and I slept untroubled that night.

I soon obtained a copy of the King James Bible and a copy of *Science and Health* to begin my search to see how my healing of drinking had come about.

During my early study, I was healed of a body malfunction for which I had taken medicine all my life, and of a serious sinus infection that had plagued me for years. A foot condition that had been diagnosed as degenerative arthritis (two doctors had told me I would have to have surgery but would be a semi-cripple the rest of my life) was also healed, just by my reading *Science and Health.* Many years later I realized that I had also been healed of gallbladder trouble that had occurred once or twice a year and was supposed to have been hereditary. There has been no recurrence of those difficulties since I was healed twenty-eight years ago. And I have had many other healings through prayer alone.

My husband was also healed of drinking shortly after I was, and our home was free of that bondage from then on. Some of my husband's healings through prayer included those of flu and hemorrhoids. This spiritually scientific way of life has brought me blessings too numerous to relate.

JUNE MCKNIGHT PIERCE
Arlington, Texas
Christian Science Sentinel November 12, 1984

The doctor told me that I had no chance of survival.

More than nine years ago I suffered a massive heart attack. . . . I was not a student of Christian Science, but my wife, who was and is a Christian Scientist, was with me. I asked her what I could hold on to in thought, and she gave me some simple truths: "You are God's perfect child." "God's love is the only power and presence." "God is All." I repeated these to myself many times as I was taken by ambulance to the hospital.

At the hospital the doctor told my family that nothing could be done for me. He said I would probably not last through the day. I knew without a doubt that my wife didn't accept this as true and she was knowing the truth all the time, that I was spiritual—that I reflected God as His creation, man.

Several hours later I was moved to another hospital, a large metropolitan one with the newest equipment and considered the best in heart care. The next morning I woke up in the intensive care section of this hospital. The first thing I noticed was that I was not afraid. There was no pain, and the nurses were all amazed that I was aware of everything that was going on. My wife and our children came in to see me, and I realized how much I really loved all of them.

In the days that followed I was able to listen to tapes about healing spiritually that my wife brought to me. I read the Bible and Mary Baker Eddy's writings when I could, and I listened to tapes when I could not read. Through the long nights I would think about the messages I had my wife write on the palms of my hands, such as "I am God's perfect child" and "God loves me."

The second or third day, the doctor told me that I had no chance of survival. He said they could not do a bypass operation because my heart was essentially destroyed. When the nurse who had been in constant attendance to that point heard this, she went to my wife and said, "I don't know what you have been doing for him, but keep doing it."

From then on, my wife and I diligently studied the Bible and *Science and Health* by Mary Baker Eddy. Fifteen days later, I decided it was time to go home.

When the doctor in charge came in, I told him what I was going to do. He tried everything to get me to stay, as he felt I would not live. Then he left, and in a few minutes returned with five different prescriptions. When I told him I did not need them, he said there was no chance at all if I did not take the medicine. But I knew I was all right, and eventually the doctor just wished me well. (While I was in the hospital, the doctors insisted that I take medication, about thirty pills a day. But they had no effect on me. I took no medicine at all once I left the hospital.)

My wife drove me home, where the rest of the family greeted me with great joy. They had not known I would be coming home that night. Love filled the house. Two days later I went back to work.

It is now a little over nine years, and I have not been restricted in any way. Snowmobiling, fishing, working, I have done all in perfect freedom.

My gratitude is deep for my wife and for all those who listen to God and are helping others to grow in understanding Him. By the way, there was another healing at that time. For twenty-five years I had worn trifocal glasses. A few days after I started reading the Bible Lesson outlined in the *Christian Science Quarterly,* I was having trouble seeing and thought my glasses needed to be changed. When I raised them up and the fine print was clear, I was astonished. I have continued to do a lot of reading and studying, which I have always done, and I read with ease to this day without glasses. My cup runneth over.

NORBERT E. UPDIKE

I would like to verify my husband's testimony. The morning he became ill, I asked him if he wanted me to call a Christian Science practitioner for healing prayer. He said yes. The call was made, but no one was there. During the next fifteen or twenty minutes, the situation worsened noticeably, but I felt absolutely clear that my husband was untouched as God's spiritual, complete image, man. At this time he asked me to call an ambulance.

It was later, when my husband was enroute to the hospital, that I was able to reach a practitioner. He said he would support the praying I was doing, and he gave me some references to study from the Bible and from *Science and Health.*

On arrival, our grown children and I were told by the doctor that it was not possible for my husband to live. He said he didn't know how my husband was alive now.

In comforting the children, I told them that we didn't have to fear but rather hold to God's law of perfect harmony, which was governing every aspect of the situation.

Later the same day my husband was taken to another hospital. The heart surgeon there was amazed at my husband's condition. He said the attack had been horrendous. The indications were such that, to their knowledge, he should be dead. Instead, he was talking and asking questions. To me this was clear proof of God's law prevailing over so-called physical law. God's law is in reality the only law and all, I knew, that we had to obey. I read to my husband from *Science and Health* the following lines: "Do not believe in any supposed necessity for sin, disease, or death, knowing (as you ought to know) that God never requires obedience to a so-called material law, for no such law exists. The belief in sin and death is destroyed by the law of God, which is the law of Life instead of death, of harmony instead of discord, of Spirit instead of the flesh" (p. 253).

A big step forward for my husband was learning that God truly loved him, that he was not a miserable sinner, but that God loves and cares for each and all of His children continuously. Also he began to realize that nothing could separate him from God or God's love, because man actually lives in God.

When my husband left the hospital, all the way home he kept expressing joy for the comfort and well-being he felt. At home he walked up the steps and into the house on his own. We sat and talked for over two hours with the children. This happened during the Christmas season, and the joy, harmony, and gratitude we all felt told us we had experienced the true coming of Christ. We all agreed it was the best Christmas ever.

My gratitude for the understanding I have gained has no bounds.

Lorelei Updike
Indianapolis, Indiana
The Christian Science Journal June 1992

The closer I got, the louder the roar of the water became.

I am submitting this testimony because of an overwhelming desire to express my thanks to God for evidence of His wonderful care during a moment of extreme danger.

Years ago we built a home on a piece of property that had a deep drainage ditch at the back of the lot. At the time, I welcomed having the ditch, thinking that the children (there were four then) would enjoy scrambling up and down its banks. They did, but after about two years the city decided to pave the ditch. It was paved in a U shape of concrete with a five-foot opening leading from a newly laid culvert at the high end of our property. This proved to be one of the main drainage avenues for the whole area where we lived.

Late one morning after I had picked up the children from swimming, we returned home unaware that the rainstorm we had driven through had actually resulted in a flash flood in our vicinity. When we reached our home, the children begged to run out back and check on how their ditch was doing in the rain. Always before, they had enjoyed playing and wading there during and after light rains. I agreed to their going but told them not to put even a toe into the water until I got an umbrella and joined them there.

When I came back outside with the umbrella, I was met by our oldest daughter, who was then ten years old. She was running toward the house, crying, "Mamma, where are my books?" (She was referring to her copies of the Bible and *Science and Health.*) She then frantically told me that her little sister and one of her younger brothers were gone. I did not fully understand, and I asked her what she meant. She indicated that the two children had each put a foot in the water and had then been swept away.

I ran toward the ditch, and the closer I got, the louder the roar of the water became. I cannot describe the dread that I felt. When I reached the edge of the rushing, angry water, our other son was standing there in great fear. It was certainly a time for us to affirm spiritual truths of God and man.

My next thought was to feel deeply grateful that our children had been taught both at home and in Sunday School that God was always with them, guiding and guarding them. I simply knew that they were aware of this right at that moment. I raced back to the house. There I told our daughter to call a Christian Science practitioner, tell him what had happened, and ask him to pray for us right away.

I had come to a firm realization that the human measurement of time is certainly not God's measurement. As the Apostle Paul wrote, "Now is the accepted time; behold, now is the day of salvation" (II Corinthians 6:2). So I clung to the realization that no matter what seemed to have happened, right now the children were in the loving care of their Father-Mother God.

Later I learned that all along the ditch, men were rapidly putting up sandbags to try to stop the violent flow of water. Two homes were already flooded. Also, water was rushing over the heavy bridges that residents had built across the ditch to enable them to enjoy the woods on the other side of their properties. As our two children were swept wildly along, the men stopped their work to race to their aid, but they could not catch up with them. At that point large slabs of concrete were being forced to the surface by the pressure of the water. At the end of a city block the ditch took an extreme left turn, and the water was crashing into a retaining wall. This was the route our children were traveling.

I took our car and drove to the end of the block. All the while I was praying to hear the thoughts of assurance and comfort that I knew were coming to me from God. By the time I got there I was feeling a calmer certainty of God's presence with our children. When I reached the turning point in the ditch several of the men had arrived before me. I heard them saying repeatedly that it was a miracle.

When I looked across the roaring water, I saw our two children on the opposite bank. They had made the sharp turn, passed the retaining wall, and were clinging to two little vines hardly the size of pencils. The men said that they couldn't possibly get to the children from where we were standing but that they would drive several blocks to reach them on the other side. To me the children's rescue from this situation was not a miracle; it was evidence of God's omnipresence. I will never forget my sense of awe and deep gratitude for this wonderful proof of God's love and power to care for His children under any human condition.

Later, when I had the children at home, I saw that there was practically nothing left of their bathing suits except the double stitched straps and leg openings. And yet they had only a few scratches on their bodies, as though they might have brushed against a rosebush. I asked both of these little ones separately about what they had done during their ordeal, and each responded with the same statements. Each told of coming to the top of the water and crying, "God is Love," before being pulled back under. When they had passed the sharp turn in the ditch, each had reached out and caught a little branch and then come to rest on the sandy bank. Until that time, neither had been aware that the other was in the water. Once again, enormous gratitude to God was uppermost in my thoughts.

JANE W. KITTRELL
Fairhope, Alabama
Christian Science Sentinel October 7, 1985

Our family has always helped one another in times of crisis, and through prayer.

My name is Matthew Hulen. I am eleven years old and in the sixth grade. I would like to tell you what happened to me during one spring break. I was home, blowing some pin darts through a straw, and I wanted to see how far I could shoot one. So I took a deep breath. But the dart went down my throat. [A pin dart is a long straight pin.]

I began to cough blood but the dart didn't come up. Then I started to say "the scientific statement of being" to myself. Soon after this, my dad walked in the house from work.

["The scientific statement of being" referred to is from *Science and Health,* page 468:

"Question.—What is the scientific statement of being?

"*Answer.*—There is no life, truth, intelligence, nor substance in matter. All is infinite Mind and its infinite manifestation, for God is All-in-all. Spirit is immortal Truth; matter is mortal error. Spirit is the real and eternal; matter is the unreal and temporal. Spirit is God, and man is His image and likeness. Therefore, man is not material; he is spiritual."]

When I told him what had happened, he helped me by saying "the scientific statement of being" out loud in a strong voice. Then he called a Christian Science practitioner. After he talked to the practitioner, I didn't cough as much, and I stopped spitting up blood.

Then my older brother and younger sister both prayed for me. And my dad and I started to read the Bible Lesson for that week together. Soon I was hardly coughing at all. In the last section of the Lesson there was a place where Mary Baker Eddy quotes Christ Jesus' words "If they drink any deadly thing, it shall not hurt them" (*Science and Health,* p. 328). This sounded like it was written just for me.

I called the practitioner and told her I was holding to that thought. She said to keep holding to it and that she would continue to pray for me. By this time I had almost stopped coughing altogether.

I took a nap and afterward I started to play TV games. Then my dad, who was reading the Bible, asked if I wanted to listen to a story. (By now two or three hours had passed since I'd swallowed the pin.) I went into the room where my dad was, and he read the story of Gideon to me (Judges, chapters 6–7).

We were discussing the middle of the story, when all of a sudden I felt the dart in the back of my mouth. I began to cough so my dad told me to spit it out. And I did! It was a large pin with a piece of yarn tied to it. We all rejoiced that I was healed completely!

The only time I had been afraid was at the very first, before my brother and sister had started to pray. But when we were praying, all fear left and I trusted God. I now know it is a fact that "if they drink any deadly thing, it shall not hurt them."

MATTHEW HULEN

I was coming back from fishing with my friend Joe when suddenly I heard this crash, and the next thing I remember the engine of the scooter-truck was running and my left arm was stuck and I couldn't get out. Joe stopped some people who helped me out, and they had me lie down on the grass. They were saying that I probably had internal bleeding, broken bones, and maybe even a concussion. But I knew none of this could really be true.

I kept on repeating this verse from *Miscellaneous Writings* by Mary Baker Eddy (p. 400):

Father-Mother God,
   Loving me,—
Guard me when I sleep;
Guide my little feet
   Up to Thee.

Then I heard my daddy's voice telling me to get up. I got up, and we went home. Pretty soon I was riding my bike.

PAUL M. HULEN

I wish to verify the testimony of my two sons.

Matthew's older brother and younger sister both prayed for him. Our family has always helped one another in times of crisis and, through prayer, God has always shown each of us the power of Truth.

Only after Matthew spit out the pin did I realize that he had *inhaled,* not just swallowed it. Later, the practitioner urged Matthew to write up his healing. So I had him sit down that afternoon and make an outline of the events just as they had occurred. I might also mention that his mother had told him the day before to throw away the straw and not to shoot any pin darts. He now has promised me that he won't shoot them anymore. And I am sure he won't.

Through many years of reliance on God, I have come to understand that when its rules are correctly applied, Christian Science heals with mathematical certainty.

Paul had left the house one morning to go fishing near the prison farm where I am the Protestant chaplain. I had instructed him to return around two o'clock in the afternoon because several relatives were coming to dinner, and he had assured me he would.

We were inside preparing the meal when an officer of the prison came running up to the front door and informed me that our son and his friend had been involved in a major accident and that the injuries appeared critical. According to the officer, my child was unconscious and had been trapped under the wreckage.

As chaplain to the prison it was my job to prepare a Sunday sermon each week. The Scriptural selection I had chosen for that Sunday was the healing of the Shunammite woman's son by Elisha (II Kings, chapter 4). During the week I had pored over this Bible account many times, actually trying to figure out exactly why I had selected it. As the officer spoke to me, I understood why. I immediately held fast to the thought that no matter what appeared to be, all was truly well. My wife called a Christian Science practitioner, and I left with the officer.

As we drove along I thought of how the Shunammite woman had said "It is well" (verse 26), despite the material evidence that her son had died. I held steadfastly to this thought and prayed, knowing that man is ever in God's care and that nothing can change this spiritual fact.

When we got there the scooter-truck was overturned and tangled in a barbed wire fence, and both children were lying on the ground. My son appeared unconscious, and Joe was crying. The final sentence of "the scientific statement of being" was vivid in my thinking: "Therefore man is not material; he is spiritual." I knew there was just no way that man, as a spiritual idea of God, could collide with anything or anything could collide with him. His spiritual identity remains intact, no matter what the physical evidence. As I held to this thought, a feeling of calm came over me that I really can't describe.

I knelt down by my son and whispered in his ear that God was his life and that since nothing could remove God from him, nothing could remove his life from him. It never occurred to me that he wouldn't respond. He opened his eyes and stated that he had been run down by a car. I told him that we needed just to shut the door on such a picture—nothing ever had gone on and nothing ever could go on except that which God had ordained, and accidents were no part of God's being.

When I asked him if he thought he could get up, he answered that he would try. There were several medical personnel on the scene by this time. However, nothing was said as my son rose and walked over to the pickup truck of a neighbor who had agreed to drive us home. I felt so clearly that we both were just shutting the door on the entire incident, closing it out of our thinking. I took him home and my wife cleaned him up. A matter of hours later he was out riding his bicycle. He never suffered any aftereffects.

Joe's parents were notified shortly after I was. Soon after bringing Paul home, I returned to the scene to do what I could for Joe, whose father, by now, had arrived. Before this boy was taken away by ambulance, I knelt down and spoke quietly in his ear, telling him that God loved him and would not let him out of His care. This did much to calm his crying. Joe was treated at the hospital and released that afternoon. I visited with him several times after that, while he was recovering at home. He returned to school within a short time and he still plays and goes fishing with my children.

Although these are vivid examples of God's healing love, I have come to expect good as a natural and constant part of my life.

David B. Hulen
Rosharon, Texas
The Christian Science Journal December 1982

I was so happy with my first discovery about man's spiritual nature.

I was given *Science and Health* in the spring of 1990, and in the summer of that same year I went on my first voyage abroad, to England. By that time I had read the book, and whenever I had any free time I would meditate upon the ideas that I "fished" out of it.

It happened that I had to travel first by train and then by boat, and when I was on board the ship I became seasick. So I started to think about some of the things Mrs. Eddy wrote in *Science and Health.* I said to myself, "You cannot be sick, because you are an idea of God!" Then I thought, "OK, that is fine. I am an idea. But why can't an idea be sick?"

First it appeared to be a rather puzzling question I did not know how to answer. Then suddenly, like a ray of sunlight through a cloudy sky, came a wonderful explanation, as if someone had just spoken it to me: "Suppose I had a picture of a snowflake in my mind. It would be just my idea, of course. Now, having that snowflake in my mind, I go to a sauna, where the temperature is about 100 degrees centigrade. The question is, can the heat make my snowflake melt?"

The very idea of trying to melt a "mental" snowflake by "real" temperature made me laugh. I understood that it would be just as impossible to make God's idea sick by tossing it in waves. I was so much absorbed in my considerations that I did not notice when exactly my seasickness was gone. But it was gone, and I was so happy with my first discovery about man's spiritual nature.

That insight is still invaluable to me. Whenever I am faced with a threatening circumstance I ask myself, "Can a mental snowflake be destroyed by heating it?" And this question leaves me with a smile on my lips and deep gratitude to God and to Mrs. Eddy in my heart. No man is able to count the blessings that the spiritual truths revealed in her books have already brought, and will surely keep bringing, to mankind.

ANNA SERDUKOVA
St. Petersburg, Russia
Christian Science Sentinel February 20, 1995

For eleven years I was paralyzed in both legs.

Originally written in German

For eleven years I was paralyzed in both legs and could walk only a few meters unassisted. I sought help in vain from many doctors in a number of hospitals.

I had given up all hope when a married couple who had become tenants of ours gave me a copy of *Science and Health*. Even though at that time I was no longer expecting healing, I read it. The book gave me much joy because I felt closer to God as I read and understood some of it. I gained new courage and asked a Christian Science practitioner for guidance and prayer, both of which he gave with great love and patience.

In the following five months I learned much. From my study of the Bible and *Science and Health,* it became ever clearer to me that matter is not the substance of man, that in truth he is not the offspring of two other mortals, not bound by physical and character inadequacies; rather, he is indeed, just as the Bible promises, the image and likeness of God, beloved and maintained by his creator.

The turning point came with the practitioner's earnest request that I understand myself unreservedly to be the child of God. It became clear to me that as the child of God I had the right to refuse to consent to anything not in conformity with the nature and action of God, good. Consequently I was able to, and had to, cancel out in my thinking (so to speak) the medical diagnosis that I was suffering from an incurable illness. In its place, I acknowledged Jesus' words to his disciples and followers, "Ye shall know the truth, and the truth shall make you free" (John 8:32). And this liberating truth that God has created man in His image, thus good and free, is something that I then experienced through healing. After a short time I was able to walk without a cane and without assistance. This healing occurred in 1979 and has remained permanent.

My family and I are very happy and grateful. For me, the greatest joy is having sensed God's nearness and constant presence.

Anne Marie Riegel
Nidda, Germany
Christian Science Sentinel May 3, 1993

Seventy-nine years later I can say it was the best investment I've made.

I bought my first textbook of Christian Science, *Science and Health* by Mary Baker Eddy, in 1910, when I was playing a concert in Boston. At that time Boston was full of controversy about Mrs. Eddy. The newspapers carried editorials about her. Some could not praise her enough for her contribution; others could not criticize her enough. And that is why I invested a dollar for *Science and Health,* to find out for myself what it was all about.

The first sentence got my attention. It states, "To those leaning on the sustaining infinite, to-day is big with blessings" (p. vii). I was so impressed with this statement that I continued to read. Being a concert violinist and traveling from city to city gave me plenty of time to read the textbook, in my dressing room, in railroad stations, on trains, and in hotel rooms. The more I read, the more convinced I became of the accuracy of Mrs. Eddy's scientific and spiritual interpretation of the Bible. Seventy-nine years later I can say it was the best investment I've made. Would you pay one dollar for a life of peace and happiness, free of illness?

Science and Health states: "Except for the error of measuring and limiting all that is good and beautiful, man would enjoy more than threescore years and ten and still maintain his vigor, freshness, and promise. . . . Each succeeding year unfolds wisdom, beauty, and holiness" (p. 246). When I first read this statement I found it hard to believe, but now, in my nineties, I can say, "Man should live to be fourscore years and ten and retain his faculties. In fact, he should improve with age, more like a Stradivarius violin." I have never been in a hospital for medical care. I don't wear glasses or a hearing aid, neither do I use a cane. I cut my own lawn, drive a car, just got married, and I still work and make public appearances. When people ask, "To what do you attribute your longevity?" I reply, "To Christian Science."

When I have a difficulty of any kind, I've made it a habit to turn instantly to God for guidance and healing. I've never been disappointed. One day when I was warming up before a concert, I got a cramp in my right hand. Being a violinist, I had always feared this possibility. I prayed and was able to play that night. The cramps continued to happen, however, so I called a Christian Science practitioner for prayerful help. Within a short time I was completely healed.

ARTHUR R. LANDRY
Sarasota, Florida
Christian Science Sentinel February 6, 1989

2

Spiritual healing and two books that lead the way

People interested in learning more about the Bible, about the promises of Christ Jesus, and about the practice of Christian healing have found a valuable resource in the book Science and Health with Key to the Scriptures *by Mary Baker Eddy. She wrote, "The Bible contains the recipe for all healing" (p. 406).*

As one writer in this chapter notes, "Through Science and Health, *the Bible has come to be better understood as a living, healing voice of God."*

As I held the gun in my hand, I heard my wife quietly say, "There is a better way."

A line-of-duty injury that retired me from the New York City Police Department left me a cripple for over twelve years. As with all such injuries, the finest hospital, surgical, and rehabilitative treatment was provided for me. Unfortunately, after three years of medical treatment, orthopedic surgeons advised me that the fractures to my feet had left me a permanent cripple.

I had progressed from casts on both feet, to a wheelchair, then crutches, and finally to two canes and orthopedic supports in both shoes. As one doctor put it, I had much to be grateful for. Initially, I had faced possible amputation of the left foot, with the bleak prognosis that I might never walk again. But I did walk again, in a laboring, halting manner, assisted by the two canes. For this I must thank the doctors who worked so long and earnestly in an attempt to bring recovery.

Then five years later, still leaning on the two canes and with supports in my shoes, I slipped and fell on the icy streets of the city. My doctor strongly advised me to leave New York for an area with a year-round moderate climate. When he warned that another fall could put me back in a wheelchair for life, my wife and I decided it was time to go. The following summer we moved to California.

I eventually improved my walking sufficiently to obtain new work. But one of the tragic effects of the injuries I sustained was the daily pain I had learned to live with. Aspirin, tranquilizers, and other sedatives were daily ingested. Sleep was difficult, and getting out of bed in the morning was an ordeal.

One morning, as I first put weight on my feet, the pain was so intense I fell back into bed. Tears came to my eyes. Then anger and resentment welled up against this tragedy that had crippled me and put an end to my career in the Police Department. I had been an athlete all my life and prided myself on my ability to tolerate pain. But this was too much. I reached under our bed for my service revolver. As I held the gun in my hand, I heard my wife quietly say, "There is a better way." I looked at her tender, loving face and asked, "What other way?" She replied, "You have tried everything else, why don't you try Christian Science?" We talked for a few minutes; then she handed me the Christian Science textbook, *Science and Health with Key to the Scriptures* by Mary Baker Eddy.

My wife is a lifelong Christian Scientist. Shortly after we met, she told me she was a Christian Scientist, that she believed God was Love and we were all His beloved children. I told her my God was my gun, my nightstick, and my shield and suggested she keep her religious beliefs to herself. Early in our marriage I read several portions of *Science and Health,* but found what it said incompatible with my thinking and so put it down.

A few weeks after I had again tried reading *Science and Health,* as my wife had suggested, I was in such intense pain that I threw the book across the room and told my wife, in some very coarse language, what I thought about her religion. She simply picked up the textbook and said, "You are not reading it correctly. All you want is a physical healing." My answer was: "I have been in agony all these years. I'm entitled to a healing. Why must I suffer like this?" She answered, "You must forget about yourself and find out about God and your relation to Him." I almost exploded again, but as I looked at her and felt her deep love and compassion, I knew I had to try once more. I had to find an answer to this puzzle. Is there really a God—if so, who is He? And who am I and how did I get into this awful mess?

I opened the textbook to the Preface and read Mrs. Eddy's magnificent first sentence: "To those leaning on the sustaining infinite, to-day is big with blessings" (p. vii). I had read that sentence previously without realizing its significance. But not this time. Now the words came alive with meaning. For twelve years I had leaned on doctors, hospitals, physical therapy, wheelchairs, crutches, canes, supports, and pills. Now was the time to lean on something much greater than material means and human will. I was filled with an overwhelming sense of peace; I knew that what I was searching for would be revealed to me.

As I read and reread page after page of *Science and Health* I lost all sense of time. What had once been puzzling and obscure became crystal clear. The Bible, the textbook, and a dictionary were my constant companions. This study, this search, was a daily joy. My thoughts began to dwell on the sustaining infinite, as each session of study and research poured in flood tides of divine Truth. The understanding of

God as Father-Mother, as perfect Love, and of His tender concern for all His children, including myself, began to dawn in consciousness. The truth that God is All, and that His beloved children reflect His divine perfection, became tangible fact to me.

Exactly when the healing came I never knew. The Christ so filled my days with joy and peace that time simply flew by.

One morning as I was shaving in the bathroom and humming the melody of Hymn 139 from the *Christian Science Hymnal* (which begins "I walk with Love along the way"), I realized that something was different. There was no pain! I let out a cry of joy as my wife walked by and told her I was healed. As we held each other, we knelt down and humbly thanked God for this blessing. That tragic episode of invalidism was a dream. Through the earnest study of *Science and Health,* an understanding of my oneness with God had been revealed to me.

Why had my early efforts with the textbook been fruitless? Could it be, as my wife said, I was only searching for a healing? Or possibly I had read the book with a critical thought. Whatever my former motives, when I put personal self aside and did search honestly and diligently, the truth that makes all men free came alive for me, as it will for anyone who earnestly seeks Truth.

This former police officer, who had been told he might never walk again, now runs three or four miles each day. As I begin my daily run, I thank God for His love, for His power and presence, and pray that I be guided to do whatever will bring glory to His name. Through this experience I have learned that God is All-in-all. And of equal import is the understanding that God never turns His back on us. It is we who turn away from Him. We have only to turn to Him again to feel His everlasting love.

John P. Ondrak

It is with great joy and deep gratitude to our Father-Mother God that I verify my husband's testimony. His healing took place exactly as stated and has been permanent.

The day I was called to the hospital, the first thought that came to me was to immediately acknowledge the ever-presence of God and to know that not for an instant was my husband outside His all-enveloping love.

When I arrived at the hospital, the doctor handed me a form to sign giving my consent for them to do whatever was necessary in caring for my husband. I silently prayed to God to open my eyes to anything I needed to see. My prayer was answered, for in fine print near the bottom of the consent form were the words "Permission to amputate." I told the doctor I could not give my consent to any such operation. I was then given another form that omitted the amputation clause. This form I signed, and my husband was then taken in for surgery.

I am so very grateful to have been a witness to this wonderful healing. To see my husband again run, bicycle, dance, and walk without a limp or defect of any kind after so many years of agonizing disability, has indeed proved to me that "with God all things are possible" (Matthew 19:26).

NANCY J. ONDRAK
Canoga Park, California
The Christian Science Journal September 1982

At noon I was up and well.

When I was a little girl, my parents enrolled me in a Christian school because of its good reputation. There I first became acquainted with the Bible. I loved the Bible stories, especially those relating to Jesus and the healings he performed.

As my parents were very medically oriented, and I was very often ill, I saw a doctor for even the smallest physical problem. I felt very sad, not only because I could never participate in sports and other activities, but also because of the many medicines I had to take constantly. And I often thought that if I had lived in Jesus' time, I would certainly have followed the crowds who went to him for healing.

Years later my marriage was in trouble. Our finances had become very low because several business transactions had fallen through for my husband; I was also ill with high blood pressure, and often lost consciousness.

My husband and I disagreed about religion, because although I had become a Christian, he kept his traditional religion. At that point a dear friend, knowing about our problems, gave me a copy of *Science and Health.*

Although I had to stay in bed that morning, I was healed within a couple of hours after I began reading the book. I read the chapter "Prayer" carefully, with tears of gratitude to God that spiritual healing is available now, as in Jesus' time. And I caught a glimpse of what true prayer is, not a mere rehearsing of petitions and litanies, as I was used to, but a deep yearning from the heart for repentance, reformation, and grace.

At noon I was up and well, driving my daughters to their ballet classes. The high blood pressure was permanently healed.

My husband also began studying *Science and Health.* Other healings followed. One daughter was healed of asthma, which had been pronounced by a doctor hereditary and incurable. My husband was healed of a chronic stomach disorder, fever, and the smoking habit. . . . I do not know where our family would be now if my friend had not given me *Science and Health.*

Lynn Noerhadi
Jakarta, Indonesia
The Christian Science Journal March 1994

Doctors stated that I would become more of an invalid.

I would like to express my gratitude for the healing many years ago of severe arthritis, which came through reading

Science and Health. I had been suffering from this problem for ten years, had been in and out of hospitals, where doctors had given me no hope of ever being able to walk without sticks again. They stated that I would become more of an invalid.

At that time I was very depressed. Then, one day as I was about to lean on a wall for support, I found myself looking in a window of a Christian Science Reading Room and reading these words in *Science and Health:* "When the illusion of sickness or sin tempts you, cling steadfastly to God and His idea" (p. 495). The operative word to me was *illusion.* I kept reading this over and over again, because I didn't understand it. Arthritis seemed no illusion to me.

I wanted to understand what I had read, so I went into the Reading Room and asked the librarian if I could read that book. I started at the beginning, and I returned again and again to the Reading Room to read until I bought my own copy. I read *Science and Health* through and studied different passages. I wanted to understand these statements because I was manifesting much the opposite to what was stated in this book. One such statement was: "Ages pass, but this leaven of Truth is ever at work. It must destroy the entire mass of error, and so be eternally glorified in man's spiritual freedom" (*ibid.,* p. 118). The book and its logic so interested me. Each day I felt great benefit from what I read.

I should say that before this time I always liked reading the Bible, but I never had understood its spiritual significance until I read *Science and Health.* One passage in the Bible that was inspiring and helpful at this time was, "Be not conformed to this world: but be ye transformed by the renewing of your mind, that ye may prove what is that good, and acceptable, and perfect, will of God" (Romans 12:2). Another was Christ Jesus' words in Matthew: "Come unto me, all ye that labour and are heavy laden, and I will give you rest. Take my yoke upon you, and learn of me; for I am meek and lowly in heart: and ye shall find rest unto your souls. For my yoke is easy, and my burden is light" (11:28–30).

I came to realize that the cause of this malady was mental, not physical, and that it was a belief that had to be eliminated, since, as *Science and Health* explains, there is no matter. I found I had to change the whole basis of my thought by overcoming false traits of character, such as resentment and criticism, and to open thought to be receptive to the truth. I began to accept into it the light of Life, Truth, and Love and the reality of my *true* being.

Gradually the pain disappeared; I was able to discard the sticks and was completely healed. That was many years ago and there has been no recurrence of this problem.

Edna Hoyle
London, England
The Christian Science Journal November 1976

I was told I had an active case of tuberculosis.

At an examination for the military service I was told I had an active case of tuberculosis. This was quite a blow to a young man just out of college and starting his business career. A chest specialist confirmed the diagnosis, telling me I would have to lie flat on my back for six months to two years. He told me I would never live a normal life and would not live very long if I did not take bed rest at once.

I left the doctor's office that day very depressed and wondering what to do. Before I could enter a sanatorium I would have to wait for the papers to clear for my admittance. I went home to be with my parents while awaiting admission to a state sanatorium.

The year before, I had been given a copy of *Science and Health.* I knew it had healed others and felt there had to be some help for me in its seven hundred pages. My parents were not Christian Scientists and were very much opposed to my reading the textbook. During the day the book stayed between the mattress and the box spring, and at night, after they had gone to bed, I would read.

When I had told a friend, who is a Christian Scientist, that I could understand very little I was reading, she told me to keep reading and take what I could understand. About three days after I started reading the book, I found the basis of my thought had changed. I was thinking of perfect Father, perfect child, and perfect creation. This revelation of my perfection as God's own child began to replace the belief of an unreal law producing a state of helplessness.

On page 332 of *Science and Health* I read "Father-Mother is the name for Deity, which indicates His tender relationship to His spiritual creation." As this thought grew in strength, I was conscious of what I know today of God as Life, Truth, and Love, and that I was the perfect child of God. I had always been, and would always be, held in His love. I felt this love which at that moment was healing me and all mankind. I was very new to this concept and didn't know to call a Christian Science practitioner. I just kept reading and thinking about what this book was telling me.

A week later the doctors started to give me a second set of tests. This group was to collect information to make up a case history for the sanatorium. This time the tests were all negative. The symptoms were gone also. The X-ray still showed a tubercular shadow. The doctors were uncertain what to do. It was at this time, and for the first time, that they wanted to give me medicine, antibiotics, to help the already healing condition. It was my dad who came forward to say, "No," as they seemed unsure of the results. The doctor admitted he was not sure but wanted to help. No one knew about the little book and my nighttime reading. No drugs or medicine were ever given. I later realized this was God's protection for what He was giving me in *Science and Health.*

This healing came totally from reading *Science and Health.* I was completely healed. All I knew to do was read and pray. Later the opposition of my family was also healed. Through *Science and Health* the Bible has come to be better understood as a living, healing voice of God.

W. RILEY SEAY
Weston, Massachusetts
Christian Science Sentinel August 2, 1975

The psychiatrist reported that there was "nothing wrong with me," therefore there was no longer a basis for disability.

I had been psychiatrically evaluated as schizophrenic, manic depressive, with psychotic tendencies. For six years social security disability had been my sole support. I couldn't sleep and often sat in fear all night. When morning came, I feared the sunset.

In my search for relief I had tried many therapies, including psychiatry, naturopathy, and medication. Nothing had helped me. Finally I realized I had exhausted all my options but one—God. I had often pleaded with Him to help me, yet I came to realize that I never really felt God could help me.

At a very low point I prayed, feeling that I could not stand my troubles anymore. I said aloud, "I'll give You three days, God." I had decided that by the end of that time, if I hadn't found some peace, I would end my life. Later that day I picked up the telephone book and noticed the listing of churches. I decided to talk to someone about my problems. Then I remembered that a friend in school had given a report on Christian Science, saying it teaches that God heals. That's all I remembered, but I called a Christian Science Reading Room near my home.

During my phone conversation with the Reading Room librarian I poured out my fear that Christianity was an Armageddon-fire-and-brimstone sort of thing. The librarian assured me that God was not like that. She also told me that I was His beloved child and that He could heal me. She read me the Lord's Prayer, with its spiritual interpretation, given in *Science and Health* by Mary Baker Eddy (see pp. 16–17). She encouraged me to come to the Reading Room.

I thanked her and quickly hung up. Then I laughed to myself that I wouldn't be so easily caught up by a religious group. Immediately, though, a gentle message came to me that I had a choice to make. This was an opportunity to choose life. I broke down and cried. After a while I stopped crying and noticed my reflection in a mirror. I thought, "Well, you could at least wash your face! You look terrible!" The next thing I knew I was in clean clothes and leaving my house. Feeling greatly uplifted, I went straight to the Reading Room.

My first words to the librarian were, "I felt I was being carried down here!" "You were led," was her calm answer. I read one or two paragraphs of *Science and Health,* including these words: "The time for thinkers has come" (p. vii). Then I told the librarian, "You won't believe this, but this is what I've always been looking for!"

I bought a copy of *Science and Health* and some Christian Science pamphlets and went home to absorb as much of the strong, spiritual truths as I could understand. I held to the Scripture "God hath not given us the spirit of fear; but of power, and of love, and of a sound mind" (II Timothy 1:7).

A verse in Proverbs assures us, "When thou liest down, thou shalt not be afraid: yea, thou shalt lie down, and thy sleep shall be sweet" (3:24). That night when I went to bed I put my head down on the pillow and started to go through the usual process of trying to relax my tense facial and neck muscles. Suddenly I realized that my face was not only totally relaxed but that I was smiling too! I slept peacefully from that time on. Within three days I was aware that I hadn't had any of the symptoms of mental disorder since that first day, and a month later I could hardly believe that trouble had ever happened to me.

I got a new job involving training in graphic arts, where I could use my illustration skill. When I became employed, social security said that they would have to reevaluate me, since I was now claiming to be well. They sent me for examination to the psychiatrist who had originally diagnosed my case. He reported that there was "nothing wrong with me," therefore there was no longer a basis for disability. I was truly overjoyed at this confirmation of healing.

In the eleven years since the healing there has been no recurrence of the symptoms, and I have had many other healings. I am very grateful to God that when the heart reaches out in prayer, the need is always met by divine Love.

Name withheld at author's request
Christian Science Sentinel November 16, 1987

One day while I was reading, the pain went away.

Several years ago I had a severe pain in my back and went to a large hospital in Los Angeles. The doctors took X-rays, which showed a dislocated disk. They said the spine was deteriorating, and a nerve was being pinched, causing extreme pain. They thought I should be operated on right away. I told them I would think about it, but I did not have the operation. I went to a chiropractor and felt better for a while.

In 1986 the pain started again. I went to a chiropractor recommended by my insurance company. He told me he could not do anything to stop the pain. I was in constant pain and could only work part time because of the suffering.

Later on that year a friend came to see me. When I told her about this problem, she offered me *Science and Health.* The next day I started to read this book. One day while I was reading, the pain went away. I was so happy. I threw out all the pain pills I'd been taking and thanked God.

In one month I read all of *Science and Health.* I never liked to read before, but I do now! I feel so good and know God loves us always.

Maria Rocha
Whittier, California
Christian Science Sentinel December 12, 1988

I became more confident that God did not make a criminal.

In 1981, I found myself sentenced to prison for one to six years, as the result of a crime that I committed while under the influence of drugs. While serving my sentence, I had plenty of time to reflect on my lifestyle. I sincerely wanted to straighten out my life. During my stay at a prison in upstate New York, I went to a chapel service conducted by Christian Scientists, and there I obtained a copy of *Science and Health.*

Immediately the book captivated my thoughts because the ideas were very revolutionary, and they gave me hope. I decided that I would read this book more thoroughly, since I had plenty of time to do so. I decided to make a schedule, whereby every day I would read one hundred pages.

At first, some of the ideas seemed abstract, but as I continued to read, I began to understand the concepts explained in the book. All of the depressing thoughts that I had before gradually disappeared. The book gave me more hope; it gave me a better understanding of what I could accomplish with the help of God. I noticed that my attitude gradually changed.

In prison, there are many ways of expressing Christian love toward fellow inmates. I became more conscientious; I expressed more patience and tolerance. I also noticed that I began to use less profanity until, gradually, I didn't use profanity at all. I also learned the importance of reformation, and as I learned this, I became more confident that God did not make a criminal nor a sinner. I began to realize that I would be healed of the weaknesses that caused me to commit sin. I didn't know how or when, but I knew that I would be healed.

One idea from *Science and Health* that I held to states: "This conviction, that there is no real pleasure in sin, is one of the most important points in the theology of Christian Science. Arouse the sinner to this new and true view of sin, show him that sin confers no pleasure, and this knowledge strengthens his moral courage and increases his ability to master evil and to love good" (p. 404).

After continually reading one hundred pages a day of *Science and Health* for about six months, all desire to smoke cigarettes and drink coffee, and the craving to use drugs, just vanished. These healings occurred simultaneously, and the desire for drugs, coffee, or cigarettes has never returned. I'm extremely grateful that I used the time I had in prison constructively because I gained a better understanding of Christian Science.

"If any man be in Christ, he is a new creature: old things are passed away; behold, all things are become new" (II Corinthians 5:17). This statement from the Bible has certainly been proved true to me. I've been transformed from being a dishonest person to an honest one.

I was desperately seeking a job, and began my search at an employment agency where I was given an application. Upon its completion, an interviewer called me to ask why I hadn't entered any work history. I stated honestly that I had no prior work experience to speak of, since for most of my life, I had been engaged in illicit activity and had never had steady employment. He replied, "Well, we're going to have to doctor your résumé." This was a moment of decision for me. The first lines of a hymn describe so well my predicament at that time:

> Oft to every man and nation
> Comes the moment to decide,
> In the strife of Truth with falsehood,
> For the good or evil side.

"Sir, put the facts exactly as I've stated," I firmly countered. I knew this interviewer thought I would be unable to find a job, because it appeared I had no skills or work experience. There was a time when I would have gone along with a scheme to falsify my résumé; but because I had since grown spiritually, I found such a course of action unacceptable.

I visited another employment agency and was sent to be interviewed by a prospective employer. During the interview I was again asked why my application was blank. I explained that, quite honestly, for most of my adult life I had rarely held a steady job. The interviewer described briefly what the job entailed and the skills required to do the job. I said I had no experience in this type of work, but I quickly added that I was willing to learn. After further discussion, he said he would consider my application.

One passage I had pondered while searching for employment was written by Mary Baker Eddy: "The devotion of thought to an honest achievement makes the achievement possible. Exceptions only confirm this rule, proving that failure is occasioned by a too feeble faith" (*Science and Health,* p. 199). Wanting to earn a living legitimately is "an honest achievement," and I'd certainly given this a great deal of sincere thought. I knew I had to be completely candid about my past in order to obtain employment, and had been ready to make full disclosure. My faith in God was growing daily. With these points in mind, I felt very confident that God would lead me to suitable employment.

The next evening I received a call from the man who had interviewed me, asking me to report to work the next morning. I arrived promptly at 8:30 and began the job. I've been working for this company for nine years, am considered one of its top mechanics, and have learned a great deal about the installation, maintenance, and repair of coffee machines, soda machines, and water coolers.

This experience has been a staff upon which I lean, for whenever I'm in need of inspiration, I recall how God provided me with a job when it appeared I would be completely unable to find one. It is very reassuring to know that when I was in need of permanent work where I could learn skills, develop talents, and earn a living, prayer and honest intentions provided all three.

In a world where it appears that doing dishonest deeds often aids in advancement, my experience has proved that, by being honest, you will be justly rewarded by our heavenly Father. The adage "Honesty is the best policy" for me is now rendered "Honesty is the *only* policy."

LOUIS FUENTES
New York, New York
Christian Science Sentinel January 28, 1991,
and March 21, 1994

I was healed of smoking and malaria fever.

Before I began to read *Science and Health* I was a cigarette smoker and suffered from the effects of the habit. But all my struggles to give it up failed. I started to read issues of the *Christian Science Sentinel* in 1986 and got a copy of *Science and Health* after that. As I read this book, I became confident that I could overcome smoking, even if the habit had held me in bondage for so many years. This confidence came a result of the spiritual truths I read about God, man, and the universe. They were so true to me that I did not doubt them, and yielded to their power in consiousness.

I began to see myself as God's idea, His expression and manifestation. The word *reflection* as explained in *Science and Health* began to come to me each time I was about to smoke a cigarette, and I would then pause to ask myself whether the act of smoking reflects God. I began to see that it conflicted with what I was learning. The spiritual status of man and the love of God became so important to me that in about three weeks the desire to smoke left me. As I continued with my study, coughs, chest pains, dizziness, fatigue, and the foul odours connected with smoking were all gone. This speedy healing amazed me greatly, until I later came across this: "Truth, spiritually discerned, is scientifically understood. It casts out error and heals the sick" (*Science and Health,* p. 275).

Studying the Bible and *Science and Health* I was also healed of malaria fever and found freedom from further periodic attacks of the malady. The education I had received in secondary school taught me to believe that a parasite is responsible for the fever, and that if the disease is not arrested through the use of drugs, death may result.

But through the understanding I gained from my study, I realised that such knowledge is the "forbidden fruit" spoken of in Genesis, which God warns man neither to eat nor touch, lest he die (3:3). It is a knowledge that leads to bondage and destruction.

The laws of God made me firm in the understanding that there is only one creator, one power and presence. As I continued to study and pray, it gradually dawned in my consciousness that since God is infinite and created all things spiritually, He did not make something parasitic to cause me suffering. My beliefs about this disease started to crumble, and I began to recover my health without the use of drugs! I was healed completely and have not had any other attack of malaria fever.

Science and Health has ever been a source of inspiration, uplifting me from the mire of false beliefs regarding ethnicity, tribalism, and racial hatred. Christian Science teaches that one should have no other Mind but God. My concept of my community changed for the better. These words have been very helpful in healing problems related to personal differences: "With one Father, even God, the whole family of man would be brethren; and with one Mind and that God, or good, the brotherhood of man would consist of Love and Truth, and have unity of Principle and spiritual power which constitute divine Science" (*Science and Health,* pp. 469-470). I have begun to see my community as right in the kingdom of God. Every individual, every job, has become important and meaningful to me.

SALIFU USMAN
Otukpo, Benue State, Nigeria
Christian Science Sentinel September 26, 1994

In the morning the pain was completely gone.

While in my sophomore year at college, I was required to take a course in Western civilization. The professor lectured that civilization really began with Abraham's worship of one God. He then traced the history of the mainstream religions down to the lesser-known ones.

When we came to Christian Science, he mentioned that it presents God as a healing power. That was all he said; if we wanted to learn more about it, he suggested we do some research on our own. That was the last class of the morning. At lunch some of the students from the class discussed what our teacher had said. Nobody had ever heard of Christian Science.

At that time I had an executive position after school that helped pay my way through college. It required late hours and carried much responsibility. I didn't get much rest. One day soon after this, my back and legs gave me much pain, so much so that I went to a doctor. He prescribed some medicine, which did not help. He suggested physical therapy, but that didn't help either. I sought a second opinion from another doctor, who prescribed a strict diet. After a few weeks I asked him what the alternative was. He recommended an operation on the sciatic nerve in my back, but warned me that it might leave me crippled for life.

I went home and lay on my bed, mulling over the events of the past few months. The pain and the bleak future made me despondent, and thoughts of suicide came as a possible solution.

At work the next day I remembered the professor's remarks about Christian Science, and asked one of my co-workers if he had ever heard of it. He said he had, and directed me to a Reading Room a few blocks away. With the help of my cane, I walked there as fast as I could. The librarian who greeted me explained that *Science and Health* had healed countless numbers of people just by their reading it. I purchased the book and hurried home.

After supper I went to bed and began reading. When I came to page 14, I stopped and reread this passage: "Become conscious for a single moment that Life and intelligence are purely spiritual,—neither in nor of matter,—and the body will then utter no complaints. If suffering from a belief in sickness, you will find yourself suddenly well." I read this again and again until I had it memorized. I pondered it until I began to feel the pain leave. I continued to read the book late into the night, forcing myself to stay awake.

In the morning the pain was completely gone. I got out of bed and discarded all my medicines and physical therapy equipment, for I was completely healed. This happened some time ago, and I have never had a recurrence of that illness.

MICHAEL REDMAN
Portland, Oregon
Christian Science Sentinel September 5, 1994

I felt I was dying.

As a young boy I became ill, and although I was under medical care, my health progressively deteriorated over a period of years. A physician diagnosed my condition as one of having minimal natural bodily resistance to certain types of harmful bacteria and resultant infections, particularly streptococcal infections and staphylococcal infections. I was also diagnosed as being a meningitis carrier.

In an attempt to maintain my health, I was put on a regimen of antibiotic drug treatment, with the frequency and dosages increasing over time. Although my bodily resistance to the harmful bacteria didn't improve, the effectiveness of the antibiotics diminished and treatment was intensified.

My doctor, a kind and caring man as well as a highly reputable physician, was very concerned about the increasing dosages. So he alternated the usage of specific antibiotics in the hope of minimizing any potential negative bodily reaction.

Finally a severe crisis occurred. Within a short period of just a few weeks, I became allergic to the antibiotic drugs; the medicines I had so depended on for my health only made me sick. The physician advised my parents that my deteriorating situation was dire, that he had run out of medical answers, and that they should "prepare for the worst." Although I was not told about his prognosis, I felt I was dying.

This was the situation when a friend from school described to me how he had been healed, through prayer, of a severe condition of asthma. Needless to say, this caught my attention, and with an attitude of "anything is worth a try," I turned to Christian Science for help. (I was in college by this time.)

I studied the chapter titled "Footsteps of Truth" in *Science and Health.* What I learned totally changed my conception of God, my life, and the very basis of reality. Spiritual light and inspiration flooded into consciousness through passages I read, such as this one: "Christian Science raises the standard of liberty and cries: 'Follow me! Escape from the bondage of sickness, sin, and death!' Jesus marked out the way. Citizens of the world, accept the 'glorious liberty of the children of God,' and be free! This is your divine right" (p. 227). All symptoms of my longstanding illness and weakness disappeared. I was completely and permanently healed. This healing occurred in 1967.

Kenneth Benedict-Gill
Holliston, Massachusetts
Christian Science Sentinel April 23, 1990

I experienced none of the former withdrawal symptoms.

By the time I had graduated from college and was in my second year of teaching music, I'd come to the conclusion that I would never find an organized religion that suited me, and I made a decision to study the Bible on my own as well as to continue in my studies of philosophy. This was as close as I could get to my sense of truth. My study was incomplete, however, because it failed to offer practical proof of what I believed.

Such was the case when one day I woke to an urgent sense of fear and danger. As the day wore on I realized my discomfort seemed to center on thoughts of my brother, who was then a helicopter pilot in Vietnam. I became increasingly convinced that he was in grave danger. It was not unusual for me to sense things concerning my brother, for we had been very close during childhood and had often shared moments of great joy, love, and in this case, fear.

I felt a need to talk to someone, and I sought a fellow schoolteacher whom I barely knew, but who had exhibited qualities of calm, love, and care in her teaching. She was a student of Christian Science. We shared the evening together and talked well into the wee hours of the morning. She encouraged me to acknowledge my brother's spiritual oneness with his creator, God, who loves and protects His children regardless of the human scene. In that way my calm, loving prayer would serve to support him.

She continued to share effective healing truths, as taught in *Science and Health*. While I wasn't clear on all the terminology she used, I was sure that here was the teaching I had sought for so many years. She emphasized that truly we are created in God's image and are therefore complete, loved, and safe. Such joy! I felt as if the weight of years had been lifted from my shoulders. Instead of fatigue and disquiet, I felt buoyant and refreshed, calm and confident.

Before our parting, my friend offered the suggestion that I not try to walk both paths, the spiritual and material. She added that to do so would only cause me confusion. Little did she know how literally I would feel led to obey her words. Armed with a paperback copy of *Science and Health,* I went home to prepare for the new day of teaching. But before doing so, I emptied my medicine cabinet of the many drugs and pills I had stored and flushed them down the toilet.

I should explain that up until then I had been using medication to control a thyroid condition, amphetamines for weight control, and a tranquilizer to calm me after taking the other drugs. This had gone on for years. I was, in fact, addicted to these prescription drugs, and whenever I forgot to take them, I would experience most unpleasant withdrawal symptoms.

My decision to get rid of the medicine didn't seem particularly onerous at the time, as it was perfectly clear to me that the path of Christianly scientific metaphysics was far closer to my sense of truth than material medicine. Days passed. I continued my study of *Science and Health,* writing notes in the margins and underlining certain sentences. I experienced none of the former withdrawal symptoms, only a sweet, calm sense of spiritual awakening. What a joy to learn that what I had believed as a child to be true was confirmed in this revelation of Truth. *Science and Health* completely answered my childhood questions and taught me how practical Truth is. I was learning to live each day on the premise that I was, in reality, a perfect child of God.

As I mentioned above, not for one moment did I suffer any discomfort from the cessation of taking the drugs. I can hardly describe my gratitude for my release from this material reliance. (A few years earlier I had suffered personality changes and mental depression, which were eventually attributed to the drugs I had been taking since my teens.) The healing of addiction has been complete, as has my healing of the thyroid condition. Before my introduction to Christian Science, a specialist had been retained to treat this disorder. Later, at the insistence of my parents, I returned to this doctor one last time. There I submitted to a series of tests, which had always indicated a deficiency, but which now showed that I was normal.

Some weeks after that, I discovered that I was forgetting to wear my glasses. At first I would rush home to get them, since I was restricted to wearing glasses while driving. They were always the first things I put on in the morning and the last I removed at night. Finally it dawned on me that I was forgetting them because I no longer needed them! I have not worn glasses since that date and have passed all my driving tests without them. The healing has been permanent.

By the way, after my brother's safe return from Vietnam, we briefly spoke of the time in question. He *had* been in extreme danger, and he reported that a calm sense of direction replaced his initial fear. He was able to make decisions that helped save the lives of many men, and he was later awarded the Silver Star Medal.

JUDITH HAHNSSEN-SCHWAB
White Plains, New York
The Christian Science Journal October 1985

3

Healing through prayer—a change of thought

Because of the direct connection between thought and experience, what we think can affect our health, happiness, and well-being. How much better, as these writers have found, when one's thinking is changed and improved through God's love.

I learned that my relation to God could not be broken.

I was a medical nurse with an RN degree and a master's degree in education, with a nursing major. When I was in my final year of nursing school, there was an instant when I saw very clearly I was in the wrong place; but having invested nearly five years in an undergraduate degree program, I continued on and found that I enjoyed teaching nursing in a community college. My experience included work in obstetrics, in a tuberculosis hospital, and I was head nurse in a kidney dialysis unit. I taught operating room, intensive care and emergency room nursing, and advanced medical-surgical nursing.

In 1973 I was in the midst of a divorce. My husband was an alcoholic, and I was supporting our baby daughter by working two jobs to make ends meet. I was seeing a psychiatrist and taking tranquilizers in order to try to keep going.

One weekend when I was not scheduled to work, I was called to fill a job, and because I needed the money, I accepted. My patient had been in an automobile accident, and her sister was a Christian Science practitioner. We had many conversations.

I knew right away that this Science was what I had been searching for. I had grown up the daughter of a minister, and had left my church when I left home for college. I had continued to love God, but rejected formal religion because of the many things that bothered me about it.

Through all my nursing education and teaching, I'd seen what makes people sick. It is not germs and viruses and organisms, but rather such problems as hate, fear, greed, guilt, grief, and an expectation of mental cause and physical effect, which I could see written on people's bodies. (I had reached these conclusions long before learning of Christian Science.)

In addition, I saw no reliable theory in medicine. I'd seen nursing theory come 360 degrees, going from one extreme to another and back again, during fifteen years of work. It seemed so often that one "authority" who had written a book was contradicted by another who had also written a book. Patients who were expected to recover sometimes did not, and some of those who had been told they were terminally ill did recover! I became convinced that medicine is not a science but a compilation of opinions.

As I studied Christian Science, I began to have many healings. Once my baby had an eye infection. Previously I had been given eye salve to instill several times a day for ten days, to treat the condition. This time I asked a Christian Science practitioner to pray for her, and the whole condition was gone by morning, and it never recurred. Another time, the baby was very feverish. Again I asked a practitioner to pray for her, and immediately she was cool. All fever was gone.

Once I had broken ribs and pneumonia. The practitioner I had called came to visit me and to pray for me. During this healing I became aware that I had broken the bones on the anniversary of the marriage that had ended in divorce, and that I had previously become sick on that same date for a number of years. As a result of the practitioner's treatment, I learned that my relation to God could not be broken, and that I could never be separated from His tender love and care. The severe pain was gone that same day. Within a week I was completely healed of both pneumonia and broken ribs.

I never again suffered from the recurring physical problems, or from the grief and loneliness I had felt from the time my marriage ended.

Christian Science was especially effective in caring for my daughter as she grew up. Her healings were always very quick, and as a parent who wanted the best possible care for her child, I found this particularly impressive. In addition to physical healings, we had healings of financial, unemployment, and housing problems. Relationships have been improved and difficult business situations corrected, all through prayer.

Scientific Christian prayerful treatment goes beyond just healing symptoms. It gets to the heart of the matter and solves the real problem, which is always mental, and this always leaves me a better person. In the course of healing, I have grown spiritually. Many times character transformation has come during physical healing, and I have grown more loving, patient, and principled.

After I began to study Christian Science, I wanted very much not to be a medical nurse anymore, and eventually I was able to find another profession. Because my own life has been transformed, my greatest joy is to share this discovery with others who are searching, as I once was.

JUDITH HEPBURN
Reno, Nevada
Christian Science Sentinel March 13, 1995

The pain, redness, and swelling that had been so evident earlier were completely gone.

Over a period of a few days I began having pain in one tooth. I called a friend of mine, who is also a Christian Scientist, described the difficulty, and asked her to pray for me.

We discussed a feeling of resentment I had been unable to resolve, regarding the way one family member was treating another. I thought this might have some bearing, at least in part, on the difficulty I was having. My friend suggested a number of references for study: articles in Mary Baker Eddy's books, such as "Taking Offense" (*Miscellaneous Writings*, pp. 223–224) and "Ways that are Vain" (*The First Church of Christ, Scientist, and Miscellany*, pp. 210–213), as well as articles from the Christian Science magazines.

My friend talked about the supremacy and allness of good. She pointed out how the chapter from *Science and Health* called "Atonement and Eucharist," relates that during his crucifixion, Jesus had to heal the hatred of what he stood for, more than the pain of being on the cross.

I read in "Taking Offense" that "to punish ourselves for others' faults, is superlative folly. . . . Well may we feel wounded by our own faults; but we can hardly afford to be miserable for the faults of others." I realized I was spending far too much time focusing on the faults I saw in another individual, and on the effects I perceived those faults were having on our family, myself included.

The following day I noticed some physical improvement, and continued my study. Then the next day I had a great deal of pain and it was hard to open my mouth. My husband, who is a physician, wanted to examine my mouth. In the past he had never asked that. I agreed out of respect for his concern. He looked, but didn't discuss his conclusions, knowing that my choice was to rely on prayer.

I found it increasingly difficult to put down my fear, and called my friend again. She quickly agreed to pray some more, and I began to read from the things she suggested. I underlined and reread passages that had particular importance for me, thinking of ways in which their spiritual truths could be helpful in this situation. "Happiness consists in being and in doing good; only what God gives, and what we give ourselves and others through His tenure, confers happiness: conscious worth satisfies the hungry heart, and nothing else can. . . . The Christian Scientist cherishes no resentment; he knows that that would harm him more than all the malice of his foes" (*Message to The Mother Church for 1902,* also by Mrs. Eddy, pp. 17, 19).

After an hour or so, I was aware that the pain, redness, and swelling that had been so evident earlier were completely gone. And although the hour was late, I was filled with renewed energy.

The next morning my husband asked me how I was doing, and I told him that I was healed. I allowed him to look, which he did at some length. Then he said several times, "This is a bona fide, medically documented Christian Science healing!"

My son was listening closely to my husband. When my husband explained the difference in what he had just seen and what he would have witnessed had there been a resolution in the absence of any medical treatment, my son's reaction was that I should send a description of this healing to the *Christian Science Sentinel.*

I thank God for this healing, which our family shared in a special way. I also thank my friend, whose prayers have helped to bring about healing and spiritual growth on numerous occasions. I am also grateful, in the time since this healing occurred, to have seen improvement in the relationship of the two family members for whom I had concern.

PAMELA FAIRBANKS

My medical specialty is diagnosis and treatment of diseases of the head and neck. I examined my wife when she was experiencing pain in her mouth. She had all the signs and symptoms of a significant infection, including a discharge from the gum near the infected tooth.

The following day she had no signs of infection. Had she had a spontaneous resolution in the absence of any medical treatment whatsoever, I would have expected the process to have been gradual, involving pronounced, then slowly diminishing, evidence of abscess. It was evident that this was not the case, as the area was completely normal.

RICHARD D. NICHOLS, M.D.
Grosse Pointe Park, Michigan
Christian Science Sentinel May 1, 1995

Both doctors said a complete hysterectomy would be necessary.

Over nine years ago, to quell family concerns after a fall, I agreed to have a medical examination. Two doctors, one of them a specialist, diagnosed a large tumor behind my uterus. Both said a complete hysterectomy would be necessary. This condition was healed entirely through prayer alone. The healing did not come about immediately; however, along the way I learned many lessons and noticed a major attitude adjustment taking place.

First, fear had to be ruled out of thought. Fear is often the basis of human suffering, and healing lies in acknowledging God's omnipotence and complete, unchanging love for all His children.

In the Bible we find these words: "God hath not given us the spirit of fear; but of power, and of love, and of a sound mind" (II Timothy 1:7). Our Savior, Christ Jesus, bore witness to God's love for man as he healed sickness and sin. As part of his mission he taught his disciples how to do the same. Mary Baker Eddy observes in *Unity of Good*, "He demanded a change of consciousness and evidence, and effected this change through the higher laws of God" (p. 11).

I came to see that in my case I needed such "a change of consciousness and evidence," and that this could only be accomplished through a complete and honest evaluation of my thoughts and motives. I had been in a state of turmoil for as long as I could remember; there were many painful childhood memories that had caused me to see myself as a hapless victim. Each time I felt free of my past, something would erupt to make the unhappy and stressful experiences loom up as real once again. It became clear to me that just burying unpleasant memories wasn't enough. They must be seen for what they were, lies about man, therefore, not to be believed. Why were they lies? Because none of God's children is capable of doing wrong to another, inasmuch as we are each a perfect reflection of the divine Mind, God.

The obvious conclusion, therefore, must be that since all that God made is good, and since He made all, there can be no element of evil present anywhere, not in the form of unloving acts against another, and not in the form of a harmful growth called a tumor. This is a statement of fact based on spiritually scientific law, and there is no material law, absolutely no evidence to the contrary, except for false human belief, which is not law.

Various truths from the Bible and Mary Baker Eddy's writings helped me to realize that the mass that really needed to be removed was one of fear, hatred, and resentment, which I had cherished for a long time. I was learning to view those who I had believed to be my tormentors with Christian understanding and compassion. Forgiveness then became first a possibility, and then a present fact.

As my consciousness became purified in this way, the condition of my body just corresponded with it, until one day the undeniable fact was that I had been healed. The tumor was gone within six months of the diagnosis.

This healing meant a great deal to me, of course. But the thing for which I am most grateful is the renewed interest it brought to my study of Christian Science. Whereas before I had hung around the fringes, taking all the good it could give and giving little in return, now I felt a determination to dedicate myself to studying in earnest the spiritual truth of God, and man made in His image and likeness.

For this "change of consciousness and evidence," which has planted me solidly on the pathway that leads to eternal Truth, I am most thankful.

JOAN C. GOETZ
Aberdeen, Maryland
Christian Science Sentinel February 28, 1994

I had been in prison for nineteen years.

In 1992 a friend and teacher at the prison where I'm serving a life sentence gave me *Science and Health with Key to the Scriptures* by Mary Baker Eddy. I took it to my cell and began reading.

At first much of what I read confused me. But somewhere along the way, things began to make sense. When I would come across something that really puzzled me, I'd go back to my friend. And studying this book along with the Bible, I noticed a difference, a calm in my life that I had never felt before.

Much of my childhood had been spent in reform schools, and I ended up killing a policeman during a bank robbery. Prior to that I had accomplished nothing in my life, other than attaining a reputation as a dangerous young man. That reputation followed me into prison, and at first I lived up to those expectations so as not to let my ego or my friends down.

I had been in prison for nineteen years, and I'd been so dedicated to bitterness and hatred that I didn't want to feel God's love. But the prison instructor who gave me that book was so devoted to God that she was understanding, calm, and fearless. I had never come across anyone like her before. She was the first person who showed me how to go about "getting right with God." It seemed funny because to her it was simple to get back on track, and to me it was hopeless. It was as if she knew the secret and was eager to share it with anyone who asked. With all the awful things I had done, I couldn't imagine that God would embrace me the way He does.

Yet, after I started to read the Bible and *Science and Health,* all the hatred and bitterness that had been there for so many years just left. I don't know exactly when it happened; one day I got up and my life was different. I discovered how to talk with a loving God. I learned that forgiveness wasn't impossible; in fact, it was natural. It was good to know I wasn't trapped. I could be free from sin if I stopped thinking sinfully and committing sinful acts, and learned that I was not a slave to mortal mind. God is my Mind.

Overcoming the life I once lived hasn't been easy for me. I wasn't used to seeing myself as God's good child, and neither were other people. Sometimes it is still very hard. If I didn't have God as my "refuge and strength, a very present help in trouble" (Psalms 46:1), I'd never make it.

One of the wonderful things about God is that He has given each of us the exact ability to love in the same manner as Jesus and his followers loved. All we have to do is do it. Jesus said, "Thou shalt love thy neighbour as thyself" (Matthew 22:39). I had to learn not to look to people's skin color, nationality, religion, or job, and hold it against them. I also learned from this statement that when someone hurts you, no matter who it is, your mom, dad, friend, or a stranger, you must forgive in the same way Jesus forgave the soldiers and the cheering crowds who participated in his crucifixion.

There will be people who say, "Sure he found religion. He's sitting in jail. People like him will do anything to get out." They will call it "jailhouse religion." But no matter what anyone says, I know now that prison can't slow me down. God doesn't care where we are when we take that step toward Him; all that really matters is that we're on the way home.

I pray never to be ignorant of my oneness with God and His love, power, justice, tenderness, and mercy. If there is one thing I've learned it is this: Being ignorant of God is what causes man to do ungodly things. One of my favorite Bible accounts is about Joseph. He asked his master's wife, who was tempting him into the crime of adultery, "How . . . can I do this great wickedness, and sin against God?" (Genesis 39:9).

Name withheld at author's request
Christian Science Sentinel September 5, 1994

The solution for me started with daily *prayer for myself.*

For years I suffered off and on from deep depression and suicidal feelings. While I never actually tried to take my life, the morbid attraction to doing this was so strong at times that I can hardly imagine physical pain could be worse. For anyone who suffers like this, it's pure joy to report healing of such a condition.

Once, prior to my healing, when feeling really low, I called my Christian Science teacher and asked him to help me through prayer. Though I gained some peace, the thing I remember most about our conversation was his saying that the depression would never be really conquered until I learned more of God and my spiritual relation to Him. At the time this answer seemed a little heartless. I guess underneath I was thinking, "Rescue me from this cycle of depression and anguish and then I'll learn more about God." But my teacher knew what I needed, and when I finally saw his point and recognized the genuine Christian concern that had moved him to answer as he did, I was ready to progress.

For the mental torment simply to have been ended would have been "heavenly," a longed-for release. But it would not have given me a real sense of heaven, the bliss that is anchored in a rock-firm grasp of the truth of spiritual being. Such solidly grounded knowing is spiritual sense. *Science and Health* states, "Spiritual sense is a conscious, constant capacity to understand God" (p. 209).

The chronic depression I suffered with resulted in part from deeply rooted attitudes that cried out for change, my ignorance of God manifested in false character traits. The depression seemed to mask the real problems, and it was these deeper causes that needed to be treated, not just the painful symptoms.

The solution for me started with *daily* prayer for myself. Also I not only began to search the Bible and Mary Baker Eddy's writings to gain clearer views of God's nature, but I worked to prayerfully "lay hold" on each new insight, to work with it until it became fixed in thought, and to make a fresh, inspired tour of my growing treasure house of understanding each day. I started to see that God's nature was really the source of *my* nature; that as His dear child I reflected all that He is. And being God's reflection, I realized, did not mean that God projected His divine being into a human "me"; in reality, I was wholly spiritual and always had been, because God is Spirit. As the reflection of God, I was not a pale imitation of the original. Rather, every quality of God—life, integrity, love, wisdom, and so on—was fully expressed in me. I came to pray, "Father, because You are Life, Life is the very substance of my being and the only thing I am really made of." I did the same using the other six synonyms for God that *Science and Health* gives us on page 465, Spirit, Principle, Soul, Love, Mind, Truth.

Daily prayer for myself, far from being selfish, helped me to discover my real, spiritual nature. And instead of separating me from family and friends, this discovery of my spiritual link to the one divine source brought me closer to those around me. It also began to draw me out of the limited sense of myself into which, it seemed, I had been so tightly squeezed.

One part of the trouble had been a preoccupation with *my* needs, *my* desires, *my* views, *my* way of doing things. In other words, self-absorption. Facing it squarely, I saw how central this was to so many of my difficulties. Eventually, through my study of Christian Science I was able, happily, to let it go.

Also connected with depression was sensualism. Mary Baker Eddy points to the connection between passions and self-orientation in these two passages from *Science and Health:* "Vibrating like a pendulum between sin and the hope of forgiveness,—selfishness and sensuality causing constant retrogression,—our moral progress will be slow" (p. 22); and, "Selfishness and sensualism are educated in mortal mind by the thoughts ever recurring to one's self, by conversation about the body, and by the expectation of perpetual pleasure or pain from it; and this education is at the expense of spiritual growth" (p. 260). As these two forceful beliefs were gradually stilled and cast out through divine Love, I found true freedom.

I guess only someone who has experienced the slavery of compulsive desires and wildly swinging moods can know how sweet it is to see them fade. It is a dear-bought blessing to realize something of Mind's control over the body.

Interestingly, during these months, my appetite for food also underwent quite a change, without my even praying specifically about it. Excess pounds simply dropped away, and I have since eaten much less and truly enjoyed what I eat more.

Can any of us be grateful enough for God's bounty extended to all? When we turn with simple, wholehearted trust to our divine Father-Mother, we feel welcomed back into the warmth and security of His love. For such a spiritual homecoming, at least begun, one can only weep tears of joy and say from the heart, "Thank you, Father."

Stephen D. Helmer
Ithaca, New York
The Christian Science Journal April 1983

I am physically and mentally stronger than in many years.

One night in my eighty-eighth year, a relative found me on the floor of my bedroom, unconscious. I was suffering from a deep chest congestion and rasping out each breath with great difficulty. A Christian Science practitioner was called, and she immediately made arrangements for me to be taken to a nearby nursing home for Christian Scientists. There I was promptly given the most skilled Christian Science nursing care, which was to be continued with untiring commitment for the next three weeks. Meantime, the practitioner had continued to pray for me and to spend time at my bedside encouraging me to pray for myself.

Finally, the steadfast insistence of the practitioner that when I thought of man I was to think of God's own expression, began to awaken me. I understood that when I thought of myself I was really thinking of God's expression of good, not of a senior mortal subject to failing strength and faculties.

Pondering the foregoing left me little time for fear, loneliness, self-pity, or gloom of any kind. I began to glimpse that all that is true of myself, or of anyone I knew in my past or present, is what God knows of each one of us. Vividly realizing this spiritual fact of God's man, the only man there is, I was able to make some progress each day in radically changing my view of myself, as well as unscientific concepts of others, which I had unthinkingly clung to for over half a century.

One of my major problems at the time was having to deal with discouragement on days when I was tempted to lapse into old mental attitudes and to lose sight of my need to patiently bring, to the best of my present ability, each thought into alignment with God's spiritual idea. But at such times I was able to accept that the reason each one can work out his own salvation is because to that end God works with us. We read in the Bible, "For it is God which worketh in you both to will and to do of his good pleasure" (Philippians 2:13). As my entire mental outlook changed, so did everything in my life, and for the better. By the time I left the nursing home, I was completely healed of the physical condition that had caused me to be taken there unconscious, and I am physically and mentally stronger than in many years.

This statement in *Science and Health,* I am finding to be a most practical daily reminder: "Men and women of riper years and larger lessons ought to ripen into health and immortality, instead of lapsing into darkness or gloom. Immortal Mind feeds the body with supernal freshness and fairness, supplying it with beautiful images of thought and destroying the woes of sense which each day brings to a nearer tomb" (p. 248).

Lillian F. Hurst
San Diego, California
Christian Science Sentinel August 28, 1978

4

Healing through prayer—awakening to spiritual reality

The power that heals spiritually is God, divine Truth, acting on and changing thought, and therefore our lives. Sometimes, persistent dedication is needed in awaking to the truths of God's presence and power.

I devoted every possible moment to learning all that I could about God.

Evil truly vanishes before a spiritualized consciousness. I submit this testimony hoping to encourage someone else who may be beset by great fear. I have proved the truth of Paul's words, "To be spiritually minded is life and peace" (Romans 8:6). Some individuals may have to dig deeper or work harder than others, but victory awaits sincere effort in a spiritual direction.

In May, 1959, I had a miscarriage. Serious loss of blood was involved. The obstetrician insisted that I go to the hospital. I felt it was necessary to comply. Two other specialists were called in by the obstetrician, and they requested permission to operate the next day. I was resolved not to have surgery. As a result, I was released in four days to go home.

A week later one of the doctors called me on the telephone and asked me to come to his office for further checkups. I replied that I was sure I could take care of myself and would have no further need for medical attention. He then firmly and bluntly informed me that a malignancy was evident and that unless I accepted their attentions I would be dead within six months. He said that I should remember I had three young children and a husband to think about and that they deserved my full consideration in this matter.

I had never known any religion but Christian Science. Over the years healings had always taken place—sometimes quickly, sometimes slowly—and it was only natural for me to want to work out this problem the same way, but I couldn't seem to settle myself down or know where to begin.

At a Christian Science lecture my husband and I attended, the lecturer told of a healing of a man with an incurable disease. He had accepted this verdict about himself, but decided that before he died he wanted to know as much about God as he possibly could; so he took the Concordances to Mary Baker Eddy's writings and started to look up all the references on God. Before he was half through with this study, he found himself healed.

I felt I had received a direction in which to travel. When I later opened the Concordance to *Science and Health with Key to the Scriptures* by Mary Baker Eddy and saw all the pages of references on God, I felt momentarily confused and wondered where to start; but the angel message came: to be orderly, and to start at the beginning.

Because the material picture of illness loomed so large in my thought, it was difficult for me to concentrate on spiritual things; so I decided to write out some of the paragraphs. I wrote extensively, and this helped me to retain the message.

The spiritual education I received as a result of this work is greater than I can ever put into words. Within three weeks I was a new person, mentally and physically; I was so uplifted that although I felt free, I could not stop this study program.

After going through all the references on God, I decided to go through synonyms for God.

This spiritual growth revealed to me that the main error needing to be eliminated was "righteous indignation." In the guise of righteousness, indignation can seem very justified; but any indignation is mortal mind and must be ruled out of the human experience.

Jesus' parable of the sower (see Luke 8:4–15) became a firm rod in my hand particularly the verses that deal with the seed sown on a rock, and Jesus' explanation that this refers to those who receive the word with joy, but when tribulation comes, do not stay with it. Oh, what I learned as I read the Bible and Mrs. Eddy's writings from cover to cover. I can truly say I was reborn!

This Bible reference was especially helpful, "In returning and rest shall ye be saved; in quietness and in confidence shall be your strength" (Isaiah 30:15). I willingly accepted this instruction, and I have since considered it to be a most valuable bit of counsel that kept me going in the right direction. I gave up the outside activities I was engaged in and have never had the desire or the time to return to them, although they were humanly good. It unfolded to me that my great hunger and thirst after spiritual things should be satisfied at all costs.

For about six months I did only the most urgently needed housework. What could wait, I let wait. I did no entertaining, but devoted every possible moment to learning all that I could about God. In the early weeks of this experience I didn't sleep day or night, but after I started a definite study program, rest came. I experienced no weariness or ill effects from this. I was learning that victory can come by obeying rules, and I diligently sought out those rules. Putting them into practice was not easy, but perseverance has paid big dividends.

Jesus' instruction, "If a man keep my saying, he shall never see death" (John 8:51), led me to search the four Gospels with close scrutiny in order to become familiar with his sayings. I pondered his parables and have arrived at the conclusion within myself that strict obedience to them will solve any problem. The wisdom they contain when they are understood spiritually is priceless and beyond measure.

As a result of this healing, I had only one desire—to help others who might be floundering, to arrive at the same degree of peace which has been mine over many years and in spite of many hurdles. This desire lends purpose to my life, strengthens and lengthens my days. I don't know any idle moments, as there is much more to learn.

Antoinette Finstad
Long Beach, California
The Christian Science Journal October 1975

The doctor's first words were, "Your son will never play football."

At one point my son, Don, was invited to be on the varsity football team of his high school. This was a dream come true for him. It is required that each football player take a yearly physical examination to determine his fitness for this strenuous sport, and so my son was examined.

When I came home from the office on the day of the exam, Don told me that the doctor had not signed his release and wanted me to call him. The doctor's first words to me were, "Your son will never play football." He said that Don had an incurable heart condition and would always have to live a quiet life in order to live at all. The doctor asked me to bring Don to his clinic on Saturday for further examination to determine what limited physical activity he could engage in. I agreed to do this. Then I told Don all that the doctor had said.

"Mom, you mean I can never play football again?" This was a cry of total despair!

This happened on Wednesday. I asked Don if he would be willing to spend every spare moment until Saturday in prayer and study with me. We had a wonderful time. We studied the healings of Christ Jesus in the Bible. We saw how compassionate he was toward those he healed. We noted that Jesus had completely disregarded matter as having anything to do with man's true identity. When he healed the man at the pool of Bethesda he said, "Rise, take up thy bed, and walk" (John 5:8).

This man had not walked for thirty-eight years. Yet Jesus did not say, "Lean on me; your legs are weak because you haven't used them for a long time. I'll help you up and heal you." No! The man obeyed Jesus' command: "And immediately the man was made whole, and took up his bed, and walked" (John 5:9). What a marvelous illustration of God's law in operation, and of mankind's receptivity to it.

We explored Mary Baker Eddy's writings to see what she has to say about *heart, body, man, function,* and *life.* The research was inspiring and joyous, not heavy with the feeling that we had three days to meet this condition so that Don could play football!

One statement in *Science and Health* really stood out to us: "Correct material belief by spiritual understanding, and Spirit will form you anew. You will never fear again except to offend God, and you will never believe that heart or any portion of the body can destroy you" (p. 425).

On Saturday we went to the doctor's office. I stayed in the waiting room. In about an hour the doctor and Don came out. The doctor was carrying charts over his arm and shaking his head. He said, "What have you been doing between Wednesday and today? I have given this boy several tests, and the conclusive evidence that was there on Wednesday is just not here today. He is perfectly sound. I can release him for all the strenuous activity he wants. What has brought about this remarkable change?"

Don told him that we were Christian Scientists and that we had been praying. The doctor told him to keep it up because it obviously worked.

Don went on to play three years of varsity football in high school and four years in college. He then was assistant football coach at a college for seven years. He also played rugby and tennis. There was never a return of the condition.

How grateful we can be for this "bugle-call" when it leads us to a deeper understanding of God and to a desire to express this understanding in our daily life.

Rhea Robertson Buck
Seattle, Washington

I would like to add that this particular healing really changed my outlook on life. It opened my eyes to the fact of man's true nature, that he is not a flimsy mortal at the beck and call of every so-called mortal law; he is a spiritual idea of God.

There have been many times when this healing has reassured me and led me to learn more of God and His spiritual image, man. This has resulted in my complete reliance on God in meeting some severe physical difficulties and in the course of my daily activity.

I would like to express my heartfelt gratitude for my mother and my grandmother because of the courageous and beautiful examples they've set for me over the years. Thanks to them, turning to God directly for help has been as natural as breathing in our family.

Donald Scott Houge
Boston, Massachusetts
Christian Science Sentinel January 21, 1991

The dentist scheduled me for an appointment the very next day.

When a tooth started twinging one day after I bit down on something hard, I went to the dentist, believing a filling had loosened. To my dismay, however, his study of an X-ray led to a much different diagnosis: an abscessed condition. Feeling that removal of one tooth which he deemed too far gone to save plus a root canal operation on the two adjacent teeth constituted the best course of action, the dentist scheduled me for an appointment the very next day. Part of the fear I felt was due to my ignorance of what the condition meant. The dentist indicated there was no specific or single cause for such a condition. As he spoke, the words *curse causeless* came to my thought. I recognized them as from the Bible verse, "As the bird by wandering, as the swallow by flying, so the curse causeless shall not come" (Proverbs 26:2). Here was immediate comfort and reassurance to turn my thought in the right direction!

I was on active military duty overseas. There seemed to be no possibility of contacting a Christian Science practitioner, and I did not see how I could have the operation postponed. Alone in my barracks room, I again felt very fearful and even a bit resentful at the thought of losing a tooth. So, I prayerfully read the Bible and Mary Baker Eddy's writings until finally this phrase gave me assurance. I read in Isaiah, "In quietness and in confidence shall be your strength" (30:15). I saw that no circumstance, no matter how dire, could shake my inner conviction that a correct understanding of God would heal—would bring about whatever adjustment was necessary to restore harmony.

Praying now to realize more of this healing understanding, I found another Bible verse: "Let my mouth be filled with thy praise and with thy honour all the day" (Psalms 71:8). Although the Psalmist undoubtedly had songs of praise in thought, I chose to interpret the reference quite literally. Soon gaining peace about the situation, I turned in for a good night's rest.

The next day the dentist again made an X-ray, preliminary to the operation. Comparing it with the first, for a long minute he just stood there head cocked, one arm akimbo. Finally he turned to me and exclaimed, "I simply don't understand this! On the basis of this second X-ray there's absolutely no justification for an operation: no indication of abscess whatever." All he could do was to advise me, somewhat in amazement, to return in six months for a normal checkup. This incident occurred several years ago, and there has been no evidence that the healing has been other than complete and permanent.

For these and numerous other healing experiences, and for the attendant spiritual awakening they bring, I am indeed grateful!

Richard Lee Peters
Rockville, Maryland
Christian Science Sentinel December 5, 1977

I felt life wasn't worth living.

Early one morning a severe pain in my neck woke me. Within a few days, the pain had enveloped my whole body, and I was almost paralyzed. Although a Christian Science practitioner prayed for me for about six months, I was not diligently striving to understand the truths of Christian Science myself, and healing did not come. As I lead a very active life, the immobility was very alarming to me.

My family became concerned and insisted that I have the condition diagnosed. I dismissed the practitioner. A doctor could neither locate the illness nor identify the condition; all he could do was offer me pills for the pain, which I felt did not have any power to help me, so I did not use them. When the condition grew even worse, my family took me to another doctor. His nurse phoned later and said that she had reserved a room for me in a hospital; I was to go in the next day for more tests.

I decided not to go to the hospital but to call a relative who is a Christian Science practitioner and find out what she had to say. I'll never forget the love she expressed so naturally. What relief I felt when she simply assured me that the law of

God heals. I had previously had many such healings, and this was just what I yearned to hear.

A friend drove me the several hundred miles to my relative's home, where I stayed for several weeks. This cousin and I spent time each day discussing spiritual truths from the Bible, the authority for Mary Baker Eddy's writings. My cousin quickly zeroed in on several things that needed to be healed. One was my reluctance to study. She put me to work researching the Bible and *Science and Health* to find specific qualities of God that man expresses. She urged me to make these qualities "my own." I realized I couldn't get by with mere surface or slipshod study. She was persistent. But I was learning so much I didn't mind. I was really studying Christian Science for the first time in my life and was enjoying it.

One evening, though, the pain and fever that often accompanied this condition returned with such severity that I felt life wasn't worth living. This occurred at a time when my cousin had another commitment and was away overnight. She was, however, continuing prayerful Christian Science treatment for me. She had made arrangements for her sister to stay with me. I complained, "If this painful existence is to constitute my life, I'm just going to die." This cousin then said, "And just where do you think you're going? Let's work with the Lord's Prayer." I didn't even want to do this. I didn't want to be bothered with it. But she knew she had to awaken my thought to realize my spiritual perfection. She insisted that I declare this prayer and respond to what each phrase meant to me, little by little. Then she went to the piano and played and sang hymns. This was a turning point in my healing. When she finished her repertoire, I went to sleep and had the best night's sleep I'd had for months.

A few days later I was well enough to return home. To my surprise, I found I was reluctant to leave; I didn't want to lose all the love my cousins were surrounding me with. After my return, there still followed a few weeks of slight discomfort, but I stayed with the study. And one day, when I leaned over to put food down for my cat, I realized I was completely free of pain. I was healed! As only the cat was present, I yelled in joy and gratitude, "I'm healed! Thank you, God, for Your goodness!" That afternoon, for the first time in many months, I went out for a walk.

In retrospect I questioned myself, "Why did it take me so long to realize my freedom, when God's laws of spiritual truth had been operating all the time?" The answer came to me in this way: my awakening to the joy of *learning* the truth had come first; then had come my awakening to the need to stay alert to these truths by *declaring* them. Merely researching and learning them intellectually was not enough. These were just the first footsteps, arousing me to begin *living* these truths. I was learning that putting them into practice leads to *proving* them to be true.

I also learned the importance of patience in prayer for healing. Patience had never been one of my virtues. This healing required patient yielding to the truth that neither the body nor time governs my thinking. Only God does. I'm still praying to have and express a clearer concept of patience.

Even now, nine years later, I sometimes go back to the notes I took, and I still profit from the inspiration they bring. I am grateful for the permanency of spiritual healing.

Mary B. McKeand
Nashville, Tennessee
Christian Science Sentinel March 27, 1995

I began to realize that I was not simply trying to heal a discordant body.

During the summer between my junior and senior years at college, doctors diagnosed that I had a tumor on the pituitary gland. A few days later a friend gave me a copy of *Science and Health*. The first paragraph I read was this one: "When man is governed by God, the ever-present Mind who understands all things, man knows that with God all things are possible. The only way to this living Truth, which heals the sick, is found in the Science of divine Mind as taught and demonstrated by Christ Jesus" (p. 180).

These words gave me hope! As I continued to read *Science and Health,* I glimpsed the truth that God, Love, doesn't cause or endorse suffering. I was healed of constant back pain due to a car accident, which had troubled me for five years.

When I realized I didn't have any more pain, it occurred to me that I could apply what I had just learned about God to other problems. In the next few moments the fear of recurring tonsillitis and the desire for alcohol were destroyed. These healings have been permanent.

I was so grateful for the release from these physical difficulties, and I was thrilled and in awe of what I was learning of God. To be able to turn to God for comfort and healing was a new concept for me. The churches I had attended during high school and college, in the course of my search for answers to questions about God, held God to be distant and aloof, knowing and sometimes ordaining evil, and powerless on most occasions to save mankind from sickness and suffering.

My first healings gave me the courage to rely on the laws of God to heal the tumor. I released the doctors and wrote to a Christian Science practitioner who lived near my college to request help through prayer. While at college, I visited her frequently; and her unflinching confidence in God's power to heal was a great comfort to me.

As I prayed, I felt a transformation taking place in my character. Depression, impatience, and resentment lessened and began to be replaced by hope and forgiveness. Fear was destroyed as I began to glimpse God's love for me.

I distinctly remember coming across this sentence in *Science and Health:* "Give up the belief that mind is, even temporarily, compressed within the skull, and you will quickly become more manly or womanly" (p. 397). I saw the fallacy in believing that intelligence originates in a brain and that the amount of intelligence I could express was determined by heredity and environmental influences. Armed with trust that God, Mind, was the source of all intelligence, I was able to complete successfully all of the assignments in my double major, and my grades improved dramatically.

Over the next several months, while in graduate school, I prayed daily for myself in order to understand the fact of my spiritual identity. I based my prayer on the fact that man is created in the image and likeness of God. I denied that evil could be attached to a spiritual idea and persistently affirmed man's spiritual perfection.

It took a lot of effort for me to hold thought to the truth of a perfect God and perfect man. As I continued, however, I began to realize that I was not simply trying to heal a discordant body. I was praying to understand man's present spiritual perfection and to eradicate a dark image from my thought. This statement from *Science and Health* was very helpful: "Tumors, ulcers, tubercles, inflammation, pain, deformed joints, are waking dream-shadows, dark images of mortal thought, which flee before the light of Truth" (p. 418). As I pondered these truths, the constant worry about the tumor began to fade.

Throughout subsequent months of study and spiritual growth, I read many testimonies of healing and articles in the Christian Science magazines. I often went to a Christian Science Reading Room. One day I came to an article in which a woman shared her healing of a tumor. She had prayed to gain a clearer understanding of man's true, spiritual substance. While pondering the ideas she shared, I glimpsed that man, made in God's image and likeness, is not material at all. His substance, the essence of his being, is spiritual. I was so grateful for this truth. I was filled with joy and gained more confidence that I could be healed.

There were times when I felt discouraged and sorry for myself. But when I turned to God I was always uplifted and comforted. And I knew progress was being made because other troubles—colds, burns, painful joints, and relationship difficulties—were quickly healed through prayer.

As I continued to pray, daily headaches, narrow vision, and fatigue disappeared. I was able to participate in athletics and other activities completely free from pain. I remember clearly the time about four years ago when I realized I was completely well.

Heather Pedersen
Boston, Massachusetts
Christian Science Sentinel February 19, 1990

SECTION II

Healing and guidance in every stage of life

Prayer is practical at every stage of human experience. In this section writers of all ages tell how the problems of work and school, the heartaches of relationships, the uncertainties of health, give way to spiritual solutions. Even difficulties starting before birth are not excluded from God's law of healing.

5

Hereditary conditions healed

Hereditary diseases seem to be an unfair fact of human life. The spiritual law however, is that true heritage comes from "Our Father which art in heaven." As the Psalmist puts it, "Yea, I have a goodly heritage" (Psalms 16:6).

The condition was cystic fibrosis—believed to be hereditary, incurable, and terminal.

From the time our daughter, Laurie, was two years old, she had breathing problems. We took her to pediatricians many times, but nobody could diagnose the problem—or offer any treatment to help.

This condition eventually affected Laurie's breathing all the time. During the day, it produced noises, and she was teased about this in school. From the beginning, Laurie and I were awake nearly every night with the problem. On vacations the entire family was affected. Also, when we traveled, often Laurie would be carsick. When our daughter was eleven, Christian Science was presented to me, and with it came a glimmer of hope.

The writings of Mary Baker Eddy, especially her book *Science and Health with Key to the Scriptures*, explained that a mental change of base from the transient things of matter to the invariable, spiritual ideas of God brings healing. Years of frustration had readied me to embrace this change of heart and thought, and now I wholeheartedly stepped out into this new view as fast as I could.

There was much to learn, to ponder, to understand. *Science and Health* opened the Bible to me and made me increasingly aware of the spiritual Science that weaves its way throughout the Bible. As a matter of fact, this textbook led me to read and study the Scriptures for the first time in my life.

In the Bible I found stories that told of release from bondage. Laurie and I were pretty much homebound—because although from the time she was school age she could attend school (and, later, Sunday School), she could do little else. It seemed as though we were hostages of sorts most of the time.

The book of Acts tells about Paul and Silas being released from the prison stocks as they prayed and sang praises to God (16:25). A promise, a new idea, touched me in reading—not just one but two people were released through prayer and praise of God. It gave me hope that *both* the child and I could be freed from bondage to disease.

One other early discovery through Bible study released me from the belief that this illness was hereditary—that I was guilty somehow of inflicting this ailment on my daughter. In the ninth chapter of John is the account of the healing of the man who was blind since birth. When asked if the man or the parents had sinned, causing this blindness, Christ Jesus answered, "Neither hath this man sinned, nor his parents: but that the works of God should be made manifest in him" (verse 3). Not only was this a release from the terrible label of heredity, but it gave assurance that the manifestation of health and wholeness could be accomplished.

After this, my confidence in God just grew and grew. I began to realize that the allness of God must replace the evidences of matter and disease. And so there was a need for me to learn everything possible about God. Synonyms for God that describe His nature were studied. And particular characteristics of each synonym were studied and thought about until understood—characteristics such as the breath of Life, the ideas of Mind, the loyalty of Truth, the perfection of Love, the law of Principle, the immortality of Soul, and so forth.

During this early study, I prayed the best I knew how. But our daughter's health continued to deteriorate. One day when our daughter was fourteen, our neighbor across the street—a surgeon and longtime friend—came over and told me that our daughter was in serious trouble. From what he was observing, he said, things looked very bad for her.

My husband and I felt so grateful for this loving concern of our neighbor. The verdict of a medical diagnosis was that the condition was cystic fibrosis—believed to be hereditary, incurable, and terminal. The doctors gave no hope. Now, more than ever, I wanted to seek Christian healing for our daughter. My husband, though not a Christian Scientist, was fully supportive of this desire. He asked, however, that I take Laurie for regular medical examinations, and I did. At that time I also agreed that she sleep in a vapor tent at night, but this was no help and was discontinued after a few weeks.

Circumstances had now brought me to a point of total humility. And now I also saw that absolute dedication to this demonstration was needed.

This promoted a change in my approach to praying for our daughter. From then on, every time her condition was "updated" on visits to the medical specialist, I worked specifically to reverse, through prayerful treatment, whatever was predicted or diagnosed.

For instance, with respect to breathing I found this statement of Mary Baker Eddy's in *The First Church of Christ, Scientist, and Miscellany* that touched me deeply: "Christian Science is at length learned to be no miserable piece of ideal legerdemain, by which we poor mortals expect to live and die, but a deep-drawn breath fresh from God, by whom and in whom man lives, moves, and has deathless being" (p. 195).

I saw this statement as a spiritual explication of breathing—the life-giving inspiration of the strength and activity of God who is Life.

One night I spent many hours in study and yielding to the power of divine Mind and Life. These words from *Science and Health* seemed to cap the work: "Mind's infinite ideas run and disport themselves. In humility they climb the heights of holiness" (p. 514).

With that truth I knew with all my heart that God did not see our daughter as a little bag of bones—disabled and frail—lying in a bed, but as His very daughter, His perfect likeness. Therefore, I could go to bed knowing that the facts were as He saw them and that He forever sees what He has made.

That night, for the first time in years, I was able to put Laurie in God's hands, in the hands of eternal Life. I slept through the night; so did she.

From that time Laurie began to grow and to laugh, to come alive. She began to eat more and to gain weight. She grew taller. She laughed! The atmosphere at home became happier. The family laughed—together. Love was being expressed with hugs and time to listen. It was not pity, because there was absolutely no acceptance of disease or confinement, no "biting of the bullet," so to speak, but a freedom, a new spirit in the family. We were *all* growing and experiencing healing.

Our daughter and I also found a sense of *belonging* as we learned to view the real nature of individuals and objects as ideas, or thoughts, in Mind. It took some time to sort out the concept of being made "in the image of God," divine Mind. But we began to realize that identity needed to be seen as God's *reflection* rather than as a piece or a part of God, divine intelligence, trapped inside a body, or matter.

Studying the first chapter of Genesis opened our eyes to the allness and goodness of God's presence: "And God saw every thing that he had made, and, behold, it was very good" (verse 31). I saw the fullness of creation, Soul's reflection, as a bouquet and the identity of individuals as single flowers, each having a place in but not making up the entire bouquet. With this, I gained a new view of the spiritual family of man, as "hid with Christ in God" (Colossians 3:3).

Each specific aspect of this claim of disease about which I was told, I treated in the same manner. I would discover the spiritual counterfact to the material counterfeit and work to understand it until I felt its reality.

I saw that I had been given a Science detailed and definite enough to counter all the particulars of material education and assumption—to expose the case against Laurie and to overturn it completely. Christian Science, I was seeing so vividly, was never mere "promise" and "hope" but specific spiritual law that, when plumbed to its depths, was more than sufficient to meet and master the spirit of this world and all its manifestations.

Early on, when told by the doctors that our daughter would die within a month's time, I spoke aloud to them, "I don't believe in death. I believe in Life." That realization was for me immediate and concrete. From that point on, the doctors and medical staff saw specific symptoms disappearing or conditions changing for the better without another word being voiced. And they acknowledged this.

One day I studied this statement about God in the Old Testament, in Habakkuk: "Thou art of purer eyes than to behold evil" (1:13). Possible original meanings of the word *purer* in Hebrew I found were "clean, fair, bright, unadulterated, and uncontaminated." How could an uncontaminated spiritual idea be diseased? How can there be such a thing as incurability? I thought. A spiritual idea could never be diseased. Our daughter had in truth never been diseased. Illness had clearly been a lie about her.

Evidence of this spiritual fact kept coming until it was obvious that the healing of thought had brought about a complete physical transformation. Our daughter was healed.

Laurie graduated from high school when she was eighteen and has lived a normal life ever since. The community accepted the healing. Even the medical specialist accepted it. He said, "If I hadn't seen this with my own eyes, I never would have believed it."

Throwing out the "old garment" of the belief of man living in matter, and touching the hem of Christ's garment of spiritual truth, was the key to the scientific Christianity that the Way-shower, Christ Jesus, demonstrated for all time. It is exactly what Mrs. Eddy discovered. And she writes in *Science and Health:* "The lightnings and thunderbolts of error may burst and flash till the cloud is cleared and the tumult dies away in the distance. Then the raindrops of divinity refresh the earth. As St. Paul says: 'There remaineth therefore a rest to the people of God' (of Spirit)" (p. 288). How grateful I am to God.

SHIRLEY ANDREW ALLARD

I am the daughter of Shirley and Art Allard. The healing my mother wrote about concerning me is correct. Today I am a very active mother of two teenage boys. I would be grateful if this testimony would give the reader hope that nothing is impossible to God.

LAURIE LANDSBAUM

I am a retired physician and surgeon. The Allards have been neighbors and friends of ours (my wife and me) for many years.

As a neighbor I saw Mr. and Mrs. Allard and Laurie quite often. At one point it was evident to me that Laurie was experiencing retardation of growth, labored breathing, and physical deterioration.

Laurie's mother and father are loving, supportive parents, and I was informed that Laurie was being taken for observation and recommendations to physicians. Laurie's mother, Shirley, is a most conscientious woman and provided a tremendous amount of support and love during that period of Laurie's life.

Remarkably, as time passed, it was evident that Laurie's general health—including physical development—gradually improved. It was also evident that strong, loving support was provided to Laurie.

Today Laurie is a grown married woman and has given birth to two physically normal children, now ages seventeen and fourteen. Laurie has surmounted tremendous past obstacles and possesses an obvious great strength of spirit.

Name withheld at author's request
Des Peres, Missouri
The Christian Science Journal June 1992

What a great feeling that was—
my very first healing through reading
Science and Health!

For ten years I suffered from attacks of sinusitis. After I had taken various medicines and used nose drops and inhalations, this problem was diagnosed as chronic by a well-known specialist. He said that I would have to live with this condition because of an irregular bone growth in my nose. I was also told that I was acutely allergic to dust. (While teaching at college I had to cover the chalk with paper, as otherwise I would immediately start sneezing.)

For about seven years I also suffered from severe kidney trouble. I went through various types of medical treatment, saw specialists, had numerous X-rays, and had a minor operation. Finally I was told that I would also have to live with this problem, as it was hereditary. (My grandmother had suffered from this condition.) And as if these problems were not enough, in 1975 I was told that I had developed tuberculosis. I had medical treatment for a while, but when I came back to Bombay (earlier I had been in Madras), I was so fearful that I didn't approach a doctor. This disease and the other illnesses loomed in front of me like threatening dragons. Little did I know then that there was something far greater than all of them. Late in 1978 I learned of Christian Science through reading a copy of the *Christian Science Sentinel* shared with me by a friend.

One day at work I was having problems with my throat and could not speak. I had to write down whatever I wanted to say. I was encouraged by friends to "take something"—medicine. I drank cups of hot soup and tea, expecting them to help. But the condition remained the same.

Finally I felt led to go to a Christian Science Reading Room. There I started reading the chapter "Prayer" in *Science and Health*. When I came to page 14 of the book, I could not move beyond these lines in the second paragraph: "Become conscious for a single moment that Life and intelligence are purely spiritual,—neither in nor of matter,—and the body will then utter no complaints. If suffering from a belief in sickness, you will find yourself suddenly well."

I could not believe what I was reading. Was I suffering only from a belief? This was a new way of thinking, and I liked it! I read these sentences over and over, trying to understand the whole message.

When my lunch hour was over, I put away the book (though not the thoughts) and walked back to work, humming something. What a lovely surprise I received as I entered my office. I was asked a question by someone, and out came my reply—clearly and normally. What a great feeling that was—my very first healing through reading *Science and Health!* I had no further problems with my throat.

But the greatness of God's love and presence was revealed even more fully after this healing when I received a bonus at work. About this time, I was offered a permanent position but I was required to have a medical examination and only if I were declared physically fit could I be made a permanent employee. To my great surprise and joy, I was declared physically fit. Though I did inform the doctor of the previously named conditions when questioned, no further mention was made of them—by the doctor or me. I have remained in good health since.

Truly in "a single moment" of realizing my true identity as a child of God—pure, perfect, loved, and cherished—many false beliefs were wiped out and the mirror cleaned, whereby I saw myself as I am—the reflection of God, good. How can I not sing praises? Dear God, how great Thou art!

Neera Kapur
Bombay, India
Christian Science Sentinel March 31, 1986

She had the symptoms of an autistic child.

At the birth of our second daughter, I was aware that something was wrong. During this daughter's early development, it became evident that her motor skills and mental growth were retarded. While the case was never diagnosed by the medical profession, she had the symptoms of an autistic child. She was content to be alone in her own little world, and she developed idiosyncrasies that set her apart from other children. By the age of three she had never spoken a word. She also had an unnatural eye condition.

This period was a great trial for me. Until this time my life had been a breezy, carefree one. Marriage to a delightful husband had brought a first daughter who was unusually bright, alert, and articulate. My happy home seemed to lose much of its bloom.

One thought kept nagging me. Why had this problem come to me? This human questioning awakened me to my deep need. I knew this was now my greatest opportunity to rely unreservedly on God. I realized that I must give this child over completely to His infinite care and all-embracing love.

As I read *Science and Health* I was impressed with this sentence: "The offspring of heavenly-minded parents inherit more intellect, better balanced minds, and sounder constitutions" (p. 61). I felt encouraged to prove the reality of this statement.

Christ Jesus' words, "With God all things are possible" (Matthew 19:26), comforted me greatly. Also, when Jesus was questioned about why a certain man was born blind, he dismissed any human reasoning on the subject and took the case straight to God. In his answer there is no search for a material cause. To my thought his words point to man's true spiritual origin and perfect state intact—"that the works of God should be made manifest in him" (John 9:3).

I began to glorify God each day. I became increasingly conscious of His grandeur and goodness and of my gratitude to

Him. I was grateful to know that in God's spiritual realm this child was His reflection, never born into matter but known to Him as divine idea. I was grateful that my husband encouraged me to work this problem out in Christian Science, even though he was not studying it at that time.

Two errors in my own thought came to the surface during this period of spiritually scientific study. One was the habit of comparing this little girl to her older sister and to children her own age. The other error to be overcome was the mental plague of "What will people think?"

As I earnestly practiced seeing the child as God's full expression, a false sense of responsibility and pride lifted from me. An overly sensitive attitude and defensiveness began to fade away. People's opinions and curious remarks distressed me less. I disciplined myself to mentally ask: What is God knowing about this child?

An interesting thing happened. People stopped asking me questions about how many doctors and therapy clinics I'd consulted. Our child responded to my freshly inspired consciousness and began to improve noticeably.

We were able to enroll her in a nursery school. I will always be grateful to the school and to the teacher. Under her loving care our daughter learned to adjust to her classmates, take some part in group activity, and attend to her personal needs.

On her fourth birthday she still had not uttered a word. One afternoon a feeling of desperation so gripped me, I sobbed uncontrollably. If she never talks, I thought, she'll never have a normal school experience. I was at this time expecting our third child, and I became filled with fear for the new baby.

The heaviness of the problem prompted me to call a Christian Science practitioner immediately. With a great sense of peace and assurance in God's omnipotence she directed me to the story of Moses in the fourth chapter of Exodus. The following dialogue stirred me beyond what my own words can express: "Moses said unto the Lord, O my Lord, I am not eloquent, . . . but I am slow of speech, and of a slow tongue. And the Lord said unto him, Who hath made man's mouth? . . . have not I the Lord? Now therefore go, and I will be with thy mouth, and teach thee what thou shalt say" (Exodus 4:10–12).

As I contemplated the spiritual significance of Moses' communion with God, a great surge went through me. All fear, all doubt left me. I became conscious of God's presence as never before. I felt the power of His infinity, His absolute allness, His perfection, encompassing me and this child. I knew that a divine experience had touched my human consciousness and that all was well. It was at that moment that I knew our little girl was healed.

I continued to pray and ponder. This statement from *Science and Health* cemented the healing for me: "The influence or action of Soul confers a freedom, which explains the phenomena of improvisation and the fervor of untutored lips" (p. 89).

This took place around Thanksgiving. Our daughter began to use words naturally and with great enthusiasm from that time on. There was no struggle, no laborious effort. The words simply began to flow. By New Year's Day her vocabulary and her enunciation were comparable to those of her age level, and the following fall she qualified for the reading readiness program in her kindergarten class.

All traces of the mental and physical handicap gradually disappeared. She became a fine student earning honor grades through high school. She is now attending a university. During high school she passed the visual part of her driver's test with ease and without the use of glasses.

Anne Stearns Condon
Encino, California
Christian Science Sentinel February 6, 1978

He believed I had less than a year to live.

"Thy testimonies have I taken as an heritage for ever: for they are the rejoicing of my heart" (Psalms 119:111).

I entered the business world as a young adult with a great sense of failure because of previous serious mistakes I'd made. My past record disqualified me from pursuing certain lifelong professional goals, so I turned at last to a company with ties to my family, and they gave me a job.

I felt a heavy burden of guilt for vanished life prospects, which seemed then irretrievably lost, and for the shame and disappointment I felt I had brought on my family and friends. Mired as I was in this depressing mental state, my work at the company was halfhearted at best. I just could not seem to shake the imprisoning belief that I was unloved and unwanted.

Then I began to manifest physical symptoms of pain in breathing. I finally had two physical examinations. The first doctor, my secretary's husband, diagnosed the problem as heart disease and urged me to obtain a second opinion. Through contact with my father's side of the family who were not Christian Scientists, I was examined by an eminent heart specialist in our city. At the end of several days of testing, he confirmed the diagnosis of heart disease, mentioning that according to medical records my father's family had a history of fatal heart disease.

He told me that he believed I had less than a year to live. He urged me to resign my job immediately and avoid exerting myself, even slightly. Then he gave me some pills, saying that, at all costs, I must get one into my mouth when the next attack occurred. I looked at the pills and asked if there were any drugs or surgery that could help me permanently. He sadly shook his head, and I remember his eyes filled with tears. In desperation I asked if he could recommend something, anything at all. To my astonishment, he suggested I might try Christian Science.

I left his office, and as I walked down the street, I thought, "I don't want to die. I want to live." In my mind, the doctor's suggestion was nothing less than a clear call to return to the study of Christian Science. At that moment I had a feeling of coming home. As I reached out mentally to God—with all my heart and without reservation—I remembered the first sentence I'd read as a child from *Science and*

Health, "To those leaning on the sustaining infinite, to-day is big with blessings" (p. vii). I decided right then to rely only on God, my true Father and Mother, to save me.

I drove to the home of a Christian Science practitioner who had stood by me through all my formative years in Science. She heard me out, then talked to me about the nature of disease, saying that disease, any disease, is the human manifestation of a belief in a power apart from God, who is the one source of all real power. She also obviously sensed that I had accepted a view of myself as a fallen, defeated, lost human being—as brokenhearted. She spoke to me of the real man of God's creating, encouraging me to see that my real being was perfect in every way and always had been, and that I could prove this truth in my experience if I would reach out to God wholeheartedly.

Extreme fear kept me in great doubt about my ability to trust God, until one night a few days later I woke up, got out of bed, and threw the pills into a wastebasket. An hour later I woke up again, took the basket out to the hallway of my apartment house, and threw the contents down a trash chute.

I called the practitioner to pray for me, and a few days after that I resigned my job and began really studying Christian Science. Haltingly at first, I acknowledged my true selfhood as God's pure, perfect child. I soon began to feel that I was growing spiritually again, although I could not seem to shake my fear of death and the thought that I was just preparing myself to face it. The practitioner stuck with me night and day, with a love for and loyalty to the spiritual truths she was continually sharing with me that were a powerful inspiration.

One night I felt the symptoms of a heart attack, the most serious one I'd ever experienced. I quickly got to my bed and tried to telephone the practitioner. Her line was busy. By then, I felt I had strength to make just one more call. It was to my mother. There was no answer. I had taken my copy of *Science and Health* to the bed with me, and having by then lost the use of my arms entirely, I could only open the book with my chin. Even then I was beginning to lose consciousness. I wanted more than anything else in the world at that moment to have the privilege of reading one last sentence from this book before I died, to say goodbye to the one thing in my life that was love itself to me.

I glanced quickly down to the open page, feeling almost frantic. I read only one short sentence (which, unfortunately, I no longer recall). But what a sentence! Instead of the hoped-for statement to prepare me for death, I was astounded to read a sentence that was an immediate, dynamic call to live. It was galvanizing! It seemed to speak just to my need, with great love, and in praise of Life, of God, of living. I cried out in joy, then fainted.

When I woke, it was early morning. I had an immediate calm and very deep conviction that I was alive and well, that I was healed. I quickly rose and walked outside. I rejoiced at every sign of life: a bird, a leaf on a tree. I saw a long flight of steps in front of me. I walked over and stared at them for a moment. Then I raced up those stairs to the very top, where I bent down instinctively to prepare myself for the familiar breathing difficulties. But this time I stopped, declared with understanding that I was perfect as God's child, and straightened my body. I was not the least out of breath. I joyfully drove through town in my car, waving at people, laughing, crying.

I ended up at the beach. It was deserted. I put on some shorts and dived into the surf, always my favorite recreation. I started to swim down the coastline. Then the thought came: "Now you've gone too far. You'll have an attack out here alone in the ocean." I turned on my back, floated, and talked out loud to God, thanking Him for preserving my life. I declared aloud that I was well, perfect in every way, and that from then on my life would be devoted to expressing creativity, love for my fellowman, and gratitude. These qualities of thought, I knew, availed me of health. I turned back over and swam probably a mile to a pier, and then back again. That was the end of my fear and also the end of the symptoms of heart disease.

That was over twenty-five years ago. Not too long after this healing I started a new business, which enjoyed a wide measure of success. As president of this corporation, I was required to carry several million dollars worth of life insurance as a condition for bank financing. To apply for this insurance I had to undergo a battery of tests conducted by several heart specialists. The results all stated that though there was evidence of previous heart damage, no present damage or heart disease was apparent. The insurance companies decided not to rate me, meaning that I paid the same premium as someone without a history of heart disease.

In later years I moved to one of the most rugged mountain areas of our state, where I founded a successful resort hotel complex. I climbed the high surrounding mountains almost daily. Friends complained they could not keep up with me. Continuing insurance examinations confirm that my health is excellent.

During this healing, my view of myself changed. I saw clearly that I must increasingly understand myself to be the child of God, and then live each day as the unfallen, immortal, innocent, and free idea of God—to the best of my understanding.

I have before me the copy of *Science and Health* my mother gave me over forty years ago. She inscribed in it a familiar sentence from its pages: "Love inspires, illumines, designates, and leads the way" (p. 454). I searched at various times for some years to find the one sentence I read the night I was healed. I have never been able to find it. I cannot remember exactly what it said. But I'll never forget how I felt when I read it. I heard its proclamation of heavenly joy and power. I felt its call to me, to all of us, to come out from a mortal sense of life and be God's full, immortal expression—to live, to love, and to serve mankind. I think of the whole experience as a glorious homecoming: a coming home to the understanding of God as the only Life, as my Life.

Truly, God is the preserver of man.

LAWRENCE ALBERT SPECTOR
La Quinta, California
The Christian Science Journal November 1986

One night I had a severe asthma attack.

When I was a small child I had an asthmatic condition. My parents chose to rely on medical means. But healing eluded the best efforts of my doctors. During the many years I was under medical care, each week I attended the Christian Science Sunday School. Because of my poor health I made slow progress in schoolwork. But when I was twelve a Sunday School teacher helped me to realize that I had the ability to learn to read. He not only encouraged me; he lovingly helped me with words during Sunday School sessions without making me feel conspicuous in front of the other pupils. Then, with my developing reading skills, I began to search out and ponder truths in the Bible and in *Science and Health*.

When I was thirteen, another Sunday School teacher helped me to catch a glimpse of the spiritual meaning of this statement: "There is but one primal cause" (*Science and Health,* p. 207). I began to see that God was truly the only cause in my life. And over the next several years I often used this statement as the basis of prayer for myself.

Even though I appreciated all that the doctors who had treated me had tried to do, while I was away at college I decided to rely completely on God for healing. After that, at times I felt that my family was quite concerned for my well-being, but I still held to my decision.

Healing didn't come in a flash, but I was encouraged by the examples set by friends in the Christian Science college organization on my campus. Even though there were many moments of doubt, my life gradually improved. Then at the end of my junior year I had a healing which left no doubt in my thought that divine Science, the law of God, was the Comforter Christ Jesus promised would come in his name (see John 14:26).

One night after returning home from school for summer vacation, I had a severe asthma attack. From about ten thirty until around four in the morning I prayed as best I knew how. However, around four I was in such a weak condition that I woke my mother and asked her to materially assist my breathing. She kindly asked me when "this" (the attack) had started. Before I could even reply, these thoughts came to me: *This* didn't start last night. *This* didn't start when I was a small child. *This* didn't start at the point of conception, and *this* didn't start back along a genealogical chain with my ancestors. The only thing that ever started was, "In the beginning God created the heaven and the earth. . . . And God saw every thing that he had made, and, behold, it was very good" (Genesis 1:1, 31). Therefore, *this,* which certainly isn't "very good," didn't have a beginning or a start. Furthermore, I realized that when Jesus healed, he healed through spiritual means alone. There is no record of his using any human means to help someone.

Immediately I felt better. I asked my mother to read to me from the Bible and from the first pages of the chapter titled "Christian Science Practice" in *Science and Health.* I continued to improve, and before long I had the strength to read by myself. Then I asked for breakfast and got dressed. As I ate I rejoiced over the beauty of the sunlight and the sparkle in the droplets of water on the lawn. Prior to that morning I had never been able to eat until well after an asthmatic attack. However, I now ate most of my meal.

Still weak and struggling but feeling much better, I asked to be driven to work. Enroute I assured my mother that I'd be all right. But I promptly corrected the notion of being all right at some future point by silently affirming that I was all right at that very moment. Two statements from Mrs. Eddy's writings then formed the basis of my prayer during that ride to work. They are: "Divine Love always has met and always will meet every human need" (*Science and Health,* p. 494); and, "God gives you His spiritual ideas, and in turn, they give you daily supplies" (*Miscellaneous Writings,* p. 307). I reasoned along these lines: God, I need strength for today, and I know that You will give me the spiritual ideas that will meet that need.

It is now a good number of years later, and I have never remembered exactly what happened between the time I began this prayer of affirmation in the car and the time I arrived at work. I do recall that as I got out of the car my mother assured me that no one would be aware that I was having a hard time breathing. Her comment startled me, for I was completely free physically. In fact, I had actually forgotten the night of struggle. There had been no period of recuperation. I was totally healed. I worked eight hours with complete mental and physical strength. That evening I ate a hearty dinner and worked another six hours on a night job. This healing hasn't been just an inspiring incident from my college days. It was the beginning of demonstrating continuing good health based on a recognition and acceptance of the spiritual sense of being.

After I had married, when our daughter was about two years old she suddenly manifested the same symptoms of asthma that I had as a child. Her difficulty in breathing alarmed both her mother and me. I realized the helplessness my parents must have felt when they saw me as a small child struggling for breath. But by now I had many proofs through the years that health difficulties can be healed through prayer. Therefore I recognized this as a new opportunity to stamp out a mortal belief of limitation that would attempt to choke the buoyancy of childhood. Both my wife and I prayed to understand more clearly the fatherhood and motherhood of God. And we prayed to perceive more fully that each of His children is protected by Him. We clung to the spiritual fact that He is the only creator.

I resolved that our daughter wouldn't experience eighteen or so years of suffering as I had, and that I wouldn't go to sleep that night until I saw a healing take place. Even at that tender age, our daughter associated peace and harmony with the Bible and *Science and Health*. She'd seen us read these books, and apparently she had realized their healing power. At one point during the night while she was being cuddled in her mother's arms, she pointed to a copy of *Science and Health* and said, "Book! Book!" My wife obediently turned to the "book" for more spiritual strength. It wasn't long before healing came, and we all were peacefully asleep. And our daughter, who is now six, was not troubled again by symptoms of asthma.

DAVID REED

I am grateful to acknowledge our daughter's healing on the very night the symptoms of asthma appeared. At the time I was greatly touched by her insistence, despite the motherly comfort I offered, that I turn immediately to the "book!"

I met my husband well after his healing of asthma, and there has not been any evidence of his being troubled by that disease since I have known him.

I thank God that we are able to share this wonderful, freeing religion with our child.

NANCY GAIL REED
Albuquerque, New Mexico
The Christian Science Journal September 1983

It became clear that he had inherited all good from his Father-Mother God.

The adoption of our third child was not only a wonderful blessing, but also a demonstration of the potency of Truth and God's tender protection and care for His loved ones. The adoption agency examined our ability as Christian Science parents to properly care for the physical needs of a child. During our interviews I felt God's presence, because so often a clear and concise answer came to thought just when needed. Several times, when the queries regarded the application of our religious teachings, I answered questions by referring directly to *Science and Health* by Mrs. Eddy.

After we were approved as adoptive parents, we were told that there was an eighteen-month-old boy available for us.

A recent medical examination, however, had revealed a deformed leg bone, which it was claimed would necessitate leg braces, and also a malformation in the ear, eye, nose, and throat area, for which the doctors requested an operation. We were asked if we were willing to take this child under the circumstances.

At first, this seemed a formidable challenge. Then I realized that we were being drawn into the material picture. I had to ask myself: Are we going to accept this physical picture, or replace it with spiritual truth? I was aware that this description of the child was certainly not true of the child of God's creating—the child we had prayed to see. We joyfully brought the boy home—literally and figuratively.

Our understanding was that we would be allowed to handle this problem with Christian Science. I began a thorough search and study of Mrs. Eddy's writings. These words from *Science and Health* were most helpful: "Bones have only the substance of thought which forms them. They are only phenomena of the mind of mortals" (p. 423); also, writing of the Adamic concept of man, Mrs. Eddy says, "Divide the name Adam into two syllables, and it reads, *a dam,* or obstruction" (p. 338). And, further on the same page, "Here *a dam* is not a mere play upon words; it stands for obstruction, error, even the supposed separation of man from God, and the obstacle which the serpent, sin, would impose between man and his creator."

I recognized that nothing could separate this child from his creator, since man is forever spiritual and at one with God. Through study and prayer it became clear that he had inherited all good from his Father-Mother God; that his hearing could not be impaired, nor could matter become painful, discordant, or swollen, since mortal mind is not a lawgiver, and God maintains man in eternal perfection. Further study brought out that these truths were supported and maintained by the one omnipotent, eternal Principle, God, and could not be reversed.

Two months later the adoption agency requested that we follow through with the recommendation of an operation and also consult a specialist regarding the child's legs. Since he was not yet legally ours, we had to agree to this. Upon examination, the ear, eye, nose, and throat specialist found no evidence of an obstruction or abnormality in the suspected area; he therefore advised no surgery! The orthopedic doctor found no signs of bone malformation, nor could he believe that there ever had been any! Shortly thereafter we were granted permission to proceed with the legal adoption of our son.

When the caseworker heard the doctors' reports she said that she had wondered why we, being Christian Scientists, were asked to take this particular child. Then she added, "Now I know."

JEAN A. PODEYN
Southold, New York
Christian Science Sentinel July 12, 1975

6

Pregnancy and birth

God's love and care for His children are timeless—without beginning or ending. God's laws of good are always there to heal the challenges that may come during pregnancy and birth.

Doctors told me I would never be capable of giving birth.

Originally written in Danish

During a stay in Paris some years ago, I developed a severe inflammation of my reproductive organs. I was treated medically for eighteen months before the inflammation ceased. Doctors told me I would never be capable of giving birth to a child.

Later on I became interested in Christian Science and consulted a Christian Science practitioner. As I studied the Bible and *Science and Health,* I began to understand the spiritual fact that God is our Father and Mother, the only creator.

Some time later I found I was pregnant. When I was examined for the first time, a doctor stood holding my case sheet. Having read it over, he could not understand how I could have become pregnant, and he spontaneously exclaimed: "You must indeed be good at healing yourself." I thought of Mary Baker Eddy's words in *Science and Health:* "If God heals not the sick, they are not healed, for no lesser power equals the infinite All-power; but God, Truth, Life, Love, does heal the sick through the prayer of the righteous" (p. 231). Early in 1992 I gave birth to a wonderful little daughter, and in 1993 I had a fine, healthy boy.

CHRISTINE HERMANSEN
Copenhagen, Denmark
Christian Science Sentinel September 5, 1994

He felt nothing could be done to save the baby.

"Thoughts unspoken are not unknown to the divine Mind. Desire is prayer; and no loss can occur from trusting God with our desires, that they may be moulded and exalted before they take form in words and in deeds" (*Science and Health,* p. 1).

Many years ago, the truth of these powerful words was demonstrated to me. I was pregnant with our son at the time, and three months into the pregnancy my water bag ruptured—a sign the doctors insisted indicated an impending miscarriage. I telephoned a practitioner and insisted emphatically that I wanted life for the baby.

The doctor came to the house prepared to abort the child, but I told him I did not want him to do that. He did not pressure me in the least, but he left his medical bag at my home and said that he knew I would be calling him before daybreak. He felt nothing could be done to save the baby.

The practitioner prayed from the standpoint that only Life and perfection were real. Her declarations included the fact that God is man's Life, and that this was a law of life for both the child and me.

I did place all my trust in God. A passage that was of great inspiration to me was from Proverbs: "Trust in the Lord with all thine heart; and lean not unto thine own understanding. In all thy ways acknowledge him, and he shall direct thy paths" (3:5, 6).

All the while the doctor maintained that the pregnancy would not be carried to term, that perhaps the fetus was weak or deformed. He insisted that I was young and could have another baby. But in my simple prayer I held fast to my faith. I stayed at my mother's house, in bed, answering daily calls from the doctor to let me know he was standing by.

After about one month, I stopped hemorrhaging and felt completely healed. I even went on a camping trip.

Five months later, I gave birth to a beautiful baby, on the exact day he had originally been expected to arrive. He was delivered without complications in about twenty minutes. The doctor held him up and announced that the baby was a miracle. He gave full credit to God and said there was nothing in his medical knowledge that could explain it.

Marjorie Wall

I am the son mentioned in the testimony, and I wish to verify that I have heard rejoicing over the healing at the time of my birth for as long as I can remember.

Brent Wall
Elmhurst, Illinois
Christian Science Sentinel August 29, 1994

The doctor was very surprised to find that everything was fine.

Our first two children were born quickly and painlessly, and these were periods of spiritual growth and happiness. When we were expecting our third child, we prayed to know that

God's creation is complete and that God, not man, is the one creator. We felt great love for the child.

In order to comply with the law relating to childbirth, I visited a doctor. After an examination the doctor explained that the baby, and perhaps I myself, probably would not survive a natural delivery, because the placenta had attached in the wrong place and was completely blocking the baby's exit. He called the difficulty full placenta previa. I was told the birth would have to be by Caesarean section.

As I drove home I prayed and thought of instances described in the Bible when obstacles had been removed. For example: the times when the stone was moved from in front of Jesus' tomb, when Peter was freed from his prison chains, and when the earthquake freed Paul from prison. I also remembered the following verse from Isaiah: "Shall I bring to the birth, and not cause to bring forth? saith the Lord: shall I cause to bring forth, and shut the womb? saith thy God" (66:9).

I was taking care of two extra children that night for a friend. After I had put them all to bed and was cleaning up, I found myself singing the following lines from Hymn 148 in the *Christian Science Hymnal:* "Green pastures are before me, / Which yet I have not seen." It seemed so appropriate. I realized that the spiritual truth of man's perfection is true at every moment; I just had not been seeing it. I also picked up an issue of *The Christian Science Journal* and opened it to an article entitled "Let God's angel roll away the stone." I just was being shown what to do!

I spent the rest of the evening praying. The next morning I called a Christian Science practitioner and told him the situation. Many helpful ideas were shared in the conversation, and I gained a better sense that the material evidence was a lie, not the truth, about God's child, and that God's law is always at work, maintaining man's spiritual perfection. I saw that I must know only what God knows and hold to that perfect idea. At this point I felt completely at peace.

Prayer was continued, and I became aware one day that the obstruction was moving. This was painful at first, but with the prayerful help of the practitioner the pain quickly ceased.

When the next examination came, the doctor was very surprised to find that everything was fine. A few weeks later a dear baby girl was born normally and quickly. She is a perfect joy.

I am very grateful for this and many other proofs of God's care that we have experienced in our family.

Barbara Allen
Navan, Ontario, Canada
Christian Science Sentinel May 22, 1989

God was not only my Father-Mother, but also the baby's Father-Mother.

It is with a great deal of gratitude and pleasure that I testify to the healing power of God's law, which my husband and I witnessed with the birth of our child.

When I was eight and a half months pregnant, I was found to have a condition of acute toxemia, and the life of the child and my own life seemed to be endangered.

Understanding that God was not only my Father-Mother but also the baby's Father-Mother made me realize that God was the baby's Life and that He was my Life and we were independently dependent on Him. The promise from the Bible, "I have made, and I will bear; even I will carry, and will deliver you" (Isaiah 46:4), was a great comfort during this time. This gave me confidence that God does it all. He is the great Physician.

More than a month elapsed between the diagnosis of toxemia and the birth of our son. During that time I was in constant prayer and studied earnestly the Bible and Mary Baker Eddy's writings. The lessons I learned were innumerable. So many errors were overcome in my own life, such as hatred, lack of appreciation, fear, belief of pain, criticism, and laziness with regard to study. At this time there were also more dire medical predictions. The doctor feared he would need to do a

Caesarean, as the child had not dropped down into position, and later the doctor felt he would have to force labor, as the child's heartbeat was slowing down and I was three weeks overdue. All this fear was handled through Christian Science.

The night before delivery I spent awake reversing every fear that came to me. I refused to give in to even one evil suggestion by prayerfully considering "the scientific statement of being" in *Science and Health* (p. 468). The opening words are: "There is no life, truth, intelligence, nor substance in matter. All is infinite Mind and its infinite manifestation, for God is All-in-all." Elsewhere *Science and Health* states, "To attend properly the birth of the new child, or divine idea, you should so detach mortal thought from its material conceptions, that the birth will be natural and safe. Though gathering new energy, this idea cannot injure its useful surroundings in the travail of spiritual birth. A spiritual idea has not a single element of error, and this truth removes properly whatever is offensive" (p. 463). This was certainly proved true. The next evening our son was born with no complications. The birth was natural and beautiful with mother, father, and son in the hospital only six hours.

VERA J. MORGAN
Visalia, California
Christian Science Sentinel March 20, 1978

The child's condition was considered extremely critical.

Originally written in Indonesian

A matter of days after our second child was born, the doctor attending the birth had him transferred to the central hospital. We were told that our son had hyperbilirubinemia and so required a complete blood transfusion. The child's condition was considered extremely critical. In a panicky state I called a Christian Science friend to pray with me. He reminded me that even though medical opinion concluded that the child's blood needed to be changed or cleansed, in the beginning God established His creation in perfection. These words encouraged me, "Man is God's reflection, needing no cultivation, but ever beautiful and complete" (*Science and Health,* p. 527).

That night I was allowed to stay with the child in the hospital. It was a good opportunity for me to study and pray. I found these words of Elihu in Job, which awakened me to listen only to God, Truth: "Hearken unto me: hold thy peace, and I will speak" (33:31). What was *God* saying about this child? I recalled that he was of God's creating, which was and is perfect forever. Because of the child's innate perfection, I saw that nothing could need correcting. I closed the door of my thought to all the human opinions about a physical condition and clung steadfastly to this truth. Then I realized that because *everyone* reflects divine Mind, or God, the doctors could witness only perfection in our son.

Next to our room, a little girl was suffering from the same illness as our son. The grandmother of the girl was staying with her and appeared to be very fearful. In talking with her I mentioned that fear and worry could be replaced with calmness; the key was in perceiving the truth and standing firm with it. This, I assured her, would bring healing. Then I shared some of the passages quoted above. At this, I saw the face of the grandmother change. She accepted these statements with openness and became calm.

The next day when doctors examined our child and the little girl in the next room, they were astonished at what they saw. They found both children to be in very good condition and determined that a blood transfusion was not necessary for either one. After one more day of observation, the children were declared completely well and released from the hospital. The head doctor of the hospital said, "This is a miracle from God. These children are healed and may go home." The grandmother was very grateful and told me that her fears had vanished. This healing was evidence to both of us that scientific prayer does heal.

Djoni Darmadi
Jakarta Pusat, Indonesia
Christian Science Sentinel November 16, 1981

I looked away from the human picture of a small, frail, physical infant to see the child of God.

I was a practicing pediatrician when I learned of Christian Science. As a doctor, I thought Western, allopathic medicine was the only way to cure illness. On the other hand, I saw so many conditions for which there was no medical help available, and I sometimes wondered how it must feel to be the parent in such cases. How would I feel if I was told my child would not live beyond a few months, or would never walk, or would grow up with brain damage and never be able to study in school?

I began to read Christian Science books and literature offered by a friend for my own interest. I did not dream how vast is the scope of God's law of Love and its application to any situation.

This awakening came in an unexpected way. I was working in a public maternity hospital. A nursery had been set up to care for premature babies. One morning the nurse in charge looked very glum. When I asked the reason for it, she pointed to a little infant who was three days old, and who had been born three months too early. His birth weight was about one pound twelve ounces. The nurses were doing their best, but everyone thought he would not survive. As I looked at the wee little one, my first thought was of human pity: "Poor baby, they are all waiting for you to die." Immediately after that, without conscious effort on my part, I silently declared, "That is not true; you represent eternal Life and have the strength of the Almighty behind you." Instinctively, with absolute conviction, I knew this was the truth. Although nothing had changed physically, I was quite confident that he would do well. And he did. He remained there 'til he was feeding comfortably. The only treatment he received was tender, loving nursing care.

We followed his progress 'til he was one year old. His growth and development were perfectly normal, both mentally and physically. The basis for that healing thought was the spiritual sense of children given in *Science and Health:* "The spiritual thoughts and representatives of Life, Truth, and Love" (p. 582).

Somebody might say this child's healing would have happened anyway. It was just a coincidence, perhaps! There was much more to this experience, however, as there is to every Christian healing. Something about God had needed to be learned. What I was seeing with human eyes, and judging with the human mind, was not the reality of things as God has made them to be. Right there, the permanence of divine Life and the strength of divine Spirit were quietly being expressed, as they have been through eternity.

Many similar experiences occurred during the rest of my career in the medical field. On many occasions I was faced with dire situations. All the medical help available had been given, and yet the child was going downhill. It seemed so wrong, so unjust! Something in me rebelled. Then I'd ask myself, What is truly going on right here? As I looked away from the human picture of a small, frail, physical infant to see the child of God—strong and whole, already perfect—the infant would recover. I was learning to acknowledge God's very tangible presence and goodness and was seeing the effect of such spiritualized thought. Ultimately, I came to the conclusion that God is the only healer, and I made the decision to stop the medical practice altogether.

Jesus healed consistently. To him nothing was incurable, because he knew that to God all things are possible. He accepted the scientific fact that God is always present, maintaining all His children in their perfect state. Can we prove this consistently? Yes, we can, because it is true and because this fact is law. Mrs. Eddy discovered this truth as she studied the Bible. Many of her healings were instantaneous. One such healing was of a child with ankylose joints. The bones in his knee joint seemed to have solidified. The medical verdict was that he would never be able to walk again. After Mrs. Eddy prayed for him, however, he could run and play with other children. (*Twelve Years with Mary Baker Eddy,* pp. 55–56.)

Medical theory is the product of human thought. All its reasoning is from effect to cause. The illness is accepted as real, and then a possible cause is presumed to have resulted in that effect. This presumption is then accepted as law. Because sickness is accepted as real, a great deal of fear ensues. But when you look away from the physical body and reason that perfect God could produce only perfect effect, you feel His presence and power. The certain effect is healing.

These facts, understood, helped a young woman who was herself at the time a practicing pediatrician. She was curious to find out why I had left the medical profession for something called Christian Science. She had never heard of it before. She asked many questions and was glad to accept some copies of the *Christian Science Sentinel.* She read them and telephoned sometimes to ask questions. A year or so later, her son, not quite five years old at the time, fell ill. For some days he was feverish, rejected food, and presented signs that made her very fearful. From the physical evidence she made a mental diagnosis of tuberculous meningitis. During her student days, she had seen several children suffering from this disease. They either did not survive or, if they did, had severe mental and physical disabilities. The laboratory test that would have confirmed or ruled out the diagnosis is a painful one, and not free from risk, so she did not want to subject her son to it.

At this time of extreme fear, she telephoned, asking for help through prayer. She was assured that God was the real Father and Mother of the child. He was completely safe in his Father-Mother's care. There is no destructive force in all of God's kingdom, and that is where the child existed. God is Love. She, as a human mother, would do all she could to keep her son well. How much more does God express His love,

His infinite, powerful love for all His offspring! They are governed by spiritual laws that do not recognize disease.

While talking to me, she did not mention the name of the disease, but from her description, the cause of the fear was obvious. During the conversation, theories regarding infection, susceptibility to bacterial invasion, and the inevitable downward trend of the disease were denied as not being part of divine order. Consciousness is governed by Mind; it is holy, not something in a brain. Therefore, it cannot be lost or dimmed, but must always be clear and alert. Activity is an expression of Life, buoyant, vital, inexhaustible. It cannot be restricted by any physical law.

She drank in these truths because they promised a lifeline for the child, help that she knew she would not get from medicines. She turned to God with all her heart, without reservation, trusting in the Almighty. The one thought she grasped firmly was that God loved the child and had never created anything to hurt him. Less than twenty-four hours later, he woke up fully, smiled his usual bright smile, and asked for something to eat. From then on, his behavior was completely normal. The mother was deeply grateful and, of course, wanted to learn how her son had been healed. She earnestly began the study of Christian Science. The boy has grown up to be a very bright teenager. . . .

This one and only God is the Father-Mother of us all, the one supreme Parent of every single child without exception. Therefore, all are completely safe. We can turn unhesitatingly to God in caring for ourselves and our children.

Jer Master
Bombay, India
The Christian Science Journal March 1994

7

Children and prayer

No one is too young to feel God's love. Children find that prayer brings healing, and that their own prayers heal themselves and others. Even the simplest prayer brings results.

The laboratory reported a very rare bacillus.

Soon after my son-in-law moved his family to a large, populous state because of his business, my three-and-a-half-year-old granddaughter became quite ill. Alarmed, her parents consulted a pediatrician. The child was submitted to a battery of tests, then finally treated with an antibiotic and brought home.

In a few days my granddaughter seemed much better. So it was a blow to my daughter when the doctor telephoned and asked that the child be brought in for more tests. He said these were needed to substantiate the laboratory reports of the presence of a very rare bacillus which, if unchecked, could cause serious or even fatal kidney damage. He further explained that the condition was beyond his scope in medicine, and he recommended a specialist in a nearby city whom he would call and apprise of the situation.

When my daughter was able to reach me, I encouraged her to obtain a copy of *Science and Health with Key to the Scriptures* by Mary Baker Eddy and to study the book. Meanwhile I would prayerfully support her. We based our prayerful work on the idea of man's spiritual perfection as God's child, looking up many selections on this subject. In frequent telephone calls my daughter and I shared the spiritual truths that prayer had revealed to us.

By this time my granddaughter was so happy and active that she was enrolled in a preschool kindergarten, where daily she energetically joined in all activities.

One day my daughter received a phone call from the office of the child specialist recommended to her and my son-in-law. They were concerned the child was at serious risk.

The child's father felt that medical advice should now be sought. My daughter told me that they had decided to make the appointment. I reassured her that the doctor could find the child well, since in her true nature she was really God's perfect, spiritual child; moreover God was always with her, no matter where she might be.

The appointment was kept, but the parents resisted the idea that a happy, bouncing, exuberant little girl should be admitted immediately into a hospital to begin extensive, complicated tests. No medical treatment was given, and no other medical diagnosis was sought.

Several months later, the school my granddaughter attended requested a medical certificate from all pupils, in line with a new policy. The same pediatrician my daughter and her husband had first consulted couldn't believe that this was the same child he had examined earlier. He asked to be permitted to do some basic tests, and my daughter allowed this.

A couple of days later the doctor called my daughter and said, "We doctors like to give out happy news, too. It doesn't seem possible, but there is no sign of any bacillus infection. Your daughter is perfectly healthy." My daughter and I thanked

God for His glorious spiritual truth. As her favorite hymn expresses it, "He holds us perfect in His love, / And we His image bear."

GLENICE M. ROBINSON
Sandy, Utah
Christian Science Sentinel January 29, 1990

The boy said, "I want God."

Our little three-year-old woke one morning with chills and an extremely high fever. For a moment I was panic-stricken and didn't know what to do. But when the boy said, "I want God," I assured him that God was always with him, and that he could never be separated for an instant from God. Then I put him back in his crib, still not knowing exactly what to do until he said, "Get the book." So I got *Science and Health* and started looking up references to *fever, fear,* and *children.* And when I would stop my study of the references, he would say, "Read." This went on for quite some time until he fell into a peaceful sleep and I felt assured he was safe and secure in God's love.

He woke early in the afternoon completely free of any fever or illness. I was overwhelmed with the wonder of it, and kept saying to myself, "You'd never know he had been so sick." Two days later the fever returned, though in a milder form. I prayed and studied some more, and very soon he was well again.

When the fever returned again in another two days, I called a Christian Science practitioner. When I explained the situation to her, she asked an interesting question: If I had a dream that my son was playing in the mud, would I give him a bath the minute I woke up? I realized what I had been doing; I had been so grateful for the healing, and so in awe of the power of Truth, that I had not fully understood that the unreality of the illness, like the unreality of events in a dream, cannot have any consequences. He was healed then, once and for all.

This taught me the valuable lesson that we must always be grateful, of course, for every healing, but that we must never make a reality out of an illness, even after it has been healed.

Margaret Shays
Darien, Connecticut
Christian Science Sentinel October 31, 1994

What I know about God

God is good, and
He is everywhere.
God doesn't "pow" you.
God doesn't knock you down.
He picks you up.
And God doesn't need a band-aid.

You can't see God,
but you can feel His angels—
He talks to you with good thoughts.
You better listen.
God makes you
be obedient, because
God just loves you, loves you, loves you.

Shelley Henderson

When I asked Shelley, age three, what "pow you" meant, she said the boys at her school sneak up on the girls with their hands held like a gun and yell "POW" very loud when the girls are not looking. She said it scares her. After further discussion of this, Shelley decided the poem meant God doesn't do anything that would scare His children.

MARY S. HENDERSON
Fremont, California
Christian Science Sentinel September 14, 1988

I don't know what you've been doing, but keep it up.

When my son entered kindergarten, his teacher noticed that he had a hard time following what was being said in class. She put him in the front row, and requested that we have his ears tested. We did. The results showed an almost complete loss of hearing in one ear, and a substantial loss in the other. The doctors insisted that hearing aids would be the only means of compensating for this situation. We politely declined, called a Christian Science practitioner for prayer, and diligently considered the description of *ears* in the Glossary in *Science and Health,* which says in part, "Not organs of the so-called corporeal senses, but spiritual understanding" (p. 585). We prayed to recognize that our son's hearing was never dependent on physicality, that it was spiritual, and had always been intact.

When we went for the next checkup required by the school, the hearing specialist said, "I don't know what you've been doing, but keep it up." Later tests by another doctor, conducted for insurance coverage, revealed "perfect hearing" in both ears. Our son, who is now in college, has for fourteen years had perfect pitch and has been a violinist and violist.

MONTY HOYT
Bernardsville, New Jersey
Christian Science Sentinel March 6, 1995

I am so happy to be over those "bad nights."

When our daughter was about five years old, she would periodically wake up terrified during the night and come wake me. I would carry her back to bed and reassure her that God was with her, that there is no place where God isn't, because God is everywhere. She would feel comforted and go back to sleep; but we would have to leave the hall light on for her, and she never closed her bedroom door. This is how she slept for several years.

Then she really began having "bad nights." Besides her fear of the dark and the terrible nightmares, she began to suffer from sleeplessness and would toss and turn until the early morning hours. This made it hard for her to get up for school the next day.

She never could say what scared her. Her father and I tried to explain to her that there wasn't anything in the room with her to be afraid of, but nothing seemed to help. Human love and reasoning didn't bring any permanent solution.

I knew God is ever available, and I knew it was time for a complete healing. It was right for our daughter to be free from this fear. I knew that God is omnipotent, omnipresent Love and that we could trust in Him with all our hearts.

One Bible promise that was so helpful was "When thou liest down, thou shalt not be afraid: yea, thou shalt lie down, and thy sleep shall be sweet" (Proverbs 3:24). Every night when our daughter was ready for bed, I would read to her articles and testimonies of healing from the Christian Science magazines.

Also, a poem by Mary Baker Eddy was full of wonderful ideas for us to pray with. It starts, "O gentle presence, peace and joy and power" (*Poems,* p. 4). We reasoned together that the gentle, peaceful, joy-filled presence is God and that nothing separate from Him is present or has power. This kind of reasoning always brought a sense of peace and made it possible for her to go to sleep and stay asleep through the night.

I was being blessed, too, for this prayerful work helped me to be more consecrated. I studied the Bible Lesson outlined in the *Christian Science Quarterly* more earnestly and prayed to see our daughter's true nature as the child of God's creating, whose being is spiritual and harmonious and who has God-given dominion. My spiritual understanding and love for God grew.

After about a week our daughter was able to go to bed free of fear. She wanted all the lights off, liked having her bedroom door closed, and slept peacefully every night.

As I think about this healing, which has been permanent, I can see that it is the light of Christ, Truth, that needs to be turned on in thought to destroy fear.

JACLYN MARIE FREEMAN

I am the daughter who had this healing, and I am so happy to be over those "bad nights."

This prayer for children by Mrs. Eddy also helped me a lot (*Miscellaneous Writings*, p. 400):

> Father-Mother God,
>   Loving me,—
> Guard me when I sleep;
> Guide my little feet
>   Up to Thee.

JENIFER L. FREEMAN
Ketchikan, Alaska
Christian Science Sentinel May 22, 1989

I had a healing today, you know!

Early one afternoon I received a call from our daughter's school, informing me there had been an accident on the playground. Our daughter had been climbing on a set of monkey bars when she slipped and fell, striking her leg on the lowest bar before hitting the ground. I was told she was injured and was having difficulty walking.

We are accustomed to resolving problems, physical and otherwise, through prayer to God. The school officials had been aware of our family's history of reliance on God and had not called for medical aid.

I immediately went to the school. As I was driving, I acknowledged prayerfully the fact that God is the ever-present Parent of each of His children. I felt a need to understand that our daughter was created in God's image and likeness. I also prayed to understand more clearly that her heavenly Father was watching over her at all times, and that all her activities were governed by divine Principle; therefore she could never fall outside God's care.

When I arrived at the school, our daughter was crying and in pain. One member of the staff expressed concern about internal injury. I took the child to a quiet place in the hall where we could talk. It was important that I assure her that God had not forgotten her, and that He loved her, as did we. Our conversation then turned to the day's activities, and as we talked about the games she had been playing on the playground, she stopped crying. While she was speaking, I was still praying to know the best place for her to be. There was no doubt in my mind that a healing would occur; prayer had never failed us.

Then our daughter indicated she was ready to return to her class. Although walking was still difficult for her, the bleeding had stopped, and it seemed appropriate to allow her to continue with her afternoon school schedule. I walked with her to the class and found they were settled down for their afternoon rest. After reassuring the office staff that our daughter was being taken care of, I returned home to continue praying.

I was disturbed by the pain my daughter was obviously experiencing. And the mental images kept appearing to me of the child falling and striking a steel bar.

I reached out to God for some healing idea that would bring release from this image. Almost immediately an angel thought from God came to me. I was suddenly aware that God, the divine Principle which governs His own universe, is also divine Love. Divine Love is neither cold, hard, nor unyielding.

This healing message helped me see that whatever God creates reflects the spiritual qualities He expresses. It seemed perfectly clear that since our daughter couldn't leave God's loving care and infinite protection, nothing material could bring her harm.

This prayer completely released me from feeling fearful about the child's condition. It stopped the haunting mental images of the accident. In fact, I felt completely assured that the healing had taken place.

A short while later our daughter came off the school bus and ran past me, chasing another child. As she was running down the sidewalk, she turned back and yelled, "I had a healing today, you know!" And it was true. There was simply no cut, no bruise, no mark, no soreness, no evidence of an accident at all. She was just perfect. I have also found that since this healing, the school personnel have exhibited great respect for our commitment to Christian healing through prayer.

While studying recently, I came across a statement in *Science and Health* that reminded me of this healing experience. It reads, "Jesus aided in reconciling man to God by giving man a truer sense of Love, the divine Principle of Jesus' teachings, and this truer sense of Love redeems man from the law of matter, sin, and death by the law of Spirit,—the law of divine Love" (p. 19).

I am thankful for the truer sense of God's nature as both Principle and Love, gained through prayer. And I am also glad for the feeling of complete peace that came when I knew my prayer had been answered and that our daughter was healed.

MICHELLE BOCCANFUSO
Lawrenceville, New Jersey
Christian Science Sentinel January 24, 1994

Elise's prayer

I love God and
God loves me.
Because I'm His child
God takes care of me.
God doesn't let error come—
I'm His little lamb.

ELISE RINDFLEISCH, AGE 4
Lyndhurst, Ohio
Christian Science Sentinel October 12, 1987

I didn't want to go back to school for the rest of my life.

When I was in the first grade, our school began a new lunch program. Each week a certain student was assigned to a table in the lunchroom to serve as the host or hostess of that table. There were many things to do! The food had to be carried to the table, passed around, and the table cleared. Sometimes there were even fifth- and sixth-graders at the same table!

At the very beginning of the year, one day the teacher wrote the names of the hosts and hostesses of that week. I was surprised to see my name! At lunch-time I was so scared. I went to the lunchroom, and the lunch lady told me which table was mine. I was trying to do everything right when a fifth-grader appeared at my table. He said some things to scare me, and I couldn't think of anything else to do but to go home. So I did.

This was the wrong thing to do. When I got home nobody was there. My neighbor found me and brought me to her house and called my school, and someone came and drove me back to school. Many people had been looking for me.

When my mom came home and found out what had happened, we decided to pray about it. I didn't want to go back to school for the rest of my life. I told my mom that I couldn't be a hostess anymore. My mom smiled and opened the Bible concordance. I was a student in a Christian Science Sunday School, where I had been taught how to use this huge book, and I looked up the word *hosts.* Over and over again it told us about the "Lord of hosts" (Psalms 84:1, 3, 12, for example). We decided it could mean hostesses too. On a little note card I wrote: "From God to Sarah, The Lord of Hosts and Hostesses is with you!"

The next morning I took this card in my pocket to look at during the day (especially at lunch). The day went great and I wasn't afraid at all. The fifth-grader even apologized.

If you are afraid of anything, you can use that Bible concordance book yourself. Your mom, dad, or Sunday School teacher can help you. You can carry God's messages with you always.

SARAH E. SCHEID

As background to Sarah's account: I had become a single parent, and it was important for me to have work away from home. This was very difficult for me to do. One day as I was locking my door to leave the house I thought, "I simply can't stand to leave the house one more time." Right on the heels of this came this angel message: "You can't leave your home! Your home is the consciousness of Love."

I had been thinking a lot about the twenty-third Psalm, especially Mrs. Eddy's interpretation of the last line. In *Science and Health* she writes, "Surely goodness and mercy shall follow me all the days of my life; and I will dwell in the house [the consciousness] of [LOVE] for ever" (p. 578). I thought about each of us, the children and me, as being held in this consciousness. This higher sense of home included safety, guidance, comfort, wisdom, and goodness. I turned the key, and for the first time I left with a smile.

I arrived at the Christian Science Reading Room where I was librarian for the day, and I continued to keep this new understanding of home. I found John 10 where Christ Jesus says: "My sheep hear my voice, and I know them, and they follow me" (verse 27). I also read, "And a stranger will they not follow, but will flee from him: for they know not the voice of strangers" (verse 5).

I reasoned that God, divine Mind, holds each of His ideas in Love. This Love was all that could ever be heard. No "strangers," not even fear or doubt, could voice an opinion that could not be ruled out by divine Love.

When I picked up Sarah from school that afternoon, I found out the protection she had received. She had been missing from her school for almost two hours. A man in a van had tried to talk to her as she walked home, but she remembered a notice sent home the day before that a man with the same description had tried to abduct a classmate walking to school.

Sarah ran through the backyards until she reached home. As no one was there, she rode her bicycle in the driveway until our neighbor found her and called the school. When relating her part of this story to me, our neighbor said she had tried to handle this as she felt that I would have. This touched me deeply because I could see that the motherhood I had been praying to see was always active. God's guidance and mercy are ever present, even though I cannot be with the children every moment.

For us this experience is substantial evidence of God's love and protection.

GAIL M. SCHEID
Bloomington, Minnesota
Christian Science Sentinel September 17, 1990

Someone is praying for me.

My mom was very sick. I knew that God was with everybody. That night I prayed for her. My daddy prayed, too. The next morning I told her I'd prayed for her, and she said she felt much better. I know God loves everybody.

CARYN SMITH

Caryn had just turned six. The healing occurred much as she related it.

I was feeling very ill and told my daughter that I needed to lie down for a while. Caryn went to her room; I lay down on my bed, trying to collect my thoughts to pray for myself. I hadn't even begun praying when I felt the illness begin to lift off me. I thought, "Someone is praying for me." I felt much better right away.

That night I slept soundly. In the morning when I woke, Caryn was standing beside the bed, smiling at me. I said, "You were praying for me, weren't you?" She said, "Yes." Later, I asked her what ideas came to her. She said, "I know that God is everywhere and He loves you. He made you perfect and you are." It was simple! I thanked her and praised God for His loving care.

Caryn attends a Christian Science Sunday School and is learning about man's relation to God. At home, we read the *Sentinel* articles and talk about the Bible stories in the weekly Bible Lessons. Whenever Caryn has a problem, we seek a deeper understanding of God's allness, His omnipotence, and His love for us—and for all His children.

SANDRA LEE SMITH
New Providence, New Jersey
The Christian Science Journal May 1994

My mom suggested that I pray.

There was a boy in my class who was being very mean to people. He was hitting and pushing and saying lots of words that weren't good.

One day I told Mom about him. My mom suggested that I pray and said she would pray too. I thought about the twenty-third Psalm. I know it by heart. I liked the part where it says, ". . . my cup runneth over" (verse 5).

Then, my mom told me about Psalm 91. I liked the part that says, "He shall cover thee with his feathers, and under his wings shalt thou trust" (verse 4).

Soon, the boy was very nice to the other kids. He was not being bossy when we played dodgeball. He has stayed nice ever since, and I like him a lot. He's one of my friends. He's being nice to the other kids, too. He's sharing.

This happened in first grade. Now I am in third grade, and he's not in my class anymore. But, yea! I get to see him on the playground!

SARAH PASSEMAR

I'm Sarah's mom. She had been somewhat overwhelmed by this boy's arrival in her class, especially when she found herself seated next to him.

I knew how much she loved God, and that His allness was very real to her. After we talked about the fact we are all God's children, she agreed that the next day at school she would look for evidence that this boy expressed God. Soon it was no effort to find God's lovely qualities expressed.

I didn't hear much more about how things had worked out until the end of the year when Sarah received an invitation to a party at this boy's house. His father confided that Sarah's name had been first on the list of guests.

PATRICIA BARNUM PASSEMAR
Santa Rosa, California
Christian Science Sentinel December 12, 1994

My parents realized that something was wrong.

Although my parents were not students of Christian Science, they recognized the tremendous value of my attending a Christian Science Sunday School when I was growing up. I will always be grateful they enrolled me in the Sunday School. Though my attendance was not very regular, when I did attend I felt a great sense of kindness and love.

One morning when I was eight years old I woke up and found it impossible to move. I was so terrified that all I could do was cry. When my parents came in to check on me they quickly realized that something was wrong. My dad picked me up, placed me in our car, and drove me to the local hospital. After a thorough examination and X-rays, I was diagnosed as having pneumonia and a collapsed lung. We were told that the collapsed lung had to be removed, so surgery was scheduled for two days later.

I cannot tell you how afraid I was. I had to stay in the hospital, and after my parents went home I felt completely alone. The next day my parents visited me and explained to me why I would have to have an operation. Before long all three of us were crying.

As I sat alone in my bed that night, I remembered this sentence written on the wall of the Christian Science Sunday School I attended: "God is Love." I quietly prayed. I remembered my teacher telling us that God loves His children very much. So I asked God for help. I knew a loving God would never forget even one of His children. I felt very calm. Suddenly I sat up straight. I realized that the pain was completely gone. I was absolutely thrilled!

The next morning members of the hospital staff came in to prepare me for surgery. I told them that I felt fine. They smiled and told me everything would be OK. A short while later I looked out the window and saw my dad drive up. I frantically waved to him to come to my room. When he arrived some staff members told him that I was not cooperating.

My dad came over to me, and I quietly told him that I felt fine. I will always be grateful that he listened to me. He asked to speak to the physician. The physician didn't believe my report and asked my dad if he could take another set of X-rays, which my dad agreed to. To the physician's amazement, the X-rays showed nothing wrong with the lung at all. I was soon released from the hospital and on my way home!

My favorite church work is what I'm doing now—serving as Sunday School superintendent, and in the Sunday School I attended as a child. My own four children enjoy regular attendance in this Sunday School. Because of my own Sunday School experience as a child, I am always especially glad when visitors feel welcome. The same sentence from the Bible is still on our wall: "God is Love."

JAMES LLEWELLYN HEILAND
Monterey, California
Christian Science Sentinel September 22, 1986

I had warts. . . . I cut my toe.

I started attending a Christian Science Sunday School on Easter Sunday, 1993. At that time I had warts on my fingers and toes. Before I had tried some of the stuff they sell in drugstores, but nothing worked.

I prayed to God. I prayed that I do not have warts and that the healing is complete and done. I prayed that I am filled with goodness, joy, and harmony. I was praying for about two weeks, and my mom was praying with me. The warts were getting a little smaller. Then one night when I went to bed, the warts were still on my fingers and toes. When I woke up, they were all gone and the healing was complete. I knew that God was with me.

I also had another healing that let me know that God is everywhere. I was downstairs playing in my room, and I got up to see what my brother and his friend were doing. They were playing with their toys on the floor. I stepped on some and cut my toe. At that time my mom was talking on the phone, so I knew I had to do something myself. I turned to God.

I prayed that God is everywhere and God is only good, so there can be no bad. Then I calmed down. I decided to go upstairs and get the Holy Bible and *Science and Health* out of the bookcase. I just opened them up to any page and started reading. I looked down and saw that my toe had stopped bleeding, but there was still a little bit of scab there. I kept praying, and in a few days everything was totally and completely healed and back to normal.

I am very grateful for the healings I had.

AMY SCHENCK

I am Amy's mother. She had warts for at least three years before learning of Christian Science. She stated to me that she knew she would have healings, because God is everywhere and God is perfect. At the age of eight years, Amy realized the truth, and the warts disappeared as she explains. Amy has continued to rely on prayer for anything that appears to be a challenge to her. The healing of her toe that she discusses happened quickly and without any help except her praying alone and God's love for her.

NANCY CALEFFE-SCHENCK
Evergreen, Colorado
Christian Science Sentinel February 6, 1995

This was another case of polio.

Our first child had a very beautiful healing. He had not been feeling well for two days, and the school he was attending called to say that it would be necessary for us to have the school physician examine the child since there were several communicable diseases going around, and we would have to report the presence of such a condition to the local authorities.

The doctor informed me that this was another case of polio. He told us that our son needed help right away.

Within the hour our two younger children were picked up by friends, and a Christian Science practitioner came to our home.

For four days and nights we rejoiced in the truth that God's child is spiritual because made in His likeness. We declared over and over that because he was the perfect reflection of God he could never, even for a moment, be separated from his Maker. Although the condition was very serious, we never doubted that the healing would come. Our son listened to the declarations of truth with great courage. We sang hymns and read to him almost constantly from the Bible and Mary Baker Eddy's writings and cared for his every need while praying for divine guidance.

On Friday following the doctor's examination I went to answer the doorbell, and upon returning to his room heard our son's screams of joy when he found he had feeling in his legs. He begged me to put him in the tub, and I managed to carry him into the bathroom and place him in the water. Before I could turn around he was wiggling his toes and kicking his legs and laughing and crying at the same time. I can still hear him shouting, "God did heal me, Mommy. He did heal me!"

In order for our son to be readmitted to school on Monday, it was necessary to have the doctor's approval. The teacher had been told that our son would not be back at school for the remainder of the school term. The doctor rejoiced with us that Christian Science had healed our son, and especially that there had been no long period of recovery. This young man has just completed three years in the service of his country, and there are no memories of this experience except that of deep gratitude.

SUE WHITAKER
Ocala, Florida
The Christian Science Journal June 1971

The teacher called the marvelous turnaround a miracle.

Our younger daughter was in tears because no one in our family could understand what she was saying. We knew that she had lost something from her pocket, something that was precious to her. I prayed with a desire to help her, something our family needed to do often when communicating with this child. We longed to have her healed of a serious speech difficulty. In my prayers for her, I realized that everyone with challenging speech difficulties could experience freedom. It was comforting to have faith that one's inclusive prayers would bless our child and others.

Ever since she had begun to talk, most of the time we could only guess at what this daughter was saying. I knew that the beauty and perfection of God were expressed by our child in her true being, the spiritual image of God. This divine fact had to be proved through practice of the spiritual truths.

As I prayed to help our daughter find what she had lost, I noticed a small book with a cover that portrayed a noted author and her daughter. The child in the portrait is embracing her mother. As I thought of our daughter's words that we could not fathom, the word *hugging* came to me. I then asked our daughter if she was telling us that she had lost a picture of a little girl hugging her mother. She happily nodded yes. Her tears changed to smiles when she finally received the longed-for answer and the picture.

At bedtime our two daughters prayed the following prayer for children in *Miscellaneous Writings* by Mrs. Eddy (p. 400):

Father-Mother God,
  Loving me,—
Guard me when I sleep;
Guide my little feet
  Up to Thee.

After our younger daughter listened to her sister say the prayer, she could only say in broken English, "I pray the same, God." We knew she longed to speak as well as her sister and the other little children.

I prayed for everyone, my family and the world. Such prayer for mankind has often been for me a gateway to healing, a prayer that one knows is answered because of a silent inner assurance as powerful and as convincing as spoken words.

Science and Health states, "Science declares that Mind, not matter, sees, hears, feels, speaks" (p. 485). I thought of these words of Christ Jesus' in the parable of the prodigal son: "Son, thou art ever with me, and all that I have is thine" (Luke 15:31). It was inspiring to know that this inclusive spiritual fact promises all good for everyone.

As I remembered the healing power of Hymn 136 in the *Christian Science Hymnal,* I found these lines from the first verse helpful:

In Thy clear light of Truth I rise
  And, listening for Thy voice,
I hear Thy promise old and new,
  That bids all fear to cease:
My presence still shall go with thee
  And I will give thee peace.

A statement from *Science and Health* is engraved on the wall of many branch churches, "Divine Love always has met and always will meet every human need" (p. 494). My family and I considered deeply and reverently this sacred promise with its power to heal.

My mother was coming to lunch one day when we were praying with strong trust that divine Love does "meet every human need." As my mother entered our house, she asked, "Can Patricia speak any better?" In a little while, as we gathered around the dining table, our younger daughter greatly pleased us as she said perfectly, "I can say *God;* I can say *good;* I can say *Love;* I can say anything at all." And she could! Our family was profoundly grateful for this beautiful healing of speech.

In kindergarten and first grade our younger daughter's school marks had been poor. In second grade, after her healing of defective speech, she received all *A*'s. Her teacher wrote to my husband and me saying that in all her years of teaching she had never known such a remarkable improvement in a student's speech. She called the marvelous turnaround a miracle.

When this daughter was in high school, her school chose her to represent them in a television program in the state's largest city. The officials said they chose her because of her excellent speaking and confident manner. Later her school again chose her to take part in the state's assembly of gifted speech students. The girl whose family formerly could barely understand her words was among those who received the highest honors in speech in their state.

Regarding the healing of speech, I recall this hymn:

It was the voice of God that spake
  In silence to thy silent heart,
And bade each worthier thought awake,
  And every dream of earth depart.

LOUISA VELNETT PALMER
Kent, Ohio

I do not remember all of the details of the speech difficulty. I do vividly remember sitting with my family at lunch and amusing myself with an imaginary game of cowboys and Indians, when all of a sudden I was making the sounds of hard *c*'s and *g*'s, sounds I had been unable to make before. What a joy it was!

I am of course very grateful for my mother's diligence and firm conviction in God's healing power. And I am deeply grateful for Christian Science. Today my profession, interestingly enough, is that of an English teacher!

PATRICIA P. SELLARS
Vienna, Austria
Christian Science Sentinel January 15, 1990

She felt the child had some form of learning disability.

Our daughter had been in the fourth grade just three weeks when I received a call from her teacher requesting a conference. Although in working with this child I was keenly aware that her first three years of school had been quite difficult for her, I wasn't prepared for what I was about to hear. The teacher informed me that she had observed our daughter's academic and physical activity closely. As a result, she felt the child had some form of learning disability, which appeared to be growing progressively worse. She backed up her suspicions by showing me evidence of the child's work. Not only did there appear to be a problem of comprehension, but an increasing lack of coordination in writing skills and other activities. The physical education program was also extremely difficult for her. The teacher strongly recommended that we seek help from a special education teacher and a psychologist. Otherwise, she felt, the child would be unable to remain in fourth grade. I thanked her for her interest and concern, but told her that I would prefer not to take those routes. I assured her that my husband and I would take immediate steps to do everything we could to help this youngster.

On the way home from the meeting, I reached out to God with all my heart, knowing that this precious child was enveloped in her Father's love and protective care. I firmly declared that God, divine Mind, was the source of all intelligence and activity, and that she was governed and controlled by His undeviating law of harmony.

When I arrived home, I called a Christian Science practitioner to help support our prayerful efforts. I'll always be grateful for the loving encouragement she gave our daughter and me. Almost immediately we were led to take some human footsteps. An excellent tutor was found, who worked diligently with the child. I, too, worked with her faithfully, encouraging her and helping her with her studies. Most important of all, I prayed with her and for her, continually assuring her of man's God-given abilities and intelligence.

At first, going to school every morning was a tearful struggle for her, but each day we prayed together to know that our Father-Mother God was with her every step of the way, and that never for a moment could she be separated from Him. We held closely to Hymn No. 139 from the *Christian Science Hymnal,* which begins:

I walk with Love along the way,
And O, it is a holy day;
No more I suffer cruel fear,
I feel God's presence with me here;
The joy that none can take away
Is mine; I walk with Love today.

Also, this Bible verse from Joshua was a great comfort to us both: "Be strong and of a good courage; be not afraid, neither be thou dismayed: for the Lord thy God is with thee whithersoever thou goest" (1:9). Our daughter carried this verse in her little pocketbook all through fourth grade.

As a result of consecrated prayer and study of the Bible and *Science and Health,* I became increasingly convinced of man's innate perfection and freedom. I saw more clearly than ever before that as the reflection of divine Mind, this child could not possibly lack a single intelligent idea or the means of expressing that idea—man is not limited in any direction! I recognized that God is the source of all activity, and that He coordinates all ideas in His universe in perfect harmony and freedom. I was learning to trust God and His law of infinite good to govern and control every facet of our daughter's life. I also realized as never before the meaning of this statement from *Science and Health:* "Patience must 'have her perfect work'" (p. 454).

Progress was almost immediate and continued steadily. And I'm happy to say that our daughter remained in the fourth grade! At the end of the school term, her teacher requested another conference. But this time it was to tell me that never in her many years of teaching had she seen such a transformation take place in a child and such tremendous progress made.

That year marked the beginning of progress and growth that has continued to the present day. The early predictions made by our daughter's teacher and the tutor have been proved false: that, because of mental deficiencies, our daughter would never be able to attend college. How grateful I am! She is now in her senior year in a major university and is an excellent student. What had appeared to be a lack of intelligence has been replaced by a keen sense of intelligence. The lack of coordination has been overcome, and she participates skillfully in many sports. She is an excellent swimmer. Also, the inability to carry a tune has been healed. She now sings with freedom and joy. All this has come about through consecrated prayer, through a deep conviction that as a child of God, our daughter is the recipient of the infinite good bestowed upon her by her heavenly Father-Mother God.

CARLENE BRITTON

I am happy and grateful to verify my mother's testimony. Those mornings we prayed together, acknowledging God's ever-presence, have blessed my life daily. I have continued praying each morning on my own in preparation for college and work. In college I am on the honor roll, and my work activities have always been accomplished easily. I find that my experience is progressive as I express more of the infinite qualities of Mind. I acknowledge God as the source of all the good I have received.

TERRYL L. BRITTON
Arlington, Texas
Christian Science Sentinel November 23, 1981

The tests indicated that I was allergic.

When I was seven, I often had a runny or stuffy nose. My father is not a Christian Scientist and he asked my mother to take me to a doctor. The doctor gave me tests to see if I had any allergies. The tests indicated that I was allergic to milk. At first I didn't have milk or anything which was made with milk for a month. Then I was to have milk no more frequently than every four days.

After a while, my nose was either runny or stuffy again. My father said that I had to go back to the doctor. So my mother made an appointment. The appointment was for more than a month away. My mother said that this was our opportunity to prove that God heals. I said that I certainly wanted to be healed. My mother told me to turn to God in prayer as I had learned to do and said that she would pray also. She was sure I could be healed of the allergy.

When we visited the allergist, I was again tested, because this was a different allergist (the first one was not available). The second doctor tested me for twice as many allergies as the first doctor. Then she told us that I was not allergic to anything. I was also breathing freely and my nose was not runny.

I am grateful to God for His love. He has shown me and my family His love in many ways. I have learned in Sunday School that God is my Life and the source of my intelligence. Even though I get a lot of work in school, it never seems to be too hard for me.

Joy Newton
Jamaica, New York
Christian Science Sentinel May 27, 1991

I started right away to pray sincerely.

One day I was playing with a few friends and cousins. I suddenly fell down and I got a very bad hurt.

Every time I used to go to my grandmother if I got hurt, and she would help me out by praying. But this time I kept my mind steady and I remembered what my Sunday School teacher had taught me, a prayer to say when you are in great pain.

I started right away to pray sincerely. First I said the Lord's Prayer. Not only that, but I prayed that God's children are never in pain because God is never in pain, and also that they get healed, not some time later, but right now. And while I was saying these prayers and thinking those thoughts, I didn't know when the pain disappeared.

I was happy that I was healed, because I knew God's love would always heal me. But I was more happy to know that I was healed without anyone's help.

Jenifer Kotwal
Bombay, India
Christian Science Sentinel July 25, 1994

I went off the floor limping badly.

One day when I was ten we were in the gym at school playing soccer. I was the goalie.

One person was dribbling the ball to me. And another went behind me to get a pass. The person dribbling it toward me kicked at the ball but hit the bottom of my leg. The person behind me pushed against the top of my leg. Part of my leg was going back and part of it forward.

I went off the floor limping badly. I tried to walk it off. It didn't work. So I sat down and prayed.

I thought of "the scientific statement of being" and the part where it says, "God is All-in-all." After I thought about that, I felt all right. And I went back in the game and played more.

NATE JONES

As Nate's mother, I am glad to verify his testimony. Throughout the years Nate has established a store of Christian Science treasures to use when he needs them. For instance, before he goes to sleep each night, we share a comforting thought. Often the truth that God is All-in-all is the idea he chooses to ponder before he falls asleep. So I can see why that angel thought helped him find his completeness in the soccer incident.

Also, we have read many testimonies by children in the *Sentinel.* Often we have talked about the weekly Bible Lessons and read favorite citations from the Bible and *Science and Health.* Nate has chosen to pray about many physical and social problems to find healing solutions, sometimes with the help of a practitioner.

WENDY JONES
Plover, Wisconsin
The Christian Science Journal December 1994

A CAT scan, an angiogram, and an MRI were taken.

In the spring of 1987 our eleven-year-old adopted daughter was diagnosed as having a tumor in the tissue surrounding her brain. The condition was considered to be only partly accessible to surgery, and we were told that radiation treatment would be required after surgery. A CAT scan, an angiogram, and a magnetic resonance image (MRI) were taken.

My husband is a neurophysiologist researcher at a university. A biologist, he had a strong, basic faith in the healing ability of nature. He was willing to trust Christian Science. We decided to put off the decision on having surgery. We agreed to have another MRI done at the end of three months to ascertain the condition of our daughter's head.

I called a Christian Science practitioner, and her prayer freed our daughter from the immediate symptoms of discomfort. During the summer months the practitioner prayed for her and helped me see her in her true being as God's perfect spiritual likeness. It was made clear to me that Christian Science is not a philosophy, not just another way of looking at life, but offers clear insight into the very reality of existence. I felt confident about the child, expectant of healing. She had a wonderful, healthy, and wholesome summer, full of swimming, riding, and sewing.

In September, the three months had gone by, and my husband took our daughter for the MRI scan as we had previously agreed to do. Our daughter considered it to be a checkup. My husband was allowed in the same room to help her keep still. The process seemed to take a very long time, and my husband kept looking out through the glass window to see what the doctors were doing. He saw them peering and pointing at the old pictures and then taking more new ones.

The doctor-in-charge eventually asked my husband whether we'd had surgery or radiation done on the child. My husband replied that nothing had been done for her except consecrated prayer. The doctor said that there was no sign of any growth and that because this was inexplicable, they had taken longer than usual in order to take more pictures.

This demonstration of God's power to heal even the most serious physical difficulty left us rejoicing and full of gratitude.

Janet R. Cooke
Honolulu, Hawaii
Christian Science Sentinel April 30, 1990

The doctor said the child had rheumatic fever.

There is a statement that has been proven many times in my experiences: "Only through radical reliance on Truth can scientific healing power be realized" (*Science and Health,* p. 167). The most outstanding healing we have had in our home was brought about through this radical reliance in the spring of 1966.

Our daughter, then eleven years of age, was suddenly stricken on a Thursday. A Christian Science practitioner was called. By afternoon the child was better, and we dismissed the practitioner. However, the next day the symptoms returned, and it was necessary to call the practitioner again. By Saturday we also had the services of a Christian Science nurse. The presence and help of the nurse did much to relieve the anxiety of my husband. Though this child's suffering was relieved, my husband, who is not a Christian Scientist, was still concerned and requested that a medical doctor be called.

The practitioner and nurse were dismissed and a doctor was called. After he had made his examination, he came to me and said the child had rheumatic fever. The doctor left, giving many instructions. A report was to be made to him within a certain hour the following day, and decisions would then be made. As the hours went by after the diagnosis, the condition did not improve. The following day my husband contacted both the doctor and the practitioner. After much deliberation on his part my husband gave his consent to engage the practitioner and nurse again and to dismiss the doctor.

It had been several days since the nurse had first come to our home. None of our neighbors had noticed her coming or going. That Friday evening a neighbor saw the nurse leave our home and immediately phoned us. By the next day our phone was ringing constantly, and neighbors stopped by to inquire what they could do. The following days brought gifts of flowers, toys, and food, plus equipment which would make the child comfortable and her care easier.

One morning on a Christian Science radio program, a quick spiritual healing of rheumatic fever was related. We had read testimonies of healings of this disease, but all of them took a long period of time. Whenever the thought of time crept in, Paul's words were remembered: "Now is the accepted time" (II Corinthians 6:2).

That day we had a different atmosphere in our home, although the child did not seem any better physically. Monday morning she stood with both feet on the floor, the first time in weeks. Hourly the deformity diminished in all limbs. By late afternoon, when a neighbor came in, I was able to invite her to visit with our daughter. By the end of that week the child was walking the stairs alone. Our daughter returned to school in six weeks.

The lesson best learned was that of compassion. Never for one moment could I let down in an attitude of love derived from my understanding of God and His Christ, and the standard of beholding man as Christ Jesus did—as perfect, and responsive to God—in appraising the needs of both my husband and our daughter. Holding both up compassionately taught priceless lessons.

Six weeks after this healing our daughter went to a summer camp to spend a month of her vacation. Her healing was so complete that she was able to swim, hike, and participate in all activities. Since this healing she has enjoyed all sports activities.

HILDA PHILLIPS LOWREY
Pittsburgh, Pennsylvania
The Christian Science Journal January 1972

One of our sons was hit by a car.

Last year, as one of our sons was crossing the street in front of our house, he was hit by a car. I was in the backyard at the time and heard the screech of brakes and the impact. I ran to the street, not knowing who had been hit. As I ran I declared the spiritual truth about God's creation, affirming that one idea of God cannot collide with another. It then occurred to me that our son was due home that very moment. Neighbors began to come to the scene.

When I reached the street, our son was lying there crying and trying to get up. He had landed on his head, and he told me that he could not see. I immediately declared to him that God was right there. *Science and Health* says, referring to Jesus, "He knew that matter had no life and that real Life is God; therefore he could no more be separated from his spiritual Life than God could be extinguished" (p. 51). I knew this child could never be separated from his loving Father-Mother God.

It sometimes amazes me what angel messages come to prayerful thought in times of immediate need. In this instance I remembered two passages from *Science and Health* we had discussed in my Sunday School class the previous Sunday: "Maintain the facts of Christian Science,—that Spirit is God, and therefore cannot be sick. . ." (p. 417) and "All is Mind and Mind's idea. You must fight it out on this line. Matter can afford you no aid" (p. 492). The truth of these statements came to me at that urgent moment, quickly and clearly. I decided right in the middle of the street that this was an illusion, that all I needed was one spiritual truth, or fact, and that was what I was going to stay with, not allowing any suggestion of evil to enter my thought.

I helped our son up. He was quite shaken, but very willing to hear about the truth. (The driver of the car, who was terribly upset, had used her car phone to call for paramedics.) I felt such compassion and love all around; it was a power that was defin-itely not just human. I know it was God. I also felt it was very important to forgive the driver. Our son told her he was sorry for running across the street without looking. We then went into the house, where I wanted to be alone to talk with him before the paramedics came. (I left my kind neighbors to care for the driver.)

Immediately I called my husband at work. He called a Christian Science practitioner for prayerful support, so I could continue to take care of the boy. He had contusions, as well as a very large swelling on his head. As we prayed, healing began before my eyes; bleeding stopped, the bruises began to fade noticeably, and shortly he was able to see. After I had made him comfortable on the sofa, the paramedics arrived. I was so grate-ful for the care and gentleness they expressed to us. They looked our son over and asked him some questions. When they asked him who he was, he answered (to their surprise, I'm sure), "I'm God's image and likeness." When they asked him where he lived, he answered, "In the everlasting arms of Love." It was obvious that these were the spiritual facts he was holding to.

Soon my husband arrived home. He continued praying with our son, while I attended to the young driver, who was still quite shaken up. To calm her, the paramedics assured her that they would not be leaving if they did not feel our son was going to be all right. In a short while, when a police offi-cer came to make a report, I was able to assure him that the paramedics had taken a look at him and released him.

It seemed wise to keep our son home from school for a few days. Although the bruises disappeared quickly, he was still in some discomfort at times. The practitioner asked him to study the Lord's Prayer, so we read it from *Science and Health,* along with its spiritual interpretation. When we got to "And forgive us our debts, as we forgive our debtors," and the spiritual interpretation, *"And Love is reflected in love"* (p. 17), he began to cry. I realized he hadn't forgiven himself; he had forgiven the driver but not himself. He called the practitioner back and discussed this with her. And then he did forgive himself. All discomfort ceased. He was back in school within a week, and there was no further discussion about the incident; it was as if it never happened.

Proof of the completeness and permanency of the healing came a few months later, when he played defensive line on a local tackle football team. I will always remember this healing and the spiritual lessons learned.

NANCY WALKER

I was waiting for my daughter outside the Walker's home when I heard the screech of car brakes. My first instinct was to call 911. I ran in to use the Walker's telephone while Mrs. Walker went out to check on Keith.

After phoning, I went out to see if I could help. By then Mrs. Walker was talking to Keith and helping him back to their home. I was quite concerned about him but felt comforted by his mother's absolute faith in God. Nancy telephoned me later that evening and told us he was doing well.

When I saw Keith a few days later there were no signs that he had ever been hit. It was so nice to see a family's absolute faith in prayer, and the positive results from it.

JACK A. BERRIER
Northridge, California
Christian Science Sentinel April 26, 1993

Love's stability: a foster child's story

How can the effects of an abused childhood be healed? In the following interview, contributing editor for the *Journal, Sentinel, Herald*

Robert A. Johnson talks with Jerry Cook, who spent the first ten years of his life being bounced back and forth between a foster home and his natural mother. Here, Mr. Cook shares how the light of Christian Science and the example of one person's life brought him through his difficult childhood and completely healed him of any aftereffects. Mr. Cook went on to a successful career that has included military service, fatherhood, and teaching.

Jerry, from what you've told me, there was very little stability in your younger years. Can you tell us something of what you remember from those years?

My first years were spent in and out of different houses. But at age three I was placed in a foster home with a very loving family. For the next eight years I was in and out of that same foster home. This home was very orderly and yet very loving, a very stable environment. During the interims when I was living with my natural mother, it was a time of just pretty much running free on the streets, doing whatever I wanted to do. There were eight of us children in the family; very few of us had the same father. I remember once when I was with my natural mother on my sixth birthday, she allowed me to drink an entire six-pack of beer. Afterward I got up and immediately passed out. I was told that not until three days later was I coherent again.

Your early childhood years were the kind that many people say leave permanent emotional scars. How do you feel about that?

Well, I think that's part of the spiritual healing I had. I can look back on those times and, yes, I do remember them, but because of the spiritual view of life that my foster mother opened up to me, I don't have any hatred or scars.

What was it about your foster home that gave you this new view?

I think it was the sense of spiritual stability. My foster mother was a Christian Scientist, and the way she ran her home was based on her understanding of the truths taught by

Christ Jesus. I knew that when I came into that house, I was going to be loved and I was going to have rules to follow. There were never any punishments, just a sense of love and of belonging. Starting at about age eight, I began attending the Christian Science Sunday School whenever I was in the home. I was a part of that family, I was totally accepted. And I was only one of eighteen foster children that my foster family had over the years!

Was there a special event that caused you to leave your natural mother and stay with your foster mother?

When I was about ten years old, my mother no longer had a place to stay, so we moved to Colorado for about six months to live with one of her daughters, who had five kids of her own. The situation was very tense. There was a sense of not belonging there. At that time I was old enough to recognize the deeper, spiritual nature of the love and caring that I had in my foster home. After that summer I said, "Send me home to my foster family or I will leave; I will just run away." I knew where I belonged.

That was a rather courageous action for a ten-year-old to take.

Well, it's like a flower that turns to the sun. Once you've felt genuine love, you will return to it. I can say that's where I had my family, and I had to return to it.

I think the protection I was turning to relates to the twenty-third Psalm, which we studied in Sunday School. *Science and Health* has an interpretation of it that really opened up this psalm to something I felt I could use daily. It begins, "[DIVINE LOVE] is my shepherd; I shall not want. [LOVE] maketh me to lie down in green pastures: [LOVE] leadeth me beside the still waters" (p. 578). I think I was beginning to feel my oneness with divine Love.

I can tell that the sense of Love's being your Father-Mother is very important to you, Jerry. How did your foster mom help give you this conviction?

Well, she really put Christian healing into practice in her daily life. I never knew anything else. I remember, when I was nine, a cat getting caught in the fan belt of our car; everybody had pretty much given up and felt that it should be put out of its misery. My foster mother put it in the basement and prayed for it, and in three days the cat was completely healed. Animals, anything that was hurt, seemed to know that she was the one who would take care of them. She loved everything. Nothing went wanting in our neighborhood.

As a teenager, did you have any healings that stand out to you?

Yes. One summer when I was a senior in high school, I was working on a farm weeding bean fields with eight or nine other boys. One of them accidentally brought his machete down on my hand as I was digging out a sunflower. I immediately covered it up and asked to be taken home. Of course, they all said I needed to go to the hospital and wanted to look at it. And I said, "No, I'll be fine, just take me home." I can remember it was "the scientific statement of being" from *Science and Health,* that I thought about as I walked the three quarters of a mile out of that field. That statement begins, "There is no life, truth, intelligence, nor substance in matter. All is infinite Mind and its infinite manifestation, for God is All-in-all" (p. 468).

When I got home, my foster mother met me at the door with no fear. She met everything in our life with no fear because she knew where it was at—that there was no room for fear because there is no fear in God. She was well founded on man's relation to God. She knew I was under the shelter—in the loving arms—of God, Love.

Needless to say, in just a few days I was out and about. In fact, we took a vacation and I went swimming with no effect from that incident.

Your foster mother's example really was what brought you out of any sense of having a difficult childhood, wasn't it? Her example of meeting every challenge with confidence?

Exactly. There never seemed to be a problem with her. And things weren't easy for her, either, but I didn't know it until I was grown up. My foster dad passed on when I was eleven; I didn't know that the only income we had was from his Social Security. But there was never any want. If something was needed, it was always there. As I say, it was fearless and total acceptance of God's care.

The final step of my healing came after I was married and had a child of my own. I still harbored a bit of sadness over not having grown up with my own family. But as I grew spiritually, I realized that, as God's offspring, we're all one family of man. I saw that because the Father-Mother God is our real Parent, I had never really missed anything. I didn't have to harbor any feeling of loss, because I had never been separated from God, Love, and the fullness of His care for me. When I was able to accept that and could see what it meant, my healing was complete. I was even able to go back and establish contact with some of my natural sisters whom I had not seen for years.

Thank you so much for sharing your story, Jerry.

Well, it needs to be shared. It's part of the complete healing—giving my gratitude for it.

Jackie Sommers is the daughter of Jerry's foster mom. In verifying her foster brother's experience for the *Sentinel,* she shared with us an insight into what shaped her mother's unshakable reliance on God as the only Father-Mother. She said that when she was born prematurely, her mother was told that her baby was in such ill health that she would not live through the night, and that if she did, she would never walk properly because her legs were deformed. Her mother called a Christian Science practitioner that day to pray for the baby and also turned wholeheartedly to God's power, affirming that "Jackie is God's child, not mine, but God's." The baby's health was quickly restored, and by age two her legs were perfectly straight. It was that healing that taught her mother the certainty of God's love and care, said Jackie, and impelled her in her work with foster children.

"My mother felt that the real Parent these foster children had was God, and that God was the provider of everything they needed—health and supply," Jackie said. "And it was never an apron-strings type of love she had for these children; she could love them for two months—or two years—and send them on their way with joy. She knew that their only real tie was with their Father-Mother God."

Christian Science Sentinel April 3, 1995

8

Growing up and "finding ourselves"

Young people face difficulties in all areas of their lives as serious as those of any adult. They, too, find prayer is effective, and that God's love is there for them.

The doctor gave a preliminary diagnosis of mononucleosis.

Late in June 1984 our son woke on a Saturday morning feeling ill. By that evening he was feeling much pain in his neck and finding it difficult to breathe and swallow. A Christian Science practitioner was called for help through prayer.

Throughout Sunday and into Monday there was swelling and he was feverish. The next morning his father wished to have a diagnosis, after observing the difficulty our son was having in breathing. The doctor gave a preliminary diagnosis of mononucleosis, and blood tests were taken. He said that there is no medicine to cure this disease, but he offered painkillers and a medication for the feverish condition. Our son chose not to take these. The official results of the blood tests were to come from the laboratory later.

We had been praying for him all along, and we began to see improvement. Our son was now able to pray for himself more, but it seemed very difficult for him to feel any joy. Indeed, he was beginning to feel very discouraged and sorry for himself. He was upset that he was missing his first week of work at his summer job and was concerned that he might lose the job. He was also concerned that he was unable to "work out" for football and that he might not make the team when training camp started in August. These fears were not helped by the doctor's earlier comments that it was unlikely that he would be able to do much of a physical nature for quite some time.

Before I left on Friday afternoon to keep a previous commitment, I reminded our son that prayerful treatment does not set out primarily to change the physical condition, but to spiritualize thought, and this brings healing. As I drove up our street later that afternoon, I was astounded to see our son out mowing a neighbor's lawn. Later I asked him what had happened after I left. Apparently the fog of lethargy and self-pity had been broken as he sat down by himself and really studied ideas from the Bible and *Science and Health with Key to the Scriptures* by Mary Baker Eddy in an effort to gain a sense of joy. He said that all of a sudden he felt good and remembered that he had promised a neighbor to cut his lawn that week. So, off he went. He had not been able to eat any food since the Saturday before; yet that night he ate pizza. That was the end of the trouble.

No recuperative period of any sort was required. He started his summer job on Monday and worked the rest of the summer. He also "worked out" for football and reported to training camp the third week in August. In addition to a full academic schedule, he had a successful football season. There were no repercussions from the disease at all.

I'd like to add that on the Monday our son reported to work, someone from the doctor's office called and asked us to bring him in because the final lab report had arrived and showed him to have a severe case of mononucleosis. They wanted to check his liver for possible damage and to prescribe a special diet to minimize possible damage that comes from such a situation. We declined the examination but thanked them for their interest. We felt tremendous gratitude to God. The healing was complete.

GERTRUDE J. GRAHAM
Yarmouth Port, Massachusetts
Christian Science Sentinel January 7, 1991

The time came for another dental checkup.

At a regular dental checkup, I was informed my teenage daughter had seventeen cavities. Since she had been to the dentist six months previously, I found this hard to accept. But soon after, when she was away and complaining that her teeth hurt, she went to a dentist in another city. He found eleven cavities, and said X-rays would probably reveal more.

I had already begun to give some prayerful thought to the diagnosis after the earlier dental visit. Now I began concentrated study. One of my first thoughts was to look up references on *space* and *fill,* since according to the dictionary a cavity is an "unfilled space within a mass." Just looking at that definition alerted me to the spiritual counterfact to the problem—that God is omnipresent and fills all space.

Some of the particularly inspiring passages I found included these: "Open thy mouth wide, and I will fill it" (Psalms 81:10); "Let my mouth be filled with thy praise and with thy honour all the day" (Psalms 71:8); "The depth, breadth, height, might, majesty, and glory of infinite Love fill all space. That is enough!" (*Science and Health,* p. 520).

Very soon my daughter stopped complaining of pain. Next I began thinking about some of the commonly accepted causes of cavities. The particular concern I had to deal with was the suggestion that eating too much sugar and junk food had caused irreversible damage. Immediately I remembered

Jesus' words "Not that which goeth into the mouth defileth a man; but that which cometh out of the mouth, this defileth a man" (Matthew 15:11), which led me to the Psalmist's prayer: "Let the words of my mouth, and the meditation of my heart, be acceptable in thy sight, O Lord, my strength, and my redeemer" (19:14).

Further enlightenment came as I associated these ideas with difficulties my daughter was having in school, both academically and with friendships. Some teachers had complained that there was too much sarcasm in the school, as if the way to feel good about oneself was to tear someone else down.

I realized this attitude could be summed up in two extremes. The first was "I'm great—I know that—how can you be so stupid?" Jesus' lesson to all of us on this attitude is "I can of mine own self do nothing" (John 5:30). The other extreme was "I can't understand—I'm so stupid." Paul's answer to this is: "I can do all things through Christ which strengtheneth me" (Philippians 4:13). The laws of God teach that what heals both these attitudes is an understanding of man's spiritual nature, which subordinates human will and self-centeredness to God, the divine Mind.

No dental work was done to fill the cavities. Instead, I prayed with the help of the weekly Christian Science Bible Lessons, trying to get a better understanding of Mary Baker Eddy's definition of man as "the full representation of Mind" (*Science and Health*, p. 591). The time came for another dental checkup. After I made the appointment, I took time especially to acknowledge prayerfully that man, as God's image and likeness, is perfect, and that only that perfection can be seen. God's man can only know what God knows.

Waiting in the office while my daughter's teeth were being cleaned and checked, I felt no concern. Just prior to the appointment, I had declared to myself that she was in God's care, knowing the prayerful work was done and complete. An hour or so later she came out grinning like a commercial, with the dentist's verdict of "No cavities." The healing was complete. I then went in for my checkup and had the same report.

A side effect of this healing was that my daughter released the animosity and resentment she had felt toward another student; her grades improved, and she became a much happier person.

We often hear about the negative side effects associated with medicine. I am so grateful that spiritual treatment has only positive side effects and is always a progressive step as we work out our own salvation.

JOAN KNOWLES
Waban, Massachusetts
Christian Science Sentinel October 19, 1992

My friend ran down the mountain to get help.

A friend and I went hiking on a snow-covered mountain in southern California. Because of the combination of warm days and below-freezing evening temperatures, many of the trails were covered with a sheet of ice. While walking along one of these trails, I slipped and fell nearly a thousand feet down the slope of a rocky gorge, eventually coming to a stop when my body hit a small tree.

I suffered severe injuries, including a compound fracture to one of my legs, a broken pelvis, a broken wrist and finger, lacerations on my face and body, various internal injuries, and internal bleeding. After the fall I suffered from hypothermia.

The pain was intense, and I remember thinking momentarily that it would have been much easier had I just fallen a few more feet and got the whole thing over with. I knew, however, that I was in a position to prove that the real man is created in the image of God, obedient to the laws of God. I knew that man's true identity is not contained in flesh and bones but is spiritual. My purpose in living was, and is, to gain a greater understanding of my relationship to God.

In *Science and Health* Mrs. Eddy writes, "The relations of God and man, divine Principle and idea, are indestructible in Science; and Science knows no lapse from nor return to harmony, but holds the divine order or spiritual law, in which God and all that He creates are perfect and eternal, to have remained unchanged in its eternal history" (pp. 470–471).

My friend ran down the mountain to get help. I spent the next four hours waiting for a helicopter to come and airlift me off the side of the mountain. I remember singing Mrs. Eddy's words from the hymn "'Feed my Sheep,'" words that seemed particularly applicable (*Christian Science Hymnal,* No. 304):

Shepherd, show me how to go
  O'er the hillside steep,
How to gather, how to sow,—
  How to feed Thy sheep;
I will listen for Thy voice
  Lest my footsteps stray;
I will follow and rejoice
  All the rugged way.

The helicopter finally arrived, and I was flown to a nearby hospital. My mother and father had called a Christian Science practitioner as soon as they heard what had happened. I'm not sure of the details of the situation, as I was unconscious at times, but I do know that the practitioner continued to support my parents prayerfully in their handling of the situation.

Because I was a minor, the doctors threatened to get a court order to perform surgery for what was considered life-threatening internal bleeding. My parents had no choice, but before the surgery was completed, all bleeding had stopped. Later the doctor told my parents, "Someone got there before me and repaired everything."

The prognosis was that I would not be able to walk for many months, and that I might never be able to walk normally again. I was put in intensive care and listed in critical condition.

During my brief stay in the hospital, through prayer alone my family and I witnessed the complete healing of my severely lacerated face. The original prognosis had been for extensive plastic surgery. On one occasion a doctor demanded that I have immediate surgery to have a metal plate inserted into my broken hip. My mother and father and I rejected this and told the doctor that we would like to continue our reliance on prayer. That evening we continued to pray, considering man as the reflection of God, who is unmovable, permanent Principle. The next morning it was decided that I was well enough to have my legs removed from traction and to complete my recovery at home.

My father reminded me of the power of God-directed persistence. And during my recovery it was most definitely the power of persistent and unconditional faith in the healing power of God that forwarded the healing that took place.

My recovery was steady. This experience began in the middle of February. Within a short time I was able to move about and return to school in a wheelchair. By early summer I was walking with the aid of crutches, even taking short hikes in the mountains of Colorado. During this time the kind support of family and friends was tremendous. Even my high-school band director, who had chosen me to be the drum major shortly before this incident, never once spoke to me about the option of rescinding his decision. Seven months after the fall I was leading our marching band as drum major in a local parade. Since that time I have enjoyed the freedom to participate in a variety of athletic activities, including biking and skiing.

Science and Health states, "Every trial of our faith in God makes us stronger" (p. 410). This trial certainly made my family and me much stronger mentally, morally, and spiritually. The healing was a real turning point for me. Since that time I've seen and experienced numerous other healings. I am most grateful for all the good that has come into my life as the result of God's care of His children.

ERIC D. NELSON
Roslindale, Massachusetts
The Christian Science Journal January 1989

Our daughter continued to lose weight.

About a year ago, I noticed that our sixteen-year-old daughter seemed to be losing quite a bit of weight. When I asked her about it, she replied that she was just trying to slim down a little for the summer. I reminded her that God's child is always in perfect proportion.

During the next few months, however, she continued to lose weight. I prayed earnestly to see her in her true being—as the perfect reflection of God. But when I tried to talk with her about the weight loss, I discovered she was not always honest with me concerning what she was eating. Family and friends became alarmed at her appearance and urged me to get her to eat, which of course I had already tried to do, but to no avail. It seemed she had become a stranger, both in appearance and in attitude. Yet through all of this our daughter seemed to see no change whatever in her physical appearance, and became obsessed with the notion that she must lose still more weight. On a human level, we just could not seem to reach her.

So I continued to pray, recognizing that our daughter was actually God's child—always perfect, pure, and free from any evil influence. Many times a loving Christian Science practitioner helped me hold to these spiritual facts.

At what seemed to be a very low point, one of our daughter's teachers called to tell me that there was a possibility that the school would take legal action to have our daughter hospitalized. At this point, our daughter herself requested help from a practitioner. (She has been attending Sunday School since she was two years old.)

I prayed all that night to recognize God's all-pervading presence. I reviewed all I had studied about man's inseparability from God, his creator, and the many comforting passages from *Science and Health* that I'd worked with.

In the morning I met with the school social worker. But before entering her office, I recalled this statement by Mary Baker Eddy, "Remember, thou canst be brought into no condition, be it ever so severe, where Love has not been before thee and where its tender lesson is not awaiting thee" (*The First Church of Christ, Scientist, and Miscellany,* pp. 149–150). I felt assured that divine Love was already present. The social worker asked what we were doing for our daughter and, confidently, I told her that she was receiving dedicated prayer.

The social worker then stated the steps she thought should be taken, but added that she would not ask for a physical examination at that time. She told us we were free to proceed with our own method of treatment. She did say, however, that she wanted to see our daughter each week and that if she saw no improvement, she would reconsider her decision.

From that time on, our family, along with a Christian Science practitioner, prayed constantly to see our daughter as God had created her, whole and perfect. We recognized also the truth of this Bible verse: "And we know that all things work together for good to them that love God" (Romans 8:28). We also recognized that everyone involved, including our daughter's teacher and the social worker, wanted healing and well-being for our daughter.

For several weeks there was no visible progress, but we were encouraged by several statements from *Science and Health,* such as: "Man is idea, the image, of Love; he is not physique" (p. 475); and, "The relations of God and man, divine Principle and idea, are indestructible in Science; and Science knows no lapse from nor return to harmony, but holds the divine order or spiritual law, in which God and all that He creates are perfect and eternal, to have remained unchanged in its eternal history" (pp. 470–471).

Suddenly one morning, our daughter woke to discover that her face and body were returning to normal. She was also herself mentally and said she felt as if she had awakened from a dream. She was happy and free for the first time in a year.

How we laughed and cried with joy and praised God for this wonderful proof of His care! Progress was swift from that morning on, and the complete healing was realized within a few days. Step by step, I am seeing more clearly that even when results are not seen immediately, God, divine Truth, is ever at work "to give [us] an expected end" (Jeremiah 29:11).

Bonnie Lynn Davis
Racine, Wisconsin
Christian Science Sentinel June 13, 1983

It appeared I was becoming completely helpless.

The summer prior to my junior year in high school was for me a great learning time. I had finished my sophomore year with a fourth place in the state tennis tournament. And to my joy I had been asked to work with my high-school coach, giving summer tennis lessons. I seized the opportunity, knowing that there would be many free hours during the day to spend improving my own playing abilities. My goal for the following year was to be a state tennis champion.

Toward the end of June, however, I began to lose all feeling in my feet. Instead of refuting this lie with the truths of perfect spiritual being, I simply brushed it aside, attributing it to long hours of strenuous activity. After a time, however, my condition became much more serious. It appeared I was becoming completely helpless. One day I happened to read a magazine article describing multiple sclerosis. I realized that I was manifesting four or five of the given symptoms.

By this time I had a Christian Science practitioner praying with me daily. And I too studied and prayed for many hours each day to destroy the mesmeric suggestion of disease. An article I read on the subject of true health in *The Christian Science Journal* emphasized the need to destroy a false concept of our source of health. It brought out that a belief based on the illusion of health as a physical condition is no more reliable than a belief in sickness, for both are built on the sands of human variableness and have no foundation in truth. This helped me see that health is really spiritual and therefore it can never fluctuate, lapse, disappear, or grow old. I gained a lot from that article's enlightening passages. Because we lived in a small, close-knit community, knowledge of the difficulty and subsequent concern for me ran rampant. I was often questioned about the problem, sometimes by people who scarcely knew me. Of course I tried to calm and reassure those individuals. And while I learned to appreciate their genuine concern, at the same time I recognized that my prayer and unceasing reliance on God would go on unaffected.

As the summer progressed, the condition seemed unyielding. I studied, prayed, and wondered why I had not yet been relieved of this false belief. The first thing I had to conquer through prayer was fear. I came to associate fear with distrust in God, and saw that the persistent fear that I might have a lifetime of inactivity was essentially distrust of God's ever-present care for me, His child. Facing up to fear in this way helped me overcome it.

My parents lovingly supported me, and were patient and encouraging when I felt disappointed and discouraged. One day my father pointed out, "You are not God's child by choice; you have no choice in the matter. You are God's child and need only accept it without question." For these words of assurance and for all their loving support, I thank my mother and father.

I spent the last week of summer vacation at the home of the practitioner who was assisting me. There I studied *Science and Health,* particularly pages 390 to 393, where Mary Baker Eddy tells us clearly what to do the instant we discover symptoms of disease. Although I had failed to take such steps in the beginning, these instructions now came to my aid, and I made a daily effort to obey each of them one by one. *Science and Health* states, "Mind is the master of the corporeal senses, and can conquer sickness, sin, and death. Exercise this God-given authority. Take possession of your body, and govern its feeling and action" (p. 393). I also studied "the scientific statement of being" on page 468, which spells out man's true identity and captures the essence of all true prayer.

During that week I began to feel a buoyant gratitude for the tremendous spiritual growth I had gained in the preceding three months. As I got on the bus to go home at the end of my stay, the practitioner encouraged me to let go of the belief of illness and let God's law operate. From then on the condition began to slowly disappear until all effects of the illness were gone and I was restored to well-being.

Although I never captured a state tennis title, I received many other recognitions and was voted Female Athlete of the Year when I was a senior.

I know now, without a doubt, that God is my only Life.

Shannon Turpen Horst
Washington, District of Columbia
Christian Science Sentinel January 4, 1982

There had been an accident and it was developing into a pileup.

In preparation for the Christmas holidays one year, my younger brother and I drove throughout one night to pick up our sister. From there we were to continue on to a family gathering in the mountains. Enroute to our sister's, the weather conditions were extremely bad. It was foggy, windy, and very cold. But I had driven the route many times and was not terribly concerned.

During the night my brother and I took turns driving and sleeping. At about 5 a.m. we entered a mountain pass close to my sister's home. The freeway at that point was five lanes across, going one way. Up ahead through the fog I noticed something strange about the taillights of the cars in front of me. Suddenly I realized that there had been an accident and that it was developing into a pileup. I immediately applied my brakes but nothing happened. The road was covered with ice.

The first words out of my mouth were "God is Love; God is Love!" I was trying to keep the car from going into a spin when my brother abruptly woke up. Ahead through the fog we saw a wall of cars clear across the freeway. I quietly knew that God's man is always safe. We braced for the impact, but it never came. Somehow the car stopped just inches from the collision.

At that moment it came very clearly to me that I must move my car quickly. I threw the car into reverse and shot through the only space available to get beyond the accident to safety. A few cars managed to follow us through, but then two cars crashed, filling in the space and blocking the entire freeway. We pulled off to the side of the road. My brother and I were completely unharmed, as was the car. Never once did I feel any panic or fear.

We got out of the car and went to help. Many people were still trapped in their cars, and others were injured. My brother and I crawled over the wet vehicles and began helping people out of cars and carrying them to safety. A few lines from the poem "The Mother's Evening Prayer" kept running through my mind. The poem is by Mary Baker Eddy (*Poems,* p. 4). The words helped to keep my thoughts focused on what was true and what was really going on.

O gentle presence, peace and joy and power;
  O Life divine, that owns each waiting hour,
Thou Love that guards the nestling's faltering flight!
  Keep Thou my child on upward wing tonight.

At this point, though there was much noise and confusion, all of a sudden I heard very clearly a cry for help. I ran to the edge of the freeway, which at that point is elevated about a hundred feet above the ground. I couldn't see through the fog, but I could hear a woman calling for help from below. I yelled to her to keep calling out, while my brother went to find a way down to her. After a few minutes my brother called out from below and yelled for me to come down. I found where the road met the ground and scrambled down the steep hill. (The hill was so icy and muddy that I ended up alternately falling and crawling down the hill.) All the way I kept repeating a prayer I had learned as a child, knowing that the truth it contained was sufficient to guide my steps safely.

I know that God is where I am—
Beneath, around, above,
Providing, guarding, guiding,
Encircling me in love.

I found my brother, and before I looked at the young woman I quickly affirmed for myself her completeness as God's idea. When I came to her, I could see that her legs were badly injured. My brother and I quietly sat down and talked with her for a few moments, assuring her that she was going to be fine. She told us that she had become confused in the fog and had stepped over the guardrail to avoid being hit. In the fog she had thought there was ground where she was going to step, but instead she had fallen down the long drop.

While I sat talking with her, my brother went to gather the blankets people were dropping to us from the road above. Mentally I kept debating whether I should try to verbalize some of what I was thinking and praying. I did not want to confuse or upset her, but I definitely wanted to break the hypnotic fear and pain that seemed to be gripping her. Right then my brother walked up with the blankets and said to the woman, "You know, God is Love!" and she said, "I know." It seemed to be just the right thing. She visibly relaxed.

Finally enough people came to help us evacuate the woman to the road where an ambulance was waiting. At this point my brother and I decided we could leave, as emergency vehicles were on the scene and others had arrived to help.

When we got to my sister's house a couple of hours late, you can imagine her surprise to see her two brothers standing at the door, cold, muddy, and smiling.

I am deeply grateful, not only for the protection and freedom from fear afforded my brother, my sister, and me, but also for the help we were able to give freely to others because of the strength and peace we have come to know.

CHRIS HEINBAUGH
South Pasadena, California

The woman who had been injured recovered and returned to work. She wrote Chris that after he and his brother reached her, telling her of God's love, she knew she would be all right. "I know I made it through as well as I did," she said, "because God was protecting me and because I had two wonderful people with me to keep me calm and remind me of that."

Christian Science Sentinel December 15, 1986

The possibility that I could be God's child was so appealing.

It was the first day of my sophomore year at college. "Sarah!" three young women shouted in unison as I rounded the corner of the hall, suitcase in hand. Two of them were friends of mine from the year before—Amy and Heather. The other woman was Stacy, the only student remaining from the previous year on my dormitory floor, though I didn't know her well.

In some of our first conversations I asked Stacy what she did for various illnesses, or accidents, because she was a Christian Scientist. "I pray," she told me. "I acknowledge that God is all-powerful, ever-present good, and that I am God's child, made in His image, and therefore my true identity contains only His perfect expression of good. This brings my physical experience more in line with spiritual reality, and I am healed."

The possibility that I could be God's child was so appealing and comforting. But *spiritual and perfect!* I kept wondering, could it be true? If God exists, if He's spiritual and is infinite good, then it must be true. But I wasn't sure about trusting God. Being at college, I wondered if there was anything left to trust, since I was discovering how much human knowledge is inherently faulty.

All during that fall semester, and probably even before then, I had been yearning for something that would give me stability, comfort, peace, and hope. So what a whole new world of ideas opened up for me in these conversations with Stacy! Just weeks after the semester began, I was writing thoughts and ideas in my journal about being *spiritual.* At first, it was hard for me to imagine that I was spiritual. I felt so far from being perfect, and in fact was struggling with the whole concept of identity.

The thought "Who am I?" was constantly on my mind. "Am I spiritual?" was the question that soon replaced it. I considered what it would mean to accept God as the only power and as completely good, as my friend Stacy did. Her life certainly seemed more peaceful than mine, and more stable, without the extreme emotional ups and downs I was experiencing. I had worried sometimes that I wasn't worth much, that I made no difference in the world. Even if I did well in my studies, I wasn't satisfied, because it seemed that someone else was always better. I felt I could never be good enough.

By the end of the semester I had gone once with my friend to a church service, which I really didn't understand. There were readings from the Bible and a book by Mary Baker Eddy called *Science and Health with Key to the Scriptures,* but I didn't understand that there was a theme to the passages read. I had never read the Bible and didn't know the other book, and I found it hard to concentrate on what was said. I wasn't used to listening directly to the Bible without any paraphrasing or explanation from the person conducting the service.

I went with Stacy to an informal meeting of the Christian Science organization on campus, "CSO" as they call it. At the time, I liked this better than the church service, because the people there were my age. The students talked about problems I could relate to, and how they prayed to solve them. The meetings were casual and warm and loving, so I felt at ease and welcome.

During that January I sometimes took part in peace protests against the Gulf War. Yet still I found myself feeling more and more hopeless and depressed. I felt overwhelmed with the sense of evil being everywhere and very powerful. I was crying every day, and the world was a dark place. Toward the end of the month, I went to see a film about South Africa called *A World Apart.* The film was a vivid depiction of a white South African family deeply committed to helping the blacks in their struggle against apartheid. Their involvement tore the family apart. I was overcome with anguish and had to leave the film halfway into it. I was crying so hard I could no longer see the screen.

I tried to pull myself together and managed to get back to my dorm without crying, but as soon as I got to Stacy's room for comfort, the tears began to stream again. She hugged me and we walked down the hall to my room, where she began to tell me how evil seems to be real and powerful, but since God is everywhere and infinite and all-powerful, evil really can't be anywhere, can't have any power. She explained that because God is the only creator, the only Parent of His children, all we can really express is His goodness and love. Stacy emphasized that it is a lie that human nature has an evil side that can dominate good, since God gave us dominion over the whole earth, including the "earthy" elements in the human condition. The false conception of man as being and doing evil is not part of spiritual reality. Stacy also brought out the idea that as one of God's spiritual children, I must reflect joy, peace, and dominion; and that sorrow, fear, and helplessness are not part of me or my identity, and therefore I could reject them.

It was nearly three hours before the tears finally stopped flowing. I began to feel hopeful and consider that God might actually exist and that I did not have to feel overwhelmed by evil. Everything we had discussed during the last few months started to come together for me. I certainly didn't want to take the position that life was meaningless and hopeless, and that good was an accident. I wasn't totally sure I had faith in God, but I was willing to take a chance for good, for Spirit, and turn away from evil.

Just taking my focus off what was evil lessened its control over me. I began to feel lighter, clearer, less burdened and—for the first time in a long time—hopeful. Just before I turned out my light, my friend slipped a note under my door, to emphasize one thing she had said while trying to comfort me. The note read, "God loves *you!*" I smiled and soon fell asleep.

That night I was healed of my depression. I was so happy the next day when Stacy asked me if I would like to come with her to Sunday School to learn more about God, and myself as His image. I felt I was standing in a doorway, leaving all my old ways of thinking behind, stepping into the unknown territory of Spirit.

The healings I had in the first few months of prayer and study encouraged me to continue studying. Before long, I had read *Science and Health* through.

This experience has been a pivotal one for me, since it has turned me to Spirit and taught me how a childlike acceptance of good as real is not naive, but powerful and healing. When I need encouragement today, I go back to the basic concept that God is good, God is Love, and God loves me—and then my outlook improves. Difficult situations are resolved through prayer. I have learned the value and necessity of claiming my joy, which "no man taketh from [me]" (John 16:22).

Name withheld at author's request.
Christian Science Sentinel January 23, 1995

My first words were swear words.

Excerpted from a radio broadcast

Beulah M. Roegge: Welcome to the *Herald of Christian Science.* Our guest today is Robert Holcomb. Bob, I understand that you had some struggles in your early days being committed to life.

ROBERT L. T. HOLCOMB: Well, I certainly did. I grew up in a very difficult situation. When I was born my mother had a nervous breakdown, and my dad thought that the way you got a woman's attention was to beat her. My first words were swear words. I was more familiar with the taste of soap than toothpaste because I spoke such foul language. It was a very difficult thing when my parents finally divorced. I think I went through the typical syndrome of thinking I was responsible. I was feeling guilty because I felt somehow I had brought all this about, and it was very challenging.

BEA: That could take away any desire to really live.

BOB: Yes. Well, it went on. My mom was a desperately unhappy individual because of all she'd been through. She had to support the family in very difficult times. And she had lots of sleeping pills and things around the house, bromides and brown bottles and yellow pills, and that type of thing. She spoke frequently of suicide, but she felt responsible for my brother and me, and she said that was the only reason she didn't do it. So, naturally, that planted the thought that I could just do away with myself that way.

BEA: I've only known you as a very happy adult. What happened to make you change?

BOB: Well, there were three women in my life who made a substantial difference. Of course, my mom—I never questioned her great love for me and her sense of caring. But I also had an exceptional teacher in the Christian Science Sunday School I attended. She always saw such good in me, always loved what I brought to the class, and she had a great sense of enthusiasm and joy about life.

BEA: Your mother was a Christian Scientist?

BOB: I think she would have said that she was interested in Christian Science. I went to Sunday School throughout my childhood and teenage years. This Sunday School teacher just had a wonderful sense of caring. And I learned something very important from her. I learned that when I was unhappy, depressed, and very low, if I could do something kind for someone, if I could do something loving and thoughtful and take my thought off of how desperate my situation was, I could start to move through these very great depressions that I felt. When I did consider suicide and would get out the bottles of pills and think, "Well, is this a way of ending it all?" the thought of love and of helping others would get me through it. I was a terrible, terrible problem child in school, too. I was in the principal's office every week. I spent more time in his office than in class because I would cut up in class. When I stayed out of school, I would forge sickness excuses. I was really a difficult case because I was so unhappy and disturbed. I didn't have many friends because I was embarrassed. I really didn't want to tell people that my parents had been divorced. My life felt groundless and without roots.

This brings me to the third woman that was very significant. She was my high-school English teacher. She was as prim a New England lady as you could come across. She gathered us together on our first day of class, first period in my junior year, and she said, "You in this classroom are very capable people, and you're able to work hard, and you're going to work hard because you're able to do it." I never had anybody say anything wonderful like that about me in school before. I thought I was just a moderate kind of a student. But she turned my life around.

BEA: Was this an advanced class or just her approach?

BOB: It was just her approach—my grades would not have indicated that I was a good student at that time.

BEA: You had potential.

BOB: That teacher just awakened it, and I became a straight *A* student after that. My behavior reformed in every class. Everything changed because I saw that I had something to give, and this made a meaning and a focus to life. I started to see that I had productive things I could do.

BEA: Can you explain this to us? Just positive action like you described isn't the final, or the complete answer. What spirituality undergirds this, would you say?

BOB: Well, the benefit that I gained from my Sunday School teacher brought about in me a great desire to do the same thing myself. I wanted to learn how you could help people through knowing more about them as God's child—through being able to understand what God is and what man, as His child, must be. When I went away to college, I started really reading and studying the Bible and getting to know God. You know, the Bible has so many references to God as Life, and I started to see what that Life is, and that there is joy, strength, continuity. I started to see that God was a very meaningful force in my life. And then I had my first spiritual healing.

BEA: Tell us about it.

BOB: Well, it was kind of an interesting experience. I was singing in Handel's *Messiah.* All through my growing-up years one of the things I'd never told my mother about was that I had terrible leg cramps. I would wake up in the night and suffer greatly. The pain would remain for several days afterward. The only way I'd been able to gain relief from these cramps was to stand up. We were all sitting down singing *Messiah,* so I didn't feel that I could stand up when one of these cramps came on. I looked down at what we were singing. It was the place in the "Hallelujah Chorus" that says, "The kingdom of this world is become the kingdom of our Lord and of His Christ." And I saw that there wasn't any law of a material sort that could have prominence over God's law. And I'd come to learn more about God's law as the law of Love, the law of Life, and I saw that this was what was triumphant. This is what had the victory, and this was the law that governed my being. And instantly the pain was gone, and that was the total end of the condition.

Bea: That's wonderful. You've never suffered from leg cramps since?

Bob: No.

Bea: So your childhood has been restored in a way, hasn't it, by seeing that you're the child of God?

Bob: Yes, this happened in a very interesting way. I finally broke through depression and loneliness and, frankly, of missing having a dad, missing the approval and nurturing. I was reading a book called *No and Yes* by Mary Baker Eddy. Under the question "IS THERE A PERSONAL DEITY?" she writes: "God is Love; and Love is Principle, not person. What the person of the infinite is, we know not; but we are gratefully and lovingly conscious of the fatherliness of this Supreme Being" (p. 19). When I read that word *fatherliness* I just felt the embrace of the Father, that He loved me, He approved of me. And there was something very tender and close about that relationship I had with God in seeing Him as fatherly. And that totally erased all the sense of fear and depression and loneliness and longing, and I just felt complete. I felt I had everything I needed.

And the interesting thing is, Bea, that when I had discovered God as Father and learned what that means, I was able to be back in contact with my dad, and we really became very good friends, went on fishing trips together. Many of the things I never had as a youngster, I had as a grownup with my dad, and we had a good relationship and there was a total sense of forgiveness and forgetting and just going forward. I love my dad very much.

Bea: I'm just so grateful to hear the whole story and the hope that it holds out for all of us that any commitment to life just brings more life, and this abundant life that Jesus promised us is shown in so many different ways.

Christian Science Sentinel February 21, 1994

Four years of sowing wild oats were starting to take their toll.

"I will restore to you the years that the locust hath eaten" (Joel 2:25). Looking back is rarely progressive (which is why it's called "looking *back,*" I suppose), but in recounting my steps since graduating from college, I can honestly state that if it weren't for Christian healing I'd have "cashed in" long ago—or, less tragically, I'd still be battling very severe emotional problems.

My last semester in college was difficult; four years of sowing wild oats were starting to take their toll. I had enjoyed wild partying and social activities, but often felt unloved, and found it difficult to maintain a true feeling of self-worth. This in turn led me to hide behind an unattractive, egotistical personality.

My relationships with members of the opposite sex were strained and uncomfortable. A homosexual friend of mine had been suggesting I try his lifestyle, as he had found this a way to happiness and solutions to relationship problems. At one point I consented, but later feelings of self-condemnation and guilt were crushing. I felt very much afraid that my only resort now would be to take up permanently a gay lifestyle—something I did not choose to do. Remorse, fear, and frustration were all hammering away at me; I had spells of crying, thoughts of committing suicide, and found it harder to interact with others.

There was a counselor on the campus whom I was seeking help from regularly. His pronouncements of "You're fine, really" would only provide relief temporarily, and I didn't seem to be getting any better as I continued to hear this from him. He was a caring individual and knew his profession, but couldn't make the pain go away. I couldn't seem to shake a ghastly feeling of having done something sinful that was irreversible and had defined me for life.

I guess it was no accident when one day I realized my only answer was Christian Science. I knew about this religion from having talked with the mother of a high-school girlfriend, who had spent a great deal of time answering my questions. I had even gone to church sometimes, but had drifted away when I went to college.

I called my friend's mom just as soon as I could and told her I needed help. I said, "I want to be the best person I can possibly be." (I'm still working on *that* one!) She invited me to pay her a visit as soon as I could, and told me to start studying the Bible and *Science and Health.*

This was all just a beginning. The road to healing of my emotional problems wasn't something to be traversed overnight. My friend's mother helped me to pray to God. I struggled with many obstacles and tough times, but while the healing was slow, it was *certain.*

Gradually I became more at ease with myself and with others. A sense of humor I had always cherished began to show itself again, only in a gentler way than before. Many character flaws were healed during this time. People were beginning to find me more likable, and I was able to function socially once more.

Loving myself, though not in an egotistical manner, came with the healing. In time, I grew to forgive myself, as well as the man I had been sexually involved with. The bitterness melted away in proportion as I tried to see *everyone* as spiritual and perfect, in God's image. "The way to extract error from mortal mind is to pour in truth through flood-tides of Love" (*Science and Health,* p. 201). The torments of the past had no hold on me, they disappeared as I came to learn they had never been part of my true, spiritual being.

Healing shows us that it's also our duty to keep praying and growing, not necessarily because the old, hard times are likely to reappear, but because we become conscious of the further demands made on us when thought is spiritualized. The lessons I learned from those difficult times have proved to be invaluable, showing me that "the very circumstance, which your suffering sense deems wrathful and afflictive, Love can make an angel entertained unawares" (*ibid.*, p. 574).

I am happily married now. I am so thankful for the opportunity to bear witness to God's power, through His divine laws of restoration and adjustment.

Name withheld at author's request
Christian Science Sentinel June 13, 1994

One thought kept presenting itself—I would never again be able to think clearly.

While I was in my late teens, I was involved with what are today referred to as "recreational drugs." One evening I found myself suffering the effects of LSD, hallucinations and all. This occurred even though I had not taken that particular drug in weeks.

Although I'd had nothing to do with Christian Science for some years, I knew prayer could heal me. Many statements from the writings of Mary Baker Eddy brought encouragement in the face of great fear. On page 469 of *Science and Health* she writes: "Mind is God. The exterminator of error is the great truth that God, good, is the *only* Mind, and that the supposititious opposite of infinite Mind—called *devil* or evil—is not Mind, is not Truth, but error, without intelligence or reality."

"The exterminator of error is the great truth that God, good, is the only Mind . . ." Those words stood as a bright light at the end of what seemed a very dark tunnel. I began to learn that God, divine Mind, infinite Principle, was the exterminator of error, not me!

Throughout this ordeal one particular thought kept presenting itself. It was that I would never again be able to think clearly. This argument was countered by the realization that intelligence has its source in the divine Mind. I read on page 478 of *Science and Health,* "How can intelligence dwell in matter when matter is non-intelligent and brain-lobes cannot think? Matter cannot perform the functions of Mind. Error says, 'I am man;' but this belief is mortal and far from actual. From beginning to end, whatever is mortal is composed of material human beliefs and of nothing else. That only is real which reflects God." I recognized that in my true spiritual being I reflected the divine Mind, infinite good.

The realization of these spiritual facts sustained me through the next few months. Gradually I was able to demonstrate the spiritual conviction that I could never be separated from God. This conviction took form in my simply being able to leave my bedroom on my own, and then the house, without a sense of overwhelming fear. Finally, with great joy, I was able to attend church on my own.

What have I learned from this healing? That I had been caught up in the sensualism and materialism of that particular period. Clearly, I was mentally asleep. Since that time I've realized that I must stay alert to the subtle suggestions of the carnal mind, which always claim to be our thinking.

Science and Health states, "The intercommunication is always from God to His idea, man" (p. 284). This statement has brought me tremendous inspiration. It shows me that no matter where we are, God is there. We need no material accompaniments to listen for His guidance, just a deep desire to know His presence.

James R. Elmgren-Carlson
Hopkinton, Massachusetts
The Christian Science Journal November 1988

My friend insisted it was not too late to turn my life around.

In my late teens and in college, I investigated a number of religions and came to the conclusion that if there was a God, He was unknowable. The philosophy classes I had taken showed mankind's futile attempts to prove the existence of God on the basis of human reason and logic, and led me to investigate hallucinogenic drugs as a way of finding some deeper meaning in life. Instead I found myself physically and "psychologically" hooked on these drugs.

I wound up in jail, serving a thirty-day sentence on a drug conviction. After I was released I returned to the university where I was enrolled as a student. I had been heavily involved in the use of marijuana, LSD, and cocaine, and quickly found myself slipping back into the same pattern despite the promise I had made to myself in jail that I would "go straight" when I got out.

At that point I was introduced to Christian Science through a young woman I met on campus. She intrigued me because she had such a different and positive philosophy of life, and we had a number of conversations about her religion. In our conversations I must admit that I tried my best to convince her that she was out of touch with reality, but in retrospect it was clearly the other way around.

When I was arrested again later that year on drug charges and for assaulting the officer who tried to search my pockets, my friend did not abandon me. In fact, she came with me to court. Because of the seriousness of the charges against me, and because I was on probation following my previous confinement, my future had never looked less promising. The judge told my attorney that I would be spending a long time in jail, and I was scared.

While we were at the courthouse, my friend insisted that it was not too late to turn my life around. She told me that God loved me as His perfect child, but that I had to be willing to bring my life into conformity with His commands in order to find my true identity as the pure and beloved offspring of Spirit, God. I had to be willing to say "no" to dependence on matter, to drugs and immorality, and to turn wholeheartedly to God for my salvation. At that moment in my life my friend was offering me hope.

I didn't know if Christian Science could really help me, but I wanted another chance in life. I can still clearly remember that first moment when I mentally quit resisting this divine aid and turned to God with my humble prayer for His help.

It was just as the Bible promises: "Submit yourselves therefore to God. Resist the devil, and he will flee from you. Draw nigh to God, and he will draw nigh to you" (James 4:7, 8). From that moment some very tangible things began to happen to me. Things which I knew were not just coincidental.

The judge's attitude toward me completely changed. Rather than a long term in jail, I was given community service work to do. My seemingly uncontrollable desire to get high on drugs and alcohol just left me.

I discovered that God is indeed knowable. The synonyms for Him, as indicated in the Bible—divine Life, Truth, Love, Mind, Soul, Spirit, and Principle—and explained in *Science and Health* (587:5–8), gave me a way to know and understand God and to see His presence and power operating in my life.

As a result of my earlier experiences with the law, I had become interested in going to law school. I had taken the Law School Admission Test on two occasions, both times scoring 43 percent. With my fledgling understanding of God as the source of my true intelligence, I retook the LSAT and scored in the ninetieth percentile. This improvement was so dramatic that the testing agency held up my score in order to recheck my test and to verify with the proctors that I had not somehow cheated. The new score was then confirmed.

I went back to the university and petitioned to have a semester of failing grades, received during the time I had stopped going to class to stay high on drugs, stricken from my records. I had been advised that such petitions were seldom approved, but when the administrators recognized the transformation of my character that had taken place they granted my petition.

On the basis of my corrected academic record and the LSAT score, and with the personal intervention of the dean on my behalf, I was accepted at one of the finest law schools in my state.

After three years of law school I took the greatly feared bar examination and actually enjoyed the experience and never had any doubt about having passed. I have now been practicing law in my state for nine years, and I feel that it is time to publicly acknowledge my deep gratitude. I was given the opportunity to start anew, and my life has been transformed.

Over the course of these fifteen years my understanding and appreciation of the Science of the Christ have grown deeper and stronger, and I know that I have found the truth I had long been searching for.

I am especially thankful that my friend who had helped me so much consented to be my wife and that we now have three wonderful children who are learning to know and love God as their Father-Mother.

Kirk Randolph Wilson

I am very happy to confirm my husband's testimony. The facts are as he has related them. I could see plainly my friend's goodness, irrespective of all the negative human circumstances, and as we worked from the basis of one all-loving God guiding and governing us, the false habits very naturally disappeared. I rejoice now, as then, in knowing him as God's perfect man, and I am grateful for the spiritual growth we both gained during our early friendship.

At that time I felt compelled to study thoroughly the chapter entitled "Marriage" in *Science and Health* to understand more clearly the basis of a right relationship. This was long before we considered marrying.

Linda Rothi Wilson
Lafayette, California
Christian Science Sentinel July 6, 1987

9

Jobs, pay, and work hazards

Looking to God in prayer, we find work, rewarding employment helping ourselves and others. Even what are called "hazardous jobs" can be safe.

It took two and a half hours to clean the hot oil off me.

For forty years I was a professional big-rig truck driver. A great many of the four million miles I logged involved moving construction equipment of huge lengths up to 110 feet and weights up to 190,000 pounds. Another part of my driving experience was with tankers, transporting hot asphalt oil. This oil is maintained at about 350 degrees Fahrenheit. One time I was pumping out an underground storage tank into my tanker, when a hose broke, blowing this hot oil on my face and ear and sealing my eyes closed. I immediately turned to "the scientific statement of being" from *Science and Health with Key to the Scriptures,* which begins, "There is no life, truth, intelligence, nor substance in matter" (p. 468). As I declared the inability of matter to feel sensation, within a short time the heat and pain left. I then became conscious of myself as the spiritual idea of God, and of the fact that nothing but God, good, had ever touched me.

My company insisted that I be taken to the hospital. The staff cleaned the oil off me with ether, and there was much fear expressed for my well-being. It took two and a half hours to clean me, and this provided the opportunity to pray for myself, affirming silently the truth of my spiritual being, untouched by matter.

By the time they were through, there was no evidence of burns. A doctor examined me and asked me to come outside so he could view me in natural light. As he was looking at my face, I looked back at him (through clear eyes) and thanked him; I told him that I had been praying all that time. His answer was that whatever I was doing, I should keep it up.

A few years later I had another encounter with this hot oil. As I was filling one of the underground tanks, I was standing almost on top of the place where the hose is attached to the tank so I could check the float. I did not realize that the float was not working properly, and the tank overflowed. The hot oil spilled on my legs and down into my shoes, severely burning my feet. I wasn't as quick this time to deny the error of this accident. I found myself saying, "Why were you so stupid to let this happen again?"

My pants had to be cut off, and my feet and ankles were badly injured because the oil had filled my shoes. After realizing I had allowed thoughts of fear and self-condemnation to possess me, which did not have reality because they did not come from God, I settled down by becoming conscious of myself as spiritual and perfect, never touched by matter.

Again I was required to go to the hospital. My legs (which had also been burned) were much better by the time I got there, although they still showed a little redness. I knew I needed to destroy fear, because fear involves inflammation (see *Science and Health,* p. 586). My feet and ankles still appeared to be so severely damaged that a doctor told me they would need skin grafts. I asked her just to clean me up. She agreed, if I would sign a release. They bandaged my feet and applied nonmedicated salve so that the bandages would not stick to my skin. The doctor insisted that I return the next day to be examined for my company's insurance.

When I arrived home I was able to be quiet and study, and to become more conscious of the truth of my being. With the prayerful support of my wife, I grew peaceful and had a good night. The next morning she drove me to the hospital. The same doctor examined me. She then turned to my wife and said that if she hadn't seen my condition the day before, she would have found it hard to believe that such a healing had taken place. No more was said about the skin grafts.

Within ten days I was declared fit to return to work (actually I could have returned in five). It's wonderful to know that as our consciousness is filled with Christ, Truth, the false evidence that seemed so real, disappears.

H. THOMAS DYER

Thomas Dyer wrote at another time of his healing of addiction to prescription drugs that began when he was driving big-rig trucks long distances.

Twelve years ago I had a rewarding opportunity to serve as a chaplain at a men's jail in California. One evening while I was waiting to be escorted up to the chapel, the guard said to me, "Why do you take your time to come here? These men are not worth your time." After praying a moment I answered him, "If you were having a bad dream, a nightmare, wouldn't you be grateful if someone shook you and tried to waken you from that dream?" This conversation reminded me of a "nightmare" experience I had that lasted about eight years.

I have worked in the trucking industry for forty years. My father was in the trucking business, so I grew up in it. I had always wanted to get into specialized hauling, cranes and bulldozers and so forth. When I did get enough experience to get a job in this kind of work, I was surprised to discover what it entailed. We would sometimes work all day and then pull a load to northern California from southern California that night, a good ten-hour drive. Sometimes, this schedule would last all week.

I had quite a time staying awake, and one night I asked a fellow I worked with how he was able to stay awake. He offered me some pills that he took. I declined them, but after fighting sleep night after night I asked him for some. The first one I took kept my eyes open and made me alert. I thought these were the greatest and wondered why I had declined them before. I saw nothing wrong with taking them.

As the weeks passed, I was using more and more of the pills. When I would get into bed, I couldn't sleep, and I would take more to get through the next day. Even when I was home on weekends, my body would be so tired and I would be so grumpy that I would take them; I felt I had no source of strength other than those pills.

My wife tried for years to awaken me, offering help through prayer, but I became verbally abusive. Finally after several years she told me she could not put up with it any-more. She moved to another city and took a job. She told me she would always know what was true about me as God's child. I remember thinking to myself: At last I won't have to listen to any more Christian Science talk.

I continued on with my lifestyle, but after a while I began to dislike myself very much. It dawned on me that I had lost a lot. I tried to stop taking the pills. By this time I was using twenty-five to thirty a day. A lot of the time I wasn't even sure what or how much I was taking. I had prescriptions with two doctors, and I was buying the pills on the black market, too. I couldn't stop by my own willpower, and I became very depressed about this.

One Sunday morning I was listening to the radio when a program came on that included healings that had come about through Christian Science. A young woman told of being healed of the same addiction I had. I had thought I was the only one with this difficulty, but her addiction had been as serious as mine. Listening to her gave me hope and courage.

I later called my wife and told her what I had heard on the radio program. I asked her if she would consider returning to me, and I said that I would like to work out my problem through Christian Science. Well, she agreed to return. For the next few months she prayed with me. I had changed jobs and was home in the early afternoons. I would get the Bible and

Science and Health and smoke cigarettes as I read. After three or four weeks, one afternoon while I was studying the Bible Lesson I lighted up a cigarette. It tasted awful. I put it out, and I have never had the desire to smoke again. This healing gave me hope and inspired me to continue studying.

I carried a paperback copy of *Science and Health* with me in my truck. Page one of the chapter "Prayer" begins: "The prayer that reforms the sinner and heals the sick is an absolute faith that all things are possible to God,—a spiritual understanding of Him, an unselfed love." I didn't understand all that I read, but I thought much about absolute faith and unselfed love, and I began to believe that all things are possible to God. I also hung on to these verses from Proverbs: "Trust in the Lord with all thine heart; and lean not unto thine own understanding. In all thy ways acknowledge him, and he shall direct thy paths" (3:5, 6).

I wasn't yet able to give up the pills, but I did cut down on them. I know I was afraid to let them go. As I continued to pray, I began to feel the foundation of the Christ, Truth, under me, and before long I was able to give up the pills for good. For the first time in eight years I felt free.

I rejoiced because I realized it had been a nightmare from which I had been shaken and awakened. But there was still more to learn. While I was extremely grateful to be awakened from this addiction, I felt very ashamed that I had succumbed to such a weakness in the first place. I had always prided myself on being strong, and this situation had knocked me down very low. It was as though a scar were left on me after the healing of the addiction.

Then one day a verse in the Bible stood out to me, "Study to shew thyself approved unto God, a workman that needeth not to be ashamed, rightly dividing the word of truth" (II Timothy 2:15). I saw clearly that my job was to please God, not man. And this verse from Ecclesiastes was also helpful: "I know that, whatsoever God doeth, it shall be for ever: nothing can be put to it, nor any thing taken from it: and God doeth it, that men should fear before him. That which hath been is now; and that which is to be hath already been;

and God requireth that which is past" (3:14, 15). In that moment I saw God's perfect creation. I understood that nothing can be added to or taken from that creation, and that man can only live in the present. Yesterday belongs to God, and so does tomorrow.

I am so grateful for Christian Science and for my dear wife.

Harold Thomas Dyer
Laguna Niguel, California
Christian Science Sentinel December 12, 1994
The Christian Science Journal April 1991

The art of loving and serving others

In this interview Ardis Krainik, general director of the Lyric Opera of Chicago and a member of the company since 1954, discusses the basis of her approach to her work. Miss Krainik's achievements, among which is an artistically successful as well as a financially stable opera company, are well known in the international opera world.

Tell us a little about the Lyric Opera and about your background.

We currently produce nine operas a year at the Lyric, seventy-three performances. There are over four hundred artists and staff involved. Also we run a school. We are a $17-million-a-year enterprise. But our product is not inanimate nuts and bolts but living, breathing ever-changing music and theater, which makes things that much more complex.

At the beginning of my career I sang opera for five or six years, hoping eventually to earn my living at it, and I worked in administration at the Lyric Opera at the same time. One day I was offered the important position of assistant manager, which I accepted with alacrity; I realized that administration was what I liked best and indeed was my strongest talent.

Prior to becoming general director of the Lyric in 1981, I was offered the position of general manager of the Australian opera in Sydney. I flew to Sydney and met the chairman of the board. We got along very well, saw eye to eye on things. Later, while sitting in the hotel room, I was overcome with the thought that I didn't know what to do, and I just sat there feeling despondent and concerned. Should I accept the challenge and move to Sydney, far from family and friends, or should I play it safe and remain in Chicago as "second banana"?

Then I saw that I really had to put my hand in the Father's. In other words, I realized that I had to give up my own personal sense of what I should do. For the first time in my experience I said, "This is Yours, Father. I'll go wherever I should go. 'Thy will be done.' I will be happy, whatever is in store for me, because I know that it's going to be good." This was a great release for me; I wasn't anxious anymore.

I was a very fearful person. But I've learned to see myself as God's spiritual image. It has taught me patience, and not to be constantly worried or anxious. That has made all the difference not just in my career but in every aspect of my life.

Well, I went through the rest of my interviews and had the most wonderful time in Sydney. Then I came home. And at the precise time I came home, the general director of Lyric Opera retired and I was offered the job, which I happily accepted.

I realized through this that good is right where we are, and that progress is spiritual and goes on in thought. My progress was in giving up a limited sense of self and trusting in God for really the first time. It was a big experience in my life.

When you started as general director of the Lyric, according to one account, the company's foundation of $2.5 million was gone, there was no money in the bank, a $500,000 bank loan was outstanding, and the company was carrying a $309,000 deficit. What did it take to tackle that?

Actually, I didn't think only of the money problems when I started out. I had a company to run. We had to produce an opera season of the finest quality. That came first.

The first day that I was general director I suddenly was overwhelmed with the realization that I had to run the company. Then this wonderful angel thought came to me, the Bible story of Moses and the burning bush (see Exodus: 3–4). Essentially, God said to Moses, "You're going to take the children of Israel out of Egypt," and Moses said, "I can't do that, I'm slow of speech." And God said, "I'm going to put the words in your mouth. I'm going to be with you." And during the forty years in the wilderness, every time Moses listened to God and obeyed Him, good came to the children of Israel; the Red Sea parted, there was manna in the desert, water came out of the rock. The most incredible things happened because Moses knew he wasn't doing it himself. He was listening to God. Thinking about that story made me recognize that I was not going to do one single thing except listen to God and follow His leading.

Now, sometimes I get off track; we all do. But that powerful Bible story always pulls me back. The minute I think I'm some sort of personal creator and that this opera company is going to fall apart without me running it, I get pulled back by this story, which for me puts everything into perspective. It reminds me how important humility is. Humility isn't sitting in the corner. It is saying, "Thy will, not mine, be done"; it is listening to God and following His direction. By the way, the $309,000 deficit was all gone the first year. Not only that; we had nearly $300,000 left over, the foundation had a balance of nearly $500,000, and the bank loan had been repaid. That $1,100,000 turnaround, all in one year, seemed quite miraculous to many.

The Wall Street Journal ***did an article on your work at the Lyric and mentioned your style of leadership.***

Well, I don't think I do anything unusual except that I try to love. People want and need to be loved. I try not to love them just as *people,* though. I work very hard to see my colleagues and staff, friends and artists—everyone in the company—as perfect, spiritual expressions of the Father. My goal isn't to make happy artists; it's to see each individual as he or she really is. That frees us all to make beautiful music.

You've said that many performing artists suffer from an almost constant fear of failure. This love must help them in that respect.

What I usually will say to people if they ask is something that helps them recognize not just that I love them but that God loves them and that "underneath are the everlasting arms", supporting them and their performance (Deuteronomy 33:27).

In other words, what you say to others about God's support is, in effect, loving them.

Yes. You know I've found that people still believe in the authority of the Bible! The truth *is* true. And people recognize and believe it when they hear it.

I think of this kind of giving as sharing my treasures with others, the things that I love so much, such as "Trust in the Lord with all thine heart; and lean not unto thine own understanding. In all thy ways acknowledge him, and he shall direct thy paths" (Proverbs 3:5, 6). These are very powerful ideas. When I think that it's right to share in this way with artists and colleagues, I do. The operative word at Lyric Opera is *love.*

There's an experience I'd like to tell you, if I may, along these lines of loving. A few years ago one of my colleagues, a general director of another company, was putting on two important new productions back to back. I was there for the first night. Afterward I went backstage and complimented him on how beautifully it had been done. I told him that I was looking forward to the next night, when the second of the two was to be presented.

The stage was filled with a great many people celebrating the first night. He pulled me aside and said, "Everybody tells me you have a direct line to the guy up there." (Those were his exact words.) My first thought was to say, "Oh, no." And then I thought, this isn't why he's saying this, for me to make some coy remark in return. He has a reason for asking. So I said, "Yes."

Then he told me that he was having lots of trouble with the second show, the final rehearsal technically had not gone well at all, and he was "scared stiff" that the show wouldn't go well the next evening, and he needed help. I said, "Do you want me to pray for you?" and he said, "Yes, I do." So I said, "You can count on it. I'm starting right now." And I did.

The next morning as I studied the Bible Lesson, which includes citations from the Bible and *Science and Health,* I used it as the basis of prayer for my colleague. I started from the absolute truth of the perfection of God and His spiritual expression, man. I got all through, and I was so uplifted myself by all of this. Then the telephone rang, and it was my colleague and he said, "Have you been praying for me?" And I said, "Yes, I have." There was a long silence, and I thought, "Oh my . . . , he's expecting me to say something special to him."

All of a sudden the last Bible citation of the Lesson came to me, and I said, "I want to tell you this: I've found something perfect for general directors, 'Ye shall go out with joy, and be led forth with peace: the mountains and the hills shall break forth before you into singing, and all the trees of the field shall clap their hands'" (Isaiah 55:12). And I said, "What you're going to find is peace and joy tonight. You don't have to worry about the singers. 'The mountains and the hills are going to break forth . . . into singing.' And you don't have to worry about the audience. 'The trees of the field' are going to 'clap their hands.'" Well, he laughed!

The performance that night went without a hitch. But more important, my colleague and I were both uplifted, and there has been a wonderful camaraderie between us ever since.

Ardis, in an interview you once said, "I never liked the attitude that you work hard to be better than someone else."

That's true. I don't believe in that kind of competition. If you love others, how can you be competing with them? If you love, you recognize that everyone has the right to do his best. So you support whatever is going on that's good. If all my colleagues are doing wonderfully, and I'm doing wonderfully, then the business of opera is doing wonderfully. I want everyone to do well.

Whenever someone says something at another opera company's expense and to the Lyric's credit, it doesn't make me happy. I don't like to do that, and I don't like to see it done. That's the chaff. I want to go ahead with the wheat.

I understand, though, there is a growing belief that it is more and more competitive in opera. It costs more and more to bring in the best performers, for instance.

Well, a person can let himself just be squashed down by the belief that everybody's in competition, that some other company is going to get the artists, so you're not going to get them unless you pay more. That's just anxiety. "Be careful for nothing; but in every thing by prayer and supplication with thanksgiving let your requests be made known unto God" (Philippians 4:6). That's a very powerful and important Bible statement. You cannot be concerned about someone's being ahead of you.

Mary Baker Eddy says in *Science and Health* that God, divine Love, "fills all space" (p. 331), and I like to think of that fullness as being expressed, for instance, in an opera company filled with great singers. They may be from Bulgaria, New York, Tuscaloosa. I don't have to worry about where they're from. All I have to be concerned with is following God's leading.

Often, people in this business think that they are personal creators. That's one of the biggest difficulties. There is only one creator; there is no personal creator. We aren't the origin of the good or right ideas that come to us. God is the creator; we are the creation.

Another obstacle is fame. We are all equally perfect children of God, like the rays of the sun. The rays all shine together.

People stop you on the street and say, "Aren't you so-and-so?" and you get little feelings inside that say, "Well *yes,* I am so-and-so." It's so easy to swell up with pride. Those feelings are "the little foxes, that spoil the vines" (Song of Solomon 2:15). It's the world saying, "Just follow me. I'll put your name up in lights. You're special." But everyone is just as special as I am. It is God who makes each of us special—spiritually individual.

To become a virtuoso you keep practicing. And what you've learned, you build on and build on and build on. You don't become a virtuoso by playing scales once. You become a virtuoso violinist or pianist or singer by constantly enlarging upon what you learn each day. To me, it's the same with praying. We don't just pray once. When we've learned how to pray so that we recognize something of God, of Truth, we continue—we learn to "pray without ceasing" (I Thessalonians 5:17). And more and more we become virtuoso Christians, true practitioners of God's will. That's what I'm trying to do.

Christian Science Sentinel October 17, 1988

The school librarian said, "You have worked a miracle."

I was asked if I would teach for three weeks a small group of eleven- to fifteen-year-old children classified as mentally retarded. All had learning problems, some were volatile of nature, extremely profane and almost totally uncontrollable at times. I lacked the special training required for this work, so I was very apprehensive.

I earnestly prayed to know what to do. Finally I saw this as an opportunity to put into practice an understanding of man's perfection as God's image and likeness, and I accepted the assignment. I asked a Christian Science practitioner to support my efforts in this line, and I was grateful for her encouragement and reassurance throughout the experience.

A further source of inspiration was the study of the Bible and *Science and Health.* Passages such as the following from the Psalms were very helpful: "The Lord will perfect that which concerneth me" (138:8) and "It is God that girdeth me with strength, and maketh my way perfect" (18:32). In *Science and Health* Mary Baker Eddy writes, "Mind is not necessarily dependent upon educational processes. It possesses of itself all beauty and poetry, and the power of expressing them" (p. 89). The practitioner helped me see that because I was the reflection of this divine Mind which is God, I expressed the intelligence necessary to teach these children. I acknowledged that the children, too, reflected the one perfect Mind. I saw there could not be a retarded mind.

The first two days with this class were almost unbelievable. The violent outbursts and angry defiance seemed overwhelming, but I held to the fact that God is governing His idea, man, at all times, and that obedience is natural in the child of God's creating.

By the third day I began to see a change in attitudes and dispositions. There were still many crises, but each one subsided more quickly than the last, and I learned to express more understanding and patience. However, one morning early in the second week, there was such violent turmoil manifested that I decided I would have to give up the assignment. But as I sat alone in the classroom almost overcome with discouragement, these questions came to thought: "Can scientific, spiritual, right thinking *really* help this, or can't it?" I fervently answered in the affirmative and there came to my thought these words from one of Mrs. Eddy's hymns quoting Genesis (*Poems,* p. 7):

"Let there be light, and there was light."
  What chased the clouds away?
'Twas Love whose finger traced aloud
A bow of promise on the cloud.

Immediately the heaviness and weight of personal responsibility began to lift, and I declared with conviction, "This turmoil among the children is an illusion. Our heavenly Father made these children loving, perfect, and obedient and keeps them that way."

When the class returned, I was awed by the stillness and peace that filled the room. An hour later there was further proof of healing, for the school librarian said, "You have worked a miracle. I have never seen these children so calm and well-behaved." I told her that full credit belonged to God and explained that I had endeavored to see these children as governed by God.

The remaining days were joyous ones, and my heart was filled with genuine love for the class. Difficult problems dissolved quickly as divine Love showed a way to resolve each one. I received gentle apologies for misbehavior and promises to do better. Profanity stopped almost entirely, fighting and angry verbal barrages all but ceased, and greater cooperation and willingness to complete assignments were expressed.

Words can never express my gratitude for this opportunity, and many more I have known since, to bear witness to the spiritually perfect nature of the child of God's creation, the only child there is. Mrs. Eddy clearly saw this when she wrote: "God creates man perfect and eternal in His own image. Hence man is the image, idea, or likeness of perfection—an ideal which cannot fall from its inherent unity with divine Love, from its spotless purity and original perfection" (*The First Church of Christ, Scientist, and Miscellany*, p. 262).

Marion L. Martin
Myrtle Creek, Oregon
Christian Science Sentinel March 25, 1972

At the end of the year I would be declared redundant.

After holding an executive position in business for over twenty years, I was somewhat shocked when it became apparent that, due to an impending takeover, my services would no longer be required. The first reaction was resentment and fear of lack of employment and supply, but these were seen immediately as thoughts limiting the allness and goodness of God.

I began to realize that "divine Love always has met and always will meet every human need" (*Science and Health*, p. 494). However, fear appeared to present itself more forcibly, and I had to deal with the mesmerism of belief in age, redundancy, unemployment, inactivity, and lack. These had to be replaced to see clearly that there were unlimited opportunities for intelligent action.

My wife and I continued to do prayerful work along these lines, and the help of a Christian Science practitioner was sought. I can never express sufficiently my profound gratitude for the spiritual help, guidance, and support given.

It then became known to me that my services would terminate at the end of the year, when I would be declared redundant. I saw clearly that the only time was now, and that now my everyday needs were being met. This destroyed a sense of fear of what the future would hold for me.

As I studied the Bible and *Science and Health* with reference to "place," enlightenment came. On page 471 it says, "Man is, and forever has been, God's reflection." I reasoned, "Is not man's place, then, established by God?" And again, on page 3, I read: "Who would stand before a blackboard, and pray the principle of mathematics to solve the problem? The rule is already established, and it is our task to work out the solution. Shall we ask the divine Principle of all goodness to do His own work? His work is done, and we have only to avail ourselves of God's rule in order to receive His blessing, which enables us to work out our own salvation."

It then not only became clear that I needed and was seeking a "place" but that somewhere there was a need for those qualities I was able to reflect. Divine Principle would bring need and supply together for the good of all. God's idea is always in his right place, right here and now, and we can experience real security through Mind. Supply and demand are controlled by divine Principle, and where the demand is, there is always the supply. This gave me such a sense of peace and security that many of my close friends would not believe that I had no other appointment awaiting me. I continued to know absolutely and finally that as one door closed another would open, and that there could only be continuity of good in God's kingdom. During the few months that followed I became stronger instead of weaker in this understanding.

Three weeks before the date of the termination of my employment I received my first letter inviting me to attend for an interview, from a firm completely unknown to me and for a position new to the firm and one that had not been advertised. The requirements for this were the qualifications and experience which I had to give, and the mesmeric limitation of age was nonexistent. Within the next three weeks the appointment had been made, and the new position commenced two weeks later. This proved not only more rewarding, as progression is the law of God, but even more satisfying, and useful activity ensued.

Leonard Offer
Keston, Kent, England
The Christian Science Journal December 1971

I saw my true job as reflecting Him.

After two years of employment with a large firm I suddenly found myself in the midst of what I considered to be very unprincipled activity. Each effort I made to correct the improper actions met with resistance. It finally came to the point of my having to yield to the improper practices or quit my job. I chose the latter.

My wife and I were expecting our first child at the time, and it was my immediate concern to supply the family's income. I had left a good paying job with a growing company for something yet unknown. A statement made by Mary Baker

Eddy in *Miscellaneous Writings* comforted this concern over family responsibility: "God gives you His spiritual ideas, and in turn, they give you daily supplies. Never ask for to-morrow: it is enough that divine Love is an ever-present help; and if you wait, never doubting, you will have all you need every moment" (p. 307).

Weeks passed without my locating a suitable position. Fear began to grip me. It looked as if I might be jobless for some time to come. Many people expressed the opinion that available work in my particular profession was very scarce, while qualified individuals seeking these positions were more numerous than they had ever been. The human picture did not look pleasant. Every time fear entered my thought I clung to the passage from Isaiah: "Fear thou not; for I am with thee: be not dismayed; for I am thy God: I will strengthen thee; yea, I will help thee; yea, I will uphold thee with the right hand of my righteousness" (41:10).

Several more days passed without success, so I decided to begin each day by visiting a Christian Science Reading Room to quietly study the Bible and the writings of Mrs. Eddy, and to pray for guidance from my heavenly Father. Trying to get a clearer concept of employment, I felt that God didn't intend for me to be unemployed. I recognized that the all-knowing Mind has complete control over all of man's activity and that there isn't anything that is left to chance or failure. Man reflects God's intelligence, and since I express this intelligence, I would be led to the right employer. The words from Proverbs 3, verses 5 and 6, gave me assurance.

My morning study continued for several more days, and each day I felt a little more at ease about the situation. One morning as I sat in the Reading Room praying, a thought came to me very clearly: "My true employer is God!" I saw my true job as reflecting Him to the fullest possible degree. To be a good employee for God, so to speak, I had to exemplify vigor, intelligence, life, trust, love, and so on. I spent the entire day working as hard and faithfully as I could for God, whom I had newly discerned to be my employer.

The next day I had two interviews for positions that appealed to me. Both firms offered me interesting, challenging, well-paying jobs immediately! After some prayerful consideration I made a choice and subsequently spent many happy, productive years working for the company.

I am indeed grateful for this demonstration of God's continuing care for me; and I know He cares for all mankind. Such proof does assure me that the Father-Mother God supplies all health, all harmony, and all good.

Through this lesson I again substantiated that man's supply comes from God; I learned to seek and to listen for His guidance; and I recognized that man's purpose is to consciously reflect the qualities of God.

Michael Drumm Joy
Framingham, Massachusetts
Christian Science Sentinel November 21, 1977

We were not only without housing but without jobs and transportation.

When my three children were in their late teens, we found ourselves in a terrible predicament; we were not only without housing but also without jobs and transportation. It seemed we had "hit bottom."

In this most uncomfortable of predicaments, however, I drew on God's abundant care and knew the lack we faced could be healed. Nothing could change the facts of being, that only God's abundance was real or true. I knew that listening to angel thoughts, messages from God to man, would bring our release from inharmony.

I was at times, however, filled with despair over our lot. One morning, waking up on a friend's front porch with cats jumping all over me, I couldn't help but wonder what was to become of us all. The Psalmist says: "In my distress I called upon the Lord, and cried unto my God: he heard my voice out of his temple, and my cry came before him, even unto his ears. . . . He sent from above, he took me, he drew me out of many waters" (Psalms 18:6, 16).

I called a Christian Science practitioner to support my own prayers for deliverance. She assured me that God's provision for man is infinite and encouraged me to trust this spiritual abundance. She suggested I study the words *abundance* and *affluence* in the writings of Mary Baker Eddy. I found that God's provision for His children is no less than abundant and satisfying; He does not dole out His goodness. I prayed to overcome anxiety and fear. I also kept gratitude prominent in thought, being ever so thankful for the loving friends who took us in at the time.

With my prayer to God, I became expectant of solutions. I followed an intuition to call friends in another part of the state to ask for a place to stay temporarily. The fearful thought came, "What if they say no?" But I knew the importance of following divine leadings. I walked to a pay phone up the highway to place the call with literally my last dime. When the welcoming voice said, "Yes, you may stay here," I gave praise for this sign of God's sustaining care. One of my daughter's friends loaned us a station wagon, and we went ahead.

The idea came to me concerning our next step that "God's own hand shall guide thee there." (This is a line from a hymn.) I had no idea where "there" was, but I knew God's loving care had never left us. I endeavored to counter thoughts of sadness with joyful thoughts of God, that He loves and cares for *all* His children. I sang praises to God often for His benevolent care, knowing that I could glorify Him each moment and that this was my real job.

The idea came to begin child-care work. I became gainfully employed in this work, and in caring for the elderly as well. Many people needed this type of help, and being in God's service I never lacked anything needful. For example, though I had no car of my own, I found that clients would ask if I cared to drive their cars.

I began attending a Christian Science church in the area, and the membership expressed much love to me. Their dedication gave me renewed hope and purpose. Their reaching out to me I later realized was evidence of the loving Christ. I continued to get jobs, sometimes through these church friends.

Each of my three children pursued a different path, one that was best for that time. I had to stop feeling so responsible for them and trust God's unfailing care to be sufficient for each of us. He could do a far better job than I ever could. There was joy to be found in leaning on God each day.

Often I would study the Bible and *Science and Health* by Mary Baker Eddy for hours. This gave me a stronger foundation of spiritual understanding. When I yielded my heart to God, I felt more secure, more patient, more grateful. Centering my life more on God's will than on a larger place or better-paying job, I moved ahead, progressing in spiritual understanding, knowing all was well. I learned we can never be separate from any needful good any more than we can become separate from God. I included the whole world in my prayer.

I was able to resume my former teaching career. It was awesome to see how prayer to God in all things brought better results than human effort and planning ever could. I had never before been to the place where I applied for this job, but felt divinely led to go there. My career in teaching urban children has been wonderful.

"Never ask for to-morrow: it is enough that divine Love is an ever-present help; and if you wait, never doubting, you will have all you need every moment" (*Miscellaneous Writings* by Mary Baker Eddy, p. 307). It is my hope that anyone confronted with lack will feel encouraged to pray. No matter how complicated or tangled or hopeless a situation may seem, God is able to keep you free of turmoil and pain now.

Dorothy B. Hewitt
Paramus, New Jersey
Christian Science Sentinel December 27, 1993

We accepted the challenge to expand.

A recent advertisement I saw for *Science and Health* said this: "People have found moral and spiritual strength by reading this book. They have also had healings of mental and physical diseases, financial burdens, and unhappy relationships." I can verify those statements through healings in my own life.

I was involved in an unhappy relationship. My fiancé and I had grown up together, and plans to marry after college promised to fulfill my desire to be a wife and mother. When he told me that his future no longer included me, I felt utterly rejected.

I turned to Christian Science in hope of finding an answer to the "why" of my situation.

In the Preface of *Science and Health* I found these words: "The time for thinkers has come" (p. vii). This made a deep impression on me. I asked for the help of a Christian Science practitioner, who directed me to a statement from *Miscellaneous Writings* by Mrs. Eddy, "Immortal Mind is God, immortal good; in whom the Scripture saith 'we live, and move, and have our being.' This Mind, then, is not subject to growth, change, or diminution, but is the divine intelligence, or Principle, of all real being; holding man forever in the rhythmic round of unfolding bliss, as a living witness to and perpetual idea of inexhaustible good" (pp. 82–83).

My college preparation had been in education, and as I began my teaching career I realized that all the qualities I had associated with being a wife and mother were needed in the classroom. In my work I found increasingly that happiness is spiritual, something that comes from God and is not determined by human relationships. And although never actively seeking career changes, I received wonderful promotions.

Then after a period of twenty years, the broken relationship was renewed. With the new relationship established on a better and firmer foundation, we were married.

My husband took over his family business, which was operating at a low financial level. Not wanting to dismiss the faithful employees who had maintained the business, together we accepted the challenge to expand rather than retrench, although retrenchment appeared to be the order of the day. With the help of a practitioner, we affirmed that Mind has innumerable opportunities for man. The human need was for the right *ideas,* and we held to the spiritual fact that these ideas are always here to be discerned and utilized. Each day began with steadfast confidence that "the right way wins the right of way, even the way of Truth and Love whereby all our debts are paid, mankind blessed, and God glorified" (*The First Church of Christ, Scientist, and Miscellany* by Mary Baker Eddy, p. 232). We were able to sustain the business profitably through this prayer, and later, when we sold it, we were abundantly blessed with more than enough proceeds to cover our needs.

Miscellaneous Writings states, "The true consciousness is the true health" (p. 298). Throughout my many years of employment, I was never absent from my post, and when I retired my entire "sick leave" was intact.

From healing experiences throughout fourscore years, I can affirm that man indeed exists "in the rhythmic round of unfolding bliss (*ibid.*, p. 83)."

Elaine D. Afton
St. Louis, Missouri
The Christian Science Journal June 1994

I pondered what the bank could do to help.

In 1985 I was the head of my bank's office in a third world city. The job was undemanding, and my family enjoyed living in a very comfortable fashion. Lovely as all this was, I had an unsatisfied desire to work harder for the betterment of mankind and not just for personal gain or material comforts.

My wife and I prayed to know that God, divine Mind, governs not just our thinking but our experience as well. Impelled by what we felt was an unselfish and right desire, we made plans to return to New York even though the bank had no position open for me to take.

Shortly before we left, I pondered what the bank could do to help the country we had enjoyed so much. As I prayed, an inspiration came to me. I saw how we could substantially reduce this country's and others' interest costs on their foreign debts. We could apply commercial refinancing techniques to the country's very large loans from the United States government, where the interest rate was fixed at high levels for years to come.

A few days later I felt impelled to offer the idea in a meeting with local United States embassy officials, although I didn't yet have any idea how it would work. Just as I was being pressed for details by eager officials (and my skeptical boss), I was called out of the room for a telephone call. During the time I was out I prayed intently to know that divine Mind doesn't take us just so far and then drop us. I knew that each idea of Mind is complete and that what appeared to be the limitations of my own ability weren't relevant. It is divine Mind that governs.

On returning to the room, I heard myself describe the method to be used in the project, feeling as I spoke that I was acting as a transparency for divine Mind. Though I didn't know it then, working on this idea was to be my only assignment for the next three years. In addition, New York turned out to be the right place to be assigned because of the special financial requirements the transaction involved. We also needed to be close enough to Washington to be able to work on government approval. I felt these early steps in the experience clearly illustrated a statement in *Science and Health,* "Right motives give pinions to thought, and strength and freedom to speech and action" (p. 454).

After more than a year's work, however, I had little to show for my effort. The United States government was far from agreeing and, in any case, my bank didn't have the specialized staff necessary to underwrite the type of financing it appeared we needed. I was skipped over for a raise, and the bank began to talk about letting me go. The obstacles in front of what I felt was a divinely inspired idea didn't worry me, but my compensation and the risk of having to find another job did. As I dwelt on these "me" oriented questions, I became discouraged and lost my focus on the work.

However, I turned to prayer for help. My wife also prayed and we contacted a Christian Science practitioner to support us through prayer. My wife helped me realize that my job was to go "about my Father's business" (Luke 2:49), to use Christ Jesus' words. It was God's job to compensate me! That realization was so complete that I plunged back into work, free of the burden of selfish thinking.

Within a month I was given a raise, completely out of sequence with the normal schedule, and the discussion about letting me go was dropped. In addition, the bank soon created a department to underwrite bond issues. The new department began to take a strong interest in my work. Over the next year, in spite of numerous continuing obstacles to government approval, I held strongly to the understanding that divine Mind, not many mortal minds, governs.

After some time the United States Congress passed a bill providing the mechanism for the refinancing to take place. And it contained a surprise: instead of its draft wording, pertaining to only two countries (one of which was my original host), it made all borrowing countries eligible.

Because the inspiration for this idea had been to help mankind, as we worked together, my colleagues were influenced somewhat by this outlook. Together we did an honest job to assist the many countries who were now eligible to reduce their interest costs under this mechanism and each time won the gratitude and respect of the international and U.S. officials involved. I felt a certain moral strength in ensuring that everything on which we advised the various countries was, to the extent possible, to their benefit as well as to that of the U.S. government. In the end, this unselfish approach succeeded, as my bank was given the transactions for fully half of the countries which participated.

Though many obstacles were overcome through prayer on each transaction, the last one involving a country near my original host country particularly showed me the power of divine Mind, which had led to this opportunity in the first place. After two years of discussion and months of specific preparation, on the day of the actual underwriting, the country's delegation in New York received misleading advice and false promises from one of the banks that was supposed to be working with us in our underwriting group. Swayed by this, the delegates switched the transaction from my firm to the other, which promised to underwrite it the following morning, using the documentation, analysis, and financial structure we had spent months working on! My colleagues and I were left reeling from this type of maneuvering.

As others were banging their fists, I found a quiet office from which to call the practitioner. She assured me that there is a divine law of justice that operates. Divine Mind is present no matter how extreme the circumstances appear to be. She quoted Micah in the Bible: "What doth the Lord require of thee, but to do justly, and to love mercy, and to walk humbly with thy God?" (6:8). Finally, she reminded me that the country's delegates and the members of the other firm are God's children, as innocent and as subject to the same Mind of God as I. I was deeply moved as I listened to this clear statement of the real facts about myself, our client, and our partners. The practitioner said she would continue to pray.

I returned to a room full of outraged colleagues. The anger and desire for revenge were tangible. Though most of the people in the room were senior to me, I dissuaded them from revengeful acts, encouraging them to continue to show that we were the ones serving the country's best interests. An associate and I went to reason with the officials at a meeting that lasted until 2 a.m. But they still said they would continue with the other firm in the morning.

Nevertheless, I was now able to see them more clearly as God's children and myself as following God's directing. I was happy to follow wherever divine Mind led, even if that meant we were not to underwrite this financing in the morning. I was feeling so free that I even stayed up for a while to do some other work, which had gone unattended.

Imagine my joy when at 6 a.m. the delegation called to say that, of all the advice they were getting, ours was the advice they believed and they would proceed with us! My colleagues were as amazed by this turnaround as they had been by the apparent setback of the previous day. I could only rejoice and agree wholeheartedly with Paul, who says, "All things work together for good to them that love God" (Romans 8:28).

This experience showed me that no matter what we do for a living, there is always a way to demonstrate God's love for man and to do whatever we do in harmony with divine Mind.

Peter H. Johnson
Darien, Connecticut
Christian Science Sentinel March 11, 1991

10

Relationships and getting along

Life is full of relationships—with family, co-workers, and society in general. When just getting along seems hard or even impossible, relying on God's natural law of harmony brings peace and healing.

We integrated the apartment building, neighborhood, church, and Sunday School.

I am grateful that I learned of Christian Science early in my life at a time when I felt inconsolable. It has taught me love and appreciation for myself and others, and not to run away from problems, but to increase my understanding of God's allness and His love when situations seem insolvable.

I was without adequate income to provide for my baby daughter and myself. As all efforts to gain employment in the field for which I was trained had failed, in sheer desperation I turned to God humbly seeking His guidance. I was willing to let Him govern my life. I accepted housework by the day and attended business school in the evenings. While reading the Bible one evening the words of Psalm 121 took on new meaning. I immediately memorized this psalm and clung to it during gloomy hours, day and night. Not long afterward I took some Christian Science magazines from a distribution box at a launderette and read them. Every week while doing the laundry there I read more of the magazines. As this reading brought newfound peace and joy, I accepted it without question as God's message to me.

After several months I found employment in the business field where a co-worker gave me a copy of *Science and Health.* I was healed of nervous convulsions simply by reading it, and my life has truly been reconstructed by that book.

My employment has been progressive, supplying adequate income and good housing. I have enjoyed better health, where before I was sickly and highly sensitive. Divine Love has shown me my individual completeness.

I would like to tell how prayer replaced resentment and frustration with gratitude and cheerfulness, and enabled me to find a higher type of employment. The better employment came after I gave thorough attention and prayer to destroying in my own thought the belief in an evil mind, or animal magnetism and worldly hatred, which was claiming I was a victim of racial bigotry. As a result of my prayer I knew that love knows no barrier, that love gets fair and just things where all else fails. I was soon notified that I had been accepted for a position that took us miles from our former location for training.

When we arrived at our destination, the one responsible for helping with the housing kept trying to place me in the black ghetto area. This was not acceptable to me because I knew that God had not placed a restriction on man, and that our move was directed, protected, supplied, and sustained by God. The place God prepares for man includes and expresses His qualities. I held to the fact that man is really at home in God, that nothing can hide this from us; and I knew this fact would be manifest in a home that would meet all our needs. And the home we found did.

Three days after our arrival we were invited to spend the night with a Christian Science practitioner who was of a different race, and who introduced us to a fellow church member whose apartment we rented. The apartment not only met the immediate need for housing but also provided my daughter and me with loving friends. One of them watched over my daughter after school. The home was located one block from school and a few blocks from the branch church we attended as long as we were in that area. The apartment was unfurnished, but we were loaned enough furniture by church members to completely furnish it.

We integrated the apartment building, neighborhood, church, and Sunday School. All during this period I learned to trust God more, and to cope with fear more successfully, seeing it was powerless to condition our lives.

Betty J. O'Neal
Boston, Massachusetts
The Christian Science Journal November 1975

God never made a black man, a white man, or a brown man. He made man in His own image and likeness.

Many years ago after our family had moved into a new home, a note came which read: "We do not want any Negroes in the neighborhood." I said to my husband, "They must be made to know, as we must know, God never made a black man, a white man, or a brown man. He made man in His own image and likeness."

At that time my husband had to walk five blocks for the bus that took him to work. When he left, I was alone in the house with our five-year-old daughter. Even though the threatening note had been received earlier, no one came to our door except someone inquiring for a person living at another address.

Weeks went by without incident. Then one evening I looked out the window and saw a menacing figure in front of my house, also one across the street and one on each corner of the streets surrounding our home. From the way they were acting, there could be no doubt whatever about their intentions. I said to myself, "This must be them."

I at once got my Bible and copy of *Science and Health with Key to the Scriptures* by Mary Baker Eddy and went upstairs to study. I was not afraid, because I know that God is always with me. I was grateful, as I live to love. "Perfect love casteth out fear" (I John 4:18). There is nothing to fear where God, Love, is, and there is no place where God, Love, is not. When I came down to prepare the evening meal the picture had completely changed, and the atmosphere of Love was felt. Nothing was ever seen or heard of from this group again.

Maud Wilson
Indianapolis, Indiana
Christian Science Sentinel September 25, 1976

In the university you would hear this about promotions—one group is more favored than another.

Prayer about the situations in which we find ourselves, helps others as well as ourselves. Doctor Isaac A. O. Ojo is a senior lecturer at Obafemi Awolowo University in Ile-Ife, Nigeria.

I have found that prayer can remove any barrier. However strong the resistance may be, it can be removed. For example, in the university you would hear from members of some tribes or some ethnic groups the unanimous comment about promotions—one group is more favored than another group.

For my secondary-school days, I attended a government college. In the college there was no regional or tribal distinction among all of us. Similarly there was no class barrier; none of us was given any preferential treatment because of his parental background, whether rich or poor. With this background, it was quite natural for me to accept the method of

Christian scientific prayer to heal a departmental rift which developed as a result of a yearly promotion exercise.

At one point after a promotion exercise in my department, I was faced with this embarrassing situation. Three people were promoted. Looking at the names of the people concerned, one could easily admit that the promotion was biased in favor of one ethnic group.

Within my department some dissatisfied colleagues came to me and said, "Look, aren't you better than these people? And you are sitting down there not making any effort to change how promotions are handled." My colleagues would not accept what this would mean for me: that for the next eight years I would probably remain in the same position if I adopted this attitude of not protesting against the outcome.

But I immediately dismissed their comments. In fact, I had been seeing from what I was reading in the Bible and *Science and Health* that we are all truly perfect and what blesses one, has to bless others. I was able to tell those people who worried about me, "Let us remove this bomb of prejudice against another group of people. Until we do that, there can be no joy among us." I said, "You cannot defeat God, and you cannot bar Him. So, I have no reason why I should say to somebody, 'You are not my friend, because you were promoted.' There is no reason that I shouldn't be friendly."

I knew God wanted each one of us to bring about unity. So, I knew I had to go out of my way to talk to these people one by one. Those who were promoted I encouraged to identify with those who were still struggling within the department. Those who were unhappy, I requested to be more purposeful and more loving in their various pursuits.

The challenge came when we had to mark the exam papers for one group of students. It was a large class. And we had to come together. You know, when I brought the issue up with my friends, there was silence. Somebody said, "You mean, you are no more part of us?" I said "Yes, I am part of you. But you fail to see yourself as you are. You are actually children of God, incapable of disunity. You have to see that. Each of us is to develop his or her expertise at a pace of his or her own choice. We should learn to rejoice with those who have succeeded."

I prayed for myself. The two themes of my prayer were, promotion is of God and ". . . progress is the law of God . . ." as Mary Baker Eddy states in *Science and Health* (p. 233). I felt relieved of any human inadequacy or failure. I felt an inner peace and joy. I was looking toward the future with hope and thanksgiving. With each passing day during my prayer, I knew we had all been healed of prejudice against one another.

The following year witnessed the highest number of promotions to the grade of senior lectureship at any time within the department. I was one of those promoted to this level. In praying for myself, I have realized that I was also praying for my department.

Through prayer we can take on the world, however big the problem may be or however small it may be. If we bring our lives into accord with the divine Principle, which is God, which is Truth, which is the light of the world, we find ourselves uplifted.

Christian Science Sentinel December 3, 1990

The two gangs have voluntarily broken up.

Gangs and the hostility that usually accompany them start small—with individuals and in individual thought. And in individual thought, healing comes. Paul Douglas White experienced this in his work as a public school administrator in Southern California.

The atmosphere in my school office that afternoon was angry, tense, potentially violent, and I felt at a loss as to what to do. Before me sat four young men, representing the leadership of the two gangs on our campus who had had repeated flare-ups with each other since the school year had begun.

As the administrator in charge of student behavior, I had arbitrated their arguments on several occasions, intervened in angry confrontations, confiscated their weapons, held meetings with all of the boys involved, counseled individually, cajoled, suspended them, and threatened expulsion from school. All done to no avail.

The four sat before me now, waiting to hear just another harangue about their most recent run-in with each other. The only problem was, I had no idea what to say to them. Every good human reason for ending this kind of behavior had been explained to them: interference with their education, disruption of the school, the risk of bodily harm, possible arrest, and so on. Then totally unexpectedly, part of a statement from *Science and Health* came to thought, "One infinite God, good, unifies men and nations . . . ." [The full sentence reads, "One infinite God, good, unifies men and nations; constitutes the brotherhood of man; ends wars; fulfils the Scripture, 'Love thy neighbor as thyself;' annihilates pagan and Christian idolatry,—whatever is wrong in social, civil, criminal, political, and religious codes; equalizes the sexes; annuls the curse on man, and leaves nothing that can sin, suffer, be punished or destroyed" p. 340.]

I didn't mention this to the boys. Instead, I suddenly pulled my chair up close to them and said, "Every one of you has been to church at one time or another, right?" They had. (They were all affiliated with Christian denominations.) "And every one of you, at one time or another during that church service said something called the Lord's Prayer." I was of course referring to the prayer given to the disciples by Christ Jesus. They agreed. "And now," I added, "I need one of you to tell me what the first two words of that prayer are that you all said." Sadly enough, this took some hard thinking on the boys' part, but we finally pieced together that the first two words were "Our Father." "Notice," I told them, "it doesn't say our Indian, Mexican, white, or black Father. It just says 'our,' *all* of ours. So now, gentlemen, I want you to turn and take a new look at each other, because if God is truly *our* Father, then what relationship do you all have to each other?" The word *brothers* came softly and quizzically out of four mouths.

In closing the meeting with them, I said, "Now, all families have strong disagreements sometimes." Since in the truest sense we were all "family," I indicated that we could restore peace by realizing, "Well after all, this *is* my brother," and then forgive, forget, and go on with our lives.

This was several months ago. In the time since, the two gangs have voluntarily broken up. There have been no incidents of racial, gang-related trouble. Best of all, many of the boys on both sides have become good friends and have normal social, academic, and athletic relationships with each other at school.

Now, we shouldn't think for a moment that adequate supervision, constructive activities, and a strong structure of discipline and affection aren't necessary at this time. They are. However, we can't expect to heal through them, because they don't go far enough. That is, they don't get to the *basis* of harmony and brotherhood, which is the fact that because there is only one Father-Mother God, we (contrary to outward appearances) are not many separate, inharmonious factions but are actually one loving family under the unerring and peaceable direction of God.

Anyone who prays along these lines of divine law, the law that defines our true relation to God and to one another, can prove in his own experience the words of St. John: "Beloved, now are we the sons of God" (I John 3:2).

Afterward, several of the young men wrote they had never before thought about all people being brothers and sisters. There was also general consensus that things were more peaceful, that "being different races doesn't make that much difference now." Perhaps, the words of one express it best, "I'm happy now that everything has changed."

Christian Science Sentinel May 30, 1988

A student in my classroom had been abused.

God is Love. This fact has been demonstrated over and over again in my life. God loves His children so much that He blesses us all with limitless good. I would love to share one of these many blessings.

A student in my classroom had come to us from another school where he had been abused. He did not trust authority figures, and had outbursts when disciplined. I started praying to see that this boy and the other children in my class, indeed all children everywhere, are the reflections of God. I came to the realization that God was the teacher of these children. I read in *Science and Health,* "The entire education of children should be such as to form habits of obedience to the moral and spiritual law, with which the child can meet and master the belief in so-called physical laws, a belief which breeds disease" (p. 62). I began to see that God's children are never imperfect, but always whole and good.

Some days it was difficult to hold the child's spiritual perfection in thought because of what I saw in his actions. But I persisted in keeping my thought in line with God's idea, affirming that all I could express was love for this child. And I saw continuing improvement in his behavior. He expressed more of those inherent spiritual qualities that I understood were given to him by God. He expressed more calmness and responded in a more loving manner to those around him.

At Christmas the boy asked if his mother could bring me a present. She came in that afternoon and delivered it to me. I was so full of joy! (It was a beautiful new briefcase, which he had picked out himself because he thought I needed a nicer one.) He told me that the gift was for his "best teacher." This was a gift of love. I was so grateful to God for the love He was showing to this child and to me.

When classes resumed in January he seemed to have regressed somewhat. I immediately began to pray to keep those Godlike qualities in my own mind. One day when he was again acting up, I asked him if something was troubling him. He said he would like to share some things with me that he had experienced at his previous school. We talked in private, and he shared the awful way in which he had been treated. I knew that this was not something God could have ordained or planned for His son, and that this treatment did not have to rule the boy.

The next day his mother called the director of the school to report the better behavior she was seeing at home. She told the director that whatever the teacher was doing was working, and to keep up the good work. And she commented that her son was going through a real healing process.

When the director shared this conversation with me, and I heard the words *good work* and *healing,* I knew I could only thank God for such a blessing.

This same student learned to read in one year, and scored several levels above his grade level in annual testing. His previous school had wanted him to come back. However, after they had reviewed his test results and a report given by a child psychologist, they called the child's mother and recommended that he stay where he was, because he was "in his right place."

Phyllis G. Palmer
Houston, Texas
Christian Science Sentinel September 26, 1994

I was clinging to a variety of abusive relationships.

I had such deep feelings of insecurity, perhaps stemming from an early life in foster homes, that I was clinging to a variety of abusive relationships; I experienced rape and threats to my life. At one time I lived with a man who had jumped parole and was living under an assumed name, I was that afraid of being alone. My whole concept of love became so completely shattered that I then made efforts to cut myself off from love. Sometimes I would just hide in my room, taking sleeping pills to prolong the escape. Suicide was a constant consideration.

Although I didn't care about love anymore, I still needed to know what the truth of reality was. I had grown up in a mainstream religion that had not answered all my questions about

God, or aided me in efforts toward self-improvement. I was also in turmoil about the validity of the Bible. Finally I prayed, "God, if there is any truth to this existence, show me what it is."

There was a Christian Science Reading Room near my workplace. At the window one day, I read that God is Mind. This was news! College psychology had begun to show me how one's experiences were directly related to thought. The human mind seemed powerful, yet so limited. What about the Mind of God? Entering the Reading Room, I spoke with the librarian. How could the Bible help if I wasn't sure it was true? He simply said, "The truth is the truth, whether you believe it or not." I walked out with a copy of *Science and Health,* and read it straight through at least twice. I yearned so to be free from the bondage that limited my life and my happiness. The following lines became a sustaining force during this time: "Sooner or later we shall learn that the fetters of man's finite capacity are forged by the illusion that he lives in body instead of in Soul, in matter instead of in Spirit" (p. 223).

Then I began to feel supported by what I was learning about God. I gained much-needed strength. When my boyfriend was arrested, I decided to make a break. As I studied the Bible and *Science and Health,* I explored the spiritual qualities of home. After gaining a deeper concept of it, I was guided to a lovely new home and friends, all in one day.

Later, a Christian Science practitioner helped me to make more spiritual progress. I had always known I had a responsibility in destroying the pattern of domestic violence I found myself in. The practitioner pointed out that women who have been exploited, rejected, and abused must understand that the qualities of womanhood cannot be exploited, rejected, or abused, by themselves or by others. This helped me get a grasp on where my responsibility lay. I began a concerted effort to identify, embrace, and express the qualities of true womanhood, particularly those related to motherhood that I learned about in reading *Science and Health.* I really began to nurture my spiritual identity. It was, and continues to be, a wonderful activity.

Prayer has opened many doors in my life in the years since—this has included a fulfilling career, a variety of lovely homes, and friendships with both men and women that are based on mutual love and respect. Not a day goes by when I don't feel the spirit of this Bible verse: "Thanks be unto God for his unspeakable gift" (II Corinthians 9:15).

Name withheld at author's request
Christian Science Sentinel April 24, 1995

I prayed more earnestly about this estrangement from my sister.

The healing I am most grateful for involved an unresolvable estrangement with one of my sisters. It took place in 1990 at the time my mother passed on.

On learning the news about our mother, my younger sister and her husband immediately came to my home so that we could support one another. My brother-in-law decided to telephone my other sister, from whom I had been estranged for about eight years. There had been no communication between us, except for a very difficult episode regarding the handling of my mother's financial affairs. Litigation had resulted in an agreement, one of the terms of which involved a very large sum of money I would owe my mother's estate when she passed on. I felt this agreement was unfair and wrong.

The next morning when I read the verses from First Corinthians: "Purge out therefore the old leaven" and "Let us keep the feast, not with old leaven, neither with the leaven of malice and wickedness; but with the unleavened bread of sincerity and truth" (5:7, 8), I prayed more earnestly than ever about this estrangement with my sister, wanting to heal the hurt, bitterness, and resentment. I continued reading and came to the sentence in *Science and Health* which discusses spiritual communion, explaining that "our wine [is] the inspiration of Love, the draught our Master drank and commended to his followers" (p. 35). Many ideas about love came to my thought. I remembered something I'd read years before in a Christian Science magazine, which said that if we patiently and persistently identify ourselves as ideas of divine Love, vessels filled with love, then all that can happen when someone attempts to offend us is that love will pour forth. I recalled an interview from a Boston newspaper that was reprinted in the *Sentinel* in 1989, about a man whose family had been murdered. He said, "There is no justice in this world and life is not fair. But there is love, and in the end it is all we have. . . ."

I turned again to the Bible and read the chapter on charity from First Corinthians (chapter 13). Then I read the same chapter in *The New English Bible.* I had read these verses many times, but at that moment I was drawn closer to two ideas: "Love keeps no score of wrongs . . ." and "There is nothing love cannot face; there is no limit to its faith, its hope, and its endurance" (I Corinthians 13:6, 7).

All that week I had been reading this sentence from the Bible Lesson: "Jesus acknowledged no ties of the flesh" (*Science and Health,* p. 31). It occurred to me that anger, despair, the sense of betrayal—all the bad feelings—were "ties of the flesh," and they were not to be acknowledged or accepted as true of God or God's child.

The thought came to call my sister and invite her to be with us. I did, and it wasn't hard. She came to dinner that night, and she brought a box of strawberries. We hugged and kissed. I also had no bad feelings. We didn't talk about those terrible years. When she left, we agreed that we needed to forgive each other. That was the beginning of a profound reconciliation in our family.

A few weeks later she telephoned to propose a more acceptable financial arrangement and then waived the terms of the agreement involving the money I was to owe the estate. I had prayed about this situation for years, continually reminding myself of something a Christian Science practitioner had once told me. She said, "If it isn't God's plan for you, it will fail." I had studied all the accounts of reconciliation in the Bible. I believed them and loved them.

Now, I know they are true. Since this healing, there has not been an unkind word between my sister and me. Our relationship is good.

Name withheld at author's request
Christian Science Sentinel May 3, 1993

An impending divorce between my husband and me didn't take place.

I was under the care of a gynecologist, having exhausted the help of several witch doctors. I was told I had a womb infection. After three unsuccessful operations, doctors said the illness was incurable and wanted to remove my womb to reduce my suffering. I was most confused, afraid, and had lost all hope.

A dear friend gave me a copy of the *Christian Science Sentinel* and *Science and Health.* I commenced reading the book and found the chapter entitled "Prayer" most uplifting. A few days later the excruciating pain in my womb left me. At the end of that month about four inches of the synthetic fibre used for stitching my wounds after each operation passed from my body during menstruation, and that was the end of these problems.

I also wish to give gratitude that, as a result of my study of the Bible and *Science and Health,* an impending divorce between my husband and me didn't take place. We used to fight every day, and there were times when we would not speak to each other for up to four months, although we were living in the same house. But by mentally separating evil from man, who is made in the image and likeness of God (as stated in the book of Genesis), I was able to express more tolerance, patience, forgiveness, and love for my husband. Prayer was helping me to see him and myself from a different outlook.

I was able to see both of us as God's spiritual children, and our individual relationships to God as always intact; therefore our unity, established in God's permanency, could not be broken. I began to see good qualities in my husband that I had not seen before, and to appreciate and love him. Our home life is now harmonious and loving.

SOPHIE MOLONDOVOTI
Soshanguve, Transvaal
Republic of South Africa
Christian Science Sentinel May 3, 1993

Someone I deeply cared for treated me unjustly.

I would like to share a healing I had of a broken heart. Some years ago, while I was passing through a series of trials, someone I deeply cared for treated me unjustly by using and slandering me. When I confronted the individual, there was no response to my remarks. I found myself mentally numb to this hardened behavior. Seeking healing, I found that dedicated prayer helped me to perceive the wrongful elements in this situation, the strong self-will on another's part, and the self-pity I had been indulging in. Gradually my outlook improved.

A passage that was especially helpful to me at this time was this one in *Science and Health:* "Human affection is not poured forth vainly, even though it meet no return. Love enriches the nature, enlarging, purifying, and elevating it. The wintry blasts of earth may uproot the flowers of affection, and scatter them to the winds; but this severance of fleshly ties serves to unite thought more closely to God, for Love supports the struggling heart until it ceases to sigh over the world and begins to unfold its wings for heaven" (p. 57). I knew from reading of Mary Baker Eddy's life experience that she had demonstrated the truth of these words, and I endeavored to put them into practice in my own life.

As the numbness faded, I noticed that hatred was creeping into my thoughts. I pondered more deeply this passage from "A Rule for Motives and Acts" in the *Manual of The Mother Church* by Mrs. Eddy: "Neither animosity nor mere personal attachment should impel the motives or acts of the members of The Mother Church. In Science, divine Love alone governs man; and a Christian Scientist reflects the sweet amenities of Love, in rebuking sin, in true brotherliness, charitableness, and forgiveness" (Art. VIII, Sect. 1).

One Sunday, while I was singing a hymn during a service in church, I saw clearly the ugliness of hatred and how it is sometimes disguised as self-justification. At the same time I saw that the truth and love I was striving to express were native to my real, spiritual identity as God's child. I saw more vividly that evil is never included in God's wholly good creation. *Science and Health* states, "Human hate has no legitimate mandate and no kingdom. Love is enthroned" (p. 454).

The final step in this healing involved overcoming a persistent feeling of having a wounded, or broken, heart. I often recalled the tender phrase "heal the heart" from a hymn, and I cherished its promise. I continued to study the Bible and Mrs. Eddy's writings, read the Christian Science periodicals, and serve in church activities.

One day I lay down for a few minutes to rest, and in the stillness this assurance came peacefully to thought: "Your heart is sealed." I was grateful and felt that the next step was to demonstrate the validity of these comforting words. Interestingly, it was only a short time thereafter when I was called upon to take care of some situations that required my responding "under fire" to arrows aimed at the heart, so to speak. I found I was able to meet them with composure. I also found my sensitivities firm and strong, not delicate nor hardened. I had been entirely healed.

Name withheld at author's request
Christian Science Sentinel July 15, 1991

I learned that no person can rule my mind or my body.

I was in a state of emotional desperation. I was involved in premarital sex, smoking, and drinking and felt much lack of direction, sadness, fear, anger, and confusion.

One day I prayed for some sort of way out of this, and very soon afterward a Christian Scientist became my roommate. This living situation at once changed my mental atmosphere, and I began reading with determination the *Sentinel*s I found crowding the bookshelves in our apartment.

I decided to talk to Christian Scientists about my problems and received much helpful information. The first change I saw was my resolve to break off the premarital sex. My roommate helped me to see that refraining from sex outside of marriage is a protection from both physical and mental anguish, and that in this case I had made myself emotionally vulnerable by engaging in premarital sex. The man I was dating had been hurting me terribly, but the original mistake was my unwise decision to become so involved with him. When I told him about my resolve to end our relationship, I felt very lonely. I realized, however, that I was already complete, not lacking good in any way. I learned that no person could rule my mind or my body, and that our relationships with each other are happy only as we understand our individual relation to God. I saw that each one of His children is dependent on Him; they are not dependent on each other.

In a few months I met my husband in a most natural and expeditious way. He valued the same kind of stable family life I desired. We both have found enormous blessing in our relationship, and continue to grow.

In the following years I have found that devotion to God has heaped goodness upon me, while avoiding Him brings a great darkness. Through prayer I was able to overcome a fear of driving, to excel in college (after several years of being officially labeled "learning disabled"), to find the ability to remain in our beautiful home and raise our children, and to begin new friendships.

Early in my last pregnancy, I showed signs of a miscarriage, and was fearful and distraught because I'd miscarried several months before. I started praying. At once I found a Christian Science practitioner to help me, and we got to the root of the problem.

I realized my concept of family, and especially of marriage, needed to be spiritualized, in order to improve my situation. During the previous months, I had felt at odds with everyone I knew, some relationships were downright horrible. I had allowed myself to drift in my thinking, and felt out of sync with God, and everything good in life. Among other things, I realized I had to correct my thinking about my husband, to affirm his goodness as God's man. I also addressed a fear of my body acting independently of God. I realized that He controlled every detail of my existence, and that the baby was not depending on matter for life, but on God alone.

From that time on, the pregnancy progressed normally, and I continued talking with the practitioner. All the relationship problems, including the difficulties my husband and I had been having in our marriage, were healed during this pregnancy.

Just before the birth, another physical complication arose. I was given a twenty-four-hour time limit for the start of labor, after which it would be medically induced. One hour before the time limit was up, I resolved to rely on no one, or no thing, other than God. My resolve was not to avoid medical intervention, but to see that I was not dependent on others for my well-being in general. I saw that I was able to rely on God to meet *all* my needs. (Previously I had some concerns about being let down by others.) The labor started and ended in a few hours; the birth was natural and harmonious. I am grateful that the practitioner was with me at the hospital during labor.

Another child, a son, was healed of food allergies at the time of this pregnancy. I attribute this to having prayed every day, specifically, to know that these allergies were not real or a part of him. Perhaps some might say children simply outgrow these ailments, but our son was freed of sensitivity to umpteen different foods at the same time, in just a few weeks.

I love to study and ponder Christian Science just for the inspiration of it all. I am most thankful, however, for the practical transformations of mind, body, and daily life brought about by this study to understand God's ever-presence and guidance.

Name withheld at author's request
Christian Science Sentinel July 30, 1995

It became clear to me when and how to discipline.

For several years I often entertained the notion that I should never have been a mother. I was frequently impatient and irritated with my two children and was confused and unsure of myself as to how to discipline. It seemed I had the choice either to express love and let them walk all over me or pit my will against theirs and make them mind.

However, I got a glimpse of the truth that God is man's only parent and the mortal sense of motherhood and fatherhood must be denied.

For many months I endeavored to be more patient, loving, and understanding, thinking that the children would respond in like manner. One day when I was reading, this Bible verse leaped out at me: "I have declared, and have saved, and I have shewed, when there was no strange god among you" (Isaiah 43:12).

I then realized that I was believing that my behavior regulated that of the children and I could have either an adverse or a beneficial effect on their personalities. The one infinite Mind, God, governs man and one mortal mind can affect another only to the degree that we believe this false mentality has power.

This was a beginning. However, there were many more wonderful truths to be revealed.

My older child became increasingly difficult to manage. He was disobedient, had temper tantrums, and even destroyed things when he did not get his way. Every human effort to discipline him failed. Often when I saw one of these tantrums coming, I would brace myself and do my best not to react. What was "handling" him was also handling me and filling me with fear. I recognized the need to see myself, too, as God's perfect reflection, possessing the dominion given me by God. Realizing that I must stand up to error, I would silently declare that I was not afraid of it, as it had no power, that good was the only power. My fear began to subside.

It was absolutely necessary to separate the evil from the child's identity. And I must love, love, love, the child, love the purity, innocence, joy, and all the qualities that constitute man's spiritual being as the son of God.

I was trying earnestly to do this. One evening after a particularly trying experience with the child I felt so barren of love that I prayed humbly, "God, You love him more than I ever can. Your love is the only love there is. Whether I feel it now or not, I know this is true." A wonderful peace came over me, and I recalled the joy and happiness the child had brought me as a tiny baby. I realized that this truly was the way he was now and this was the only way I could behold him.

However, the tantrums and acts of destruction continued, and there was still fear and anxiety in my thinking.

The climax came one day when the youngster was playing with matches and accidentally set fire to the garage. I immediately called the fire department, and then, a Christian Science practitioner. She pointed out the definition of *fire* in the Glossary of *Science and Health,* which reads in part, "affliction purifying and elevating man" (p. 586). It was pointed out that this was all that was going on.

I regained my composure, and the fire was safely put out. But twenty minutes later the youngster was found in the car burning holes in the upholstery with the cigarette lighter. This was totally discouraging. After a few minutes, though, it became completely obvious to me that this could not be God's man, created in His image and likeness. The evil, swollen out of proportion, destroyed itself with this last act. The fire had separated the dross from the gold.

This was indeed the last of the temper tantrums, and the child is now loving, cooperative, and a joy to live with.

During the next few days the wonderful truth unfolded to me that the motherhood of God is always expressing itself without interruption. This released me from the personal sense of motherhood, and I began effortlessly to express more patience, love, and understanding toward the children. It has also become clear to me when and how to discipline. I understand this to be the evidence of God's father qualities—firmness, confidence, judgment, and strength. This was especially important to me, for the children had lost their father.

This experience has taught me that we never need to be discouraged. If we persist, Truth will always have the victory.

Sandra Matthes Vukov
Lake Oswego, Oregon
The Christian Science Journal September 1971

I wasn't sad anymore.

When I was little I had an aunt who always had time to be with me. She let me take blankets and drape them over furniture to play house. But most of the time I spent sitting next to her while she read to me.

When I was five years old my aunt passed on. A few nights later I was lying in bed, with my mom sitting next to me. She was explaining that my aunt was God's idea and still expressed life and love.

At first it was hard for me to understand. But then I did, and I said, "It's like when you walk down the beach and you see the shell of a crab. You think the crab is dead because he's not there, but he has really shed his shell and is still walking down the beach."

So even though I couldn't see my aunt, I knew she was still expressing life, and I wasn't sad anymore.

I've been going to a Christian Science Sunday School since I was three or four.

One day when I was in school I didn't feel well. There is a poem that I learned from the *Sentinel.* It's about effortless joy, and it says that God is singing and we're His song. I thought about the poem over and over again, and soon I felt great!

Madeline April-Erin Sweeny

I am aware of the day in school when Erin didn't feel well and worked with the poem. She continued to pray with those thoughts throughout the year and shared them with her Sunday School class.

Erin wrote this testimony on her own. In fact, she wrote it one day when she did not feel well and had stayed home from school. We spent the morning reading the Bible and *Science and Health* together. Then she returned to her room. That afternoon Erin came downstairs healed, with what she had written.

Constance E. Sweeny
Sutton's Bay, Michigan
Christian Science Sentinel March 31, 1986

I found myself struggling with the question of life after death.

My peace, joy, and confidence were shattered about fifteen years ago by the suicide of one of my sons, a young man in his early twenties; a young man of great potential. When it happened I blamed myself for not having loved enough, listened enough, and for not having had the wisdom to provide proper guidance. I couldn't sleep, dreaded meeting friends, and cried whenever I was alone, in spite of my prayers. I was First Reader in our branch church then, and my initial reaction was thinking that I must resign. But this would be bowing to the problem not God, so I carried on. The time dedicated to preparing services provided periods of freedom from thinking about self. And the readings from the Bible, and *Science and Health* that unfolded for the Wednesday testimony meetings were helpful both to me and to the congregation.

One sleepless night I went to the kitchen (where no one would hear) and allowed myself to abandon all self-control. As I was screaming and whacking things I heard a voice say, "You can't go on like this," and I felt the touch of Love. Instantly I was quiet and controlled and said, "What can I do?" Quickly the answer came: I should send my younger son to a private school, renew my teacher's license, and go back to teaching. But I found myself arguing that at this time of year the school wouldn't take a new pupil; and probably my license couldn't be renewed after thirty years of not teaching; and who would hire someone nearing the retirement age? This dialogue was repeated three times before I was convinced that I had to follow the instructions. Then I went back to bed and slept.

Early the next morning I went to the Education Office to find out what I must do to renew my license. In fact, I had nothing to do, it was renewed on the spot. The next weekend my son and I went to interview with the headmaster at the private school, who was most understanding. He said they were expecting a boy to leave after Christmas, which made it possible to accept my son. At this point I was tempted to panic, as I had no prospect of a job. But God provided this too, for I was soon asked to fill in at a secondary school for a teacher who was leaving at Christmas.

When I look back on this experience I marvel at the smoothness with which all the steps were carried out. Initially the situation had looked impossible, but, as the Bible tells us, "with God all things are possible" (Matthew 19:26).

During the next six months I was so fully occupied that there was no time for self-pity, self-condemnation, or sleeplessness. This respite from mortal thinking brought improvement. Studying at the boarding school did much for my son's self-confidence; and the school class I taught made progress, even though it was difficult at times.

Still, much of my grief went unhealed, buried beneath such a blanket of activity that there was almost no time for real thinking. Fatigue was the primary reason I experienced deep sleep at night.

For a long time after the teaching job ended, I found myself struggling with the question of life after death. Knowing that problems not solved here must be solved hereafter was no comfort to me at all. I'd think of the possibility of my son's disappointment and hopelessness to find he had not escaped his problems; of his rebellion at still being expected to overcome them; of his continuing frustration about the cruelty of world conditions. I wondered if he had committed this act to get even with me and with what I had tried to teach him. Many tears were shed during wakeful night hours.

Finally the light of Truth flooded my consciousness and I realized that my role had not ended as I had been believing. I could still help my son by denying the picture that had always seemed so real, the picture of an extremely sensitive, fearful, doubtful, overly analytical child. I could affirm my son's true likeness as God's perfect reflection, who had never suffered from depression. I could release him to his real Parent, our Father-Mother God. A great burden was lifted, and there were no more unhappy, morbid thoughts. The happiness we'd shared (and there was much); the joy he'd spread (and he was able to help many in distress); the intelligence he'd expressed (and in his work he had many triumphs) were and are the qualities that seem most real to me about him.

In Psalms 119 we read, "Thy word is a lamp unto my feet, and a light unto my path" (verse 105). What freedom is found when we apprehend the spiritual meaning of the Scriptures!

Margaret R. Bowman

As Mrs. Bowman's son, and remembering what a tangle we were in, I can appreciate how smoothly everything worked out. Everybody who had a part in the events at that time was so helpful. It was just as my mother has recounted it; as though some governing hand was guiding the pieces into place. My mother, a widow, has always held the family together through love and understanding, particularly when these qualities seemed hardest to give and were most needed. How glad I am to be her son, for no amount of riches could compare with what she has given me.

Roger A. Bowman
Halifax, Nova Scotia, Canada
Christian Science Sentinel June 7, 1982

Since childhood I had been unable to feel the love expressed by others.

As a child of five, although I did not understand what was happening at the time, I was sexually abused on two separate occasions. Both of the men who molested me were people in our neighborhood. My family never learned of the first incident, but the second time, a neighbor walked in while it was happening. She made so much noise, screaming and crying, that I became very frightened. The young man was taken into custody, and the case went to trial.

Owing to changing circumstances, I went to live with another member of my family, who may have known about the second incident but never spoke of it. I grew up feeling that I was a perverted, evil child, and I never mentioned the unpleasant episodes until I became a young woman. Throughout these years I forced myself not to think of the awful, recurring nightmares I was having. By this time I found concentration difficult. During my school years, at the request of school authorities I was sent to several psychologists, all of whom verified my above-average intelligence. My family voiced their exasperation over what they felt was an indifference on my part to schoolwork. This plunged me into further self-depreciation and condemnation. I had few friends and seemed to live in an unhappy, lonely world of my own. I experienced lapses of memory and heard music where there was none.

After I had completed the required examinations for my chosen field, I moved to a distant city, where I was isolated from the family, friends, and culture that I had grown up with. A new friend recommended that I study Christian Science. At first I was reluctant. But the gentle persuasion of this individual, whom I respected, overcame my reservations, and I began reading *Science and Health.* This awoke me to the knowledge that something was wrong in my life, that my help was to be found in this book and the new way of life it would open for me.

Utilizing the truths that I was gleaning from the Bible Lesson in the *Christian Science Quarterly,* I began to realize, as Mary Baker Eddy states, "The illusion of material sense, not divine law, has bound you, entangled your free limbs, crippled your capacities, enfeebled your body, and defaced the tablet of your being" (*Science and Health,* p. 227). As I continued on a minute-to-minute basis to pray to the best of my understanding, sincerely striving to overcome the insistent self-condemnation, I gained confidence and actually began to feel God's presence. This liberation of my consciousness was by no means a quick one, it took several years.

Reading these Bible Lessons and employing their truths, I began to trust God and to allow the hideous mental ghosts to come unrestrictedly to the forefront of my thought. I knew that as I dealt with these suggestions as honestly as I could and did not fear them, I would perceive the spiritual truth needed to annul them totally. And so it was. Many times, while I was studying and endeavoring to concentrate prayerfully on my true nature, the depressing, condemning suggestion left me, and the sunshine of the truth of God's man spread its healing warmth within. I could say about spiritual being, "It's true of me!" and know that it really was.

While I was making new friends and becoming increasingly outgoing, I still had periods of anxious concern and fear of the unknown; ugly memories would then monopolize my thinking, compelling me to withdraw within myself once more. These periods happened suddenly and without warning. One morning I was studying the Lesson when I received a wonderful assurance that my true nature was spiritual and that no one could ever really harm me. My real being was pure and incorruptible, because my true substance was spiritual. There followed the realization that I could claim spiritual authority and dominion over every situation confronting me. After this enlightenment, the periods of confusion and the fear that I might be sexually abused again gradually disappeared until they no longer recurred. The basis of my friendships became sounder, and they were lasting.

Years earlier, the woman had screamed and cried when she saw me molested. I thought her reaction meant that I was an evil little girl, and I had carried the heavy burden of this assumption. Now I realized I had misinterpreted her reaction, and that she really had been afraid and concerned for me. After this became clear, and I began to learn more of man's eternal innocence, I was able to be much kinder to myself and to forgive myself.

Over the years I have felt a continuation of mental freedom. This in turn has released me for more constructive reasoning, benefiting my own life and the lives of the people I have known. Since childhood I had been unable to feel the love expressed by others, to utilize it so that it was meaningful and nourishing to me. Finally I met a young man who expressed all the qualities to which I was drawn and could so easily love, but it took several years for his love to reach me. One day, when I felt confused and fretful about things, I glanced at him and found him looking at me with gentleness. I asked him what he was thinking, and he replied, "I'm just loving you." I could see that he was. From that moment I began not only to feel his special, unselfish, caring love, but to feel it in other degrees from those around me. This has been a most precious proof of God's love for me and His great kindness to man.

The last verse of a hymn states what Christian Science has done for me:

The freer step, the fuller breath,
   The wide horizon's grander view;
The sense of Life that knows no death,—
   The Life that maketh all things new.

Name withheld at author's request
Christian Science Sentinel March 3, 1980

Section III

Gaining control over the unexpected

Unexpected danger, an accident, a terminal disease, an addictive drug, would appear to be beyond one's control. But as the writers in this section found, God's law provides reliable solutions, protection, and healing.

11

Erasing the marks of crime, fear, and terrorism

Fear, crime, violence, and their effects are removed through the power and love of God. Prayer benefits communities as well as individuals, as these writers proved.

A man ran out of the alley with a knife in his hand.

The reliance on prayer by this police detective has not only helped him begin to remove hatred and anger but has led to more effective police work. Since his current assignment is with the homicide and assault division of a large urban police force in the United States, this interview is presented anonymously.

Before I became a detective I was a patrolman for a little short of seven years. When I had been on the force only nine or ten months, I was working in a very rough area of town. Officers in another patrol car came on the radio with a report that they had discovered a stabbing incident. They asked the fire department to treat the wounded victim, and they radioed they had made an arrest. We believed they had captured a suspect; there seemed to be no point for us to go into the area.

When the call had first come out, I had started to pray. It wasn't really any specific prayer, but it kept my thought clear and I didn't react to any of the information. As I continued to pray, I drove up one particular avenue and the thought came to me "turn left." What happened is described in the Bible in this way: "Thine ears shall hear a word behind thee, saying, This is the way, walk ye in it, when ye turn to the right hand, and when ye turn to the left" (Isaiah 30:21).

I turned left and drove down a few more blocks. I felt it was right to come to a halt at the curb in front of an alley. I remember not knowing why I was there, because the street was practically deserted. This was very late at night. Then a man ran out of the alley in front of our headlights with a knife in his hand. We jumped out of the car and chased him. After a standoff of a minute or so, he put the knife down. We captured him and made the arrest. We discovered that this was the man who had done the stabbing reported by the other unit. The officers at the scene several blocks away had arrested a suspect, but they had not captured the right person.

I think that was my first real demonstration of how useful I can be to God. I was going to say "how useful God could be to me as a policeman," but I remember being so elated that I had been led to do what I did. From then on I was able to rely more confidently on God as divine Mind. More and more I began to see that there's one divine Mind, that Mind is God. I know what I am doing is right human activity and God will show me what steps to take. I pray along those lines, and I try to listen to what God has to say to me.

I remember one night we were flying down the freeway in the patrol car to go to a section of town where a guy had been snatching purses and beating up his victims. Another incident had just occurred. The description we were given of the suspect was limited. We had no vehicle description, no direction of flight, no clothing description. We traveled about three miles on the freeway and came into the area. I decided to stop one car in particular, even though none was mentioned. The driver tried to escape. After we caught him, we found about seven purses in the back seat. The way we were sure of the identification, I thought was very apropos. I found a Bible in one of the purses. A woman's name was written in the Bible; it was the name of the person who had just been robbed.

My partner knew I was a Christian Scientist. At one point I had given him a copy of *Science and Health*. And we talked about religion off and on. One time when we were attempting to locate a holdup suspect, he asked me which way we should go. I was in a very despairing mood, and I said, "I don't know, just do whatever you want to do." He turned to me and he said, "Look, you just do whatever it is you do over there, and tell me where to go." He was telling me to pray and I did.

Prayer resulted in a physical healing that took place for me while I was a patrolman. I was on a plainclothes assignment. My partner and I were using confidential informants to work on drug cases in our district. Confidential informants (CI's) are criminals who for whatever motivation will provide the police with information that we can use to solve a case. But what always has to be understood is that they're not really doing this out of a sense of justice or righteousness. It's usually fear that's guiding them.

We discovered that one of our CI's was actively trying to find out personal details about us, where we lived, who the members of our family were, and so on. One night as I left the precinct, I realized I was being followed by a car. I took steps to lose this car, and I reported the incident to my partner. Very soon he was also followed, and he saw that our CI was tailing him.

Later my partner and I were in our car trying to decide what to do about this situation. We were still somewhat new at running investigations like this. A great deal of fear and hatred was presenting itself as my thinking. There were some very unchristian thoughts going back and forth.

At that moment I felt a pain in my head, and I reached up and touched the back of my head and I felt a lump. It was extremely painful. It may have been there for a while, but I hadn't noticed it. I know Christ, Truth, was present because a phrase came to me at that exact moment. It was ". . . let us labor to dissolve with the universal solvent of Love . . . ." The phrase is part of a sentence from *Science and Health:* "In patient obedience to a patient God, let us labor to dissolve with the universal solvent of Love the adamant of error,—self-will, self-justification, and self-love,—which wars against spirituality and is the law of sin and death" (p. 242). I knew that the only way to heal this was to love.

That night I read something Mrs. Eddy has to say in *Science and Health* about Christ Jesus: "The 'man of sorrows' best understood the nothingness of material life and intelligence and the mighty actuality of all-inclusive God, good. These were the two cardinal points of Mind-healing, or Christian Science, which armed him with Love" (p. 52).

I saw "the mighty actuality of all-inclusive God" really had to embrace everybody, including this informant. Jesus' armaments were not handguns. He didn't need a sword or any weapon to keep himself safe. That was a rebuke to me because I had more than one handgun on me earlier in my patrol car. My partner and I had been in a shootout a year or so back in which a murder suspect fired shots at us. My partner shot him while I was pinned down. So this whole atmosphere of violence was one I needed to be free of. I needed to have my thinking healed of this sense of hatred and violence.

I prayed along those lines, and I could see that my armament, my protection, was God's love, not anything physical that I did to another person. The next time I remembered to check, I discovered that this lump had completely vanished. I was healed in just a few days through prayer alone.

I've heard it said that if we're not actively loving people, then we are hating them in one degree or another. I can see that my thought toward criminals and the public in general had been very, very far from loving or Christlike. The summer after I was promoted to detective, there were three or four officers who had to shoot suspects who were trying to shoot them. I worked as an investigator in the unit I'm now in. It's a unit that handles sex crimes and child abuse cases, and we're a part of the section that also handles homicide and robbery. Every shooting is something that is studied by detectives. I remember hearing the details of one of these shootings; I just was filled with hatred for this suspect.

I realized this hatred had to be handled, and I wasn't going to achieve that through anything other than prayer, because the human senses would say I was right to hate a crook who tried to kill a policeman. But our only choice, if we're going to live the life Christ Jesus did, is to love. It's still something that I wrestle with because right now I investigate child abuse cases. The crime is so repugnant. I really have to work prayerfully to keep a spiritual point of view.

But hatred can only make the situation worse; it's a futile waste of energy. What has become clear to me is that hating someone is similar to entering a dream. There's no point in participating in a dream. I should concentrate on what God is actually doing rather than on what a dream may be claiming to do. This whole process has caused me to look to God and see more clearly that He's with me every step. I can go through my day asking for guidance as the psalms in the Bible say you can, glorifying God in everything I do.

I used to like to think of myself as a policeman, and it was very important to me that I was in the department. That has lessened; now I feel I could do just about anything in the world as long as I was doing it to serve God and to glorify Him. It's a much more peaceful way of thinking. A lot of the anger and the aggressiveness that seemed built into me for years has faded away. I am a much happier person and easier to live with.

I've found that belligerence and antagonism on my part don't really accomplish what a loving perspective does. I may never speak a word to a man; I may never appear to be kind or polite to him. Yet in my own consciousness I can say that I don't care what the senses tell me; I know that God would never allow evil to happen to His creation, that includes the crook as well as the victim.

I've spent quite a bit of time reasoning about what God's man has to be. It seems to me that when we react to man as a criminal who kills, robs, and rapes, we're blaspheming God.

We're saying God could have made man mortal and that He let man become confused. One of the major things I've learned is to hold in check the impulse to react. Instead of going ahead blindly, and all the time having hateful thoughts toward people, I can say to myself, "I have a job to do here, but I'm not going to let myself get pulled down into hating while I do it." That's made it a lot easier on me, and I think it makes for better case preparation.

As I continue to study and pray, it becomes clearer to me that ultimately this whole picture of an evil, mortal man has to be erased. Instead of regarding ourselves as mortals who are bound up in a lot of unhappy circumstances, really the whole thing has to be dropped away. It has to be for the people that we say are on the right side of the law and for those who may be considered to be on the wrong side. If God is God, He had to make each and every one of us as His individual reflections.

Even though in my contact with these individuals I may rarely see any regeneration, sooner or later they will have to change. The more I see this for myself, the more I know it has to be true for them too. This whole mortal dream is going to be erased. I think if people saw they had a choice between accepting Christ, Truth, or accepting a mortal picture of themselves, they would, once they came to understand, begin to leave this unhappy life behind. . . . The only way to free mankind completely from all this is to see man's spiritual nature, and that's going to be brought about through prayer and through healing.

Christian Science Sentinel May 27, 1991

I saw some of the most rigid, bitter, and hardened faces that I had ever seen.

Our home was situated on a corner lot, and the garage doors faced the high school across the street. For years, much to my dismay, these doors served as a billboard for messages. Gangs from outside the area would leave messages for other gangs from the school. Regardless of how many times, over a dozen or so years, we repainted those doors, the graffiti would reappear. Finally, frustrated and discouraged, we considered it a losing battle and just learned to live with it.

One Friday afternoon, breaking from my usual routine, I came home for lunch. Actually, it was my last day at my job, and I needed to make some personal telephone calls. When I arrived home, I couldn't believe my eyes. From the curb where I parked my car, up the walkway, and on the front door itself there were graffiti in bold orange paint. And to add to the insult, the offenders were standing there with paint cans in hand, lining the path to my front door. I was stunned as I made my way through their defiant glares.

Once I stepped into my home, the shock turned into anger. I don't believe I have ever felt so totally offended, so utterly used, and so intensely helpless. How dare they deface my property! How could they use my home for venting their frustration!

When I came out, they were still there. It almost seemed that they were waiting for me to come out, daring me to react. Frankly, I was so angry that I almost couldn't see straight. It seemed that all I could do was sit in my car and try to gather my composure before returning to work.

I had been studying the Holy Bible and *Science and Health with Key to the Scriptures* for just a few months. The Bible became a wonderful source for guidance. The study of *Science and Health* was shedding new light not only on the Bible but also on everything in my life. I was gleaning inspiration and direction from the words of its author, Mary Baker Eddy. I was learning, in accord with the Bible, that man's true selfhood is spiritual and good, because our creator, God, is Spirit, infinite good itself. In this light, I was eager to discover more of what God made me to be. Here was my opportunity.

As I looked out the car window, I saw some of the most rigid, bitter, and hardened faces that I had ever seen. They couldn't have been more than sixteen or seventeen years old.

I thought, How can I use what I have been learning? Is this situation beyond God's help? What am I doing? Am I joining in the hating? Wasn't the anger expressed through their graffiti the same anger that was now coming to my thought to deface their character?

I realized that the culprit was not really me or them. It was anger, misunderstanding, intolerance, ignorance, prejudice, the carnal mind, seeking acceptance and expression through any mentality that was open to its influence. Was I going to let my thought be like those garage doors, and now my walkway, a billboard for hatred? Was I going to justify the hatred of my fellowman? Was I going to let hatred mar my image of them?

I couldn't be made to label the labelers. I couldn't let public opinion—those who feel labeled or those who do the labeling—influence me. As the warmth of the sun melts ice, God's love was strong enough to melt this evidence of hatred. I could love more!

God made man to beautify, not to deface. And I wasn't going to allow any false message to deface my image of these young people. I knew these thoughts that were coming to me were thoughts of love, reflecting God's love, because they were filled with light, with goodness, and I could feel their warmth.

A sense of compassion for each one of them surged within me. Even if they didn't realize their spiritual nature, I could! I had to deny every false trait attaching itself to these kids. I couldn't let them convince me (regardless of what was going on in front of me) that they didn't have God's goodness within them. They had a right to be seen in the correct light. Someone had to care enough to know that they could be seen this way. Someone had to pray.

My prayer as I sat in my car was simple. I turned to my Father-Mother God. I recalled reading in the Bible that when one of Jesus' disciples asked him to teach them to pray, he gave them what is known as the Lord's Prayer. Most of us know how this prayer of prayers begins: "Our Father which art in heaven." In *Science and Health* Mrs. Eddy writes, giving the spiritual sense of these words, "*Our Father-Mother God, all-harmonious . . .*" (p. 16). As I turned to my

Father-Mother, it was so clear that God was also *their* Father-Mother, *our* Father-Mother, who protects and provides for us as Father, and who holds us close and unconditionally loves us as Mother.

When I arrived home that evening from work, the graffiti were completely cleaned off my property. But that was not all! The very next week, two bright and shining students from the high school came to my door, asking my permission to paint the garage doors. They explained that their art department had a campaign sponsored by the Parent-Teacher Association to beautify the neighborhood. They felt it was high time that they did something about its decaying appearance. One said, "We want to give our neighborhood some class. And don't worry if you see more graffiti; we have lots of paint."

I couldn't believe my ears! The project even attracted local television and newspapers. Best of all, when I passed through my old neighborhood recently, it was still free of graffiti, some twenty years after the incident.

Look what prayer can accomplish! I can't tell you how long those garage doors had been displaying graffiti. Yet, through a moment of spiritual insight—a moment to love more deeply, more purely, more humbly—I witnessed God's power to heal. In this light, my anger and resentment were erased, and with them the graffiti.

LAMEICE HARDING SCHIERHOLZ
Westlake Village, California
Christian Science Sentinel February 1, 1993

I silently affirmed that God's children are honest.

Originally written in German

We need to regain the childlike heart that knows only God, good, divine Love. We can increasingly succeed in doing this by denying that any fault, whether it appears to be our own or someone else's, could be part of God's infinite, good creation.

An experience I had illustrates this. One day when I was walking along a street, two men were walking in front of me, one about half a meter behind the other. As the first man turned to go into a shop, he dropped his wallet. The second man grabbed it, stopped, and checked to see how much money was in it. He then walked on. Observing this, I silently prayed, knowing most emphatically that God had never made a dishonest man. I affirmed that God's children are honest and that the evidence of the material senses is a lie; God's child can only act rightly.

I had hardly completed this line of thought when the first man rushed out of the shop with a despairing look on his face, looking for his wallet. By this time I had arrived at the spot where he had dropped it. The other man turned around, came back a few steps, and returned the wallet to the first man. He said, pointing to me, "This lady told me I should give back your wallet." I had not said a word to him. This change of heart on his part was the result of his own response to divine Truth.

KÄTE MEIER
Rio de Janeiro, Brazil
Christian Science Sentinel April 6, 1992

It was as though I were a spectator at the scene.

About eight o'clock one evening the doorbell rang. My husband was occupied upstairs, and my daughter was in the laundry at the rear of the house. So I went to answer the door. As I walked toward it, I picked up my little dog. The caller was a young man who said his car had broken down, and he asked to use the telephone to call for help. Our home is across the road from a university; frequently students have asked to use the phone.

It was quite dark and the porch light dim. I let the young man in. When I turned to indicate where the phone was, he had pulled a ski mask over his face and was pointing a gun at me. Then he went back to the door, opened it, and two more men entered, also wearing ski masks and holding guns.

At first I thought someone was playing a bad joke and said so, but I quickly realized this was no joke. I said to the men, "If it's money you want, there is my purse," which was on the hall table.

One of the men stationed himself at the foot of the stairs; another, so he could see both the living and dining room entrances. I was not frightened; it was as though I were a spectator at the scene.

As the first man emptied my wallet this statement of Christ Jesus' came to mind: "For where two or three are gathered together in my name, there am I in the midst of them" (Matthew 18:20). At first, this hardly seemed applicable to the situation, but since it was what came to me at the time, I knew this was the truth I needed. I knew God was right there in the midst of us, inseparable from His creation, man. The ninety-first Psalm came to mind, also.

I felt by this time that these young men were under the influence of drugs; their eyes were very strange looking. Instead of fear or anger, though, I had a great sense of compassion for them, of not wanting them to do this to themselves. This statement from *Science and Health* then came to mind, "Jesus beheld in Science the perfect man, who appeared to him where sinning mortal man appears to mortals. In this perfect man the Saviour saw God's own likeness, and this correct view of man healed the sick" (pp. 476–477). This perfect man I held in thought.

After the man who had emptied my wallet dumped everything out of my purse, he asked about money elsewhere in the house as well as if I had any diamonds. I was able to put off his questions, simply through trusting in God for my answer. I spoke quietly, without excitement or fear. Only the one man did the talking; the others just stared, with their guns pointed toward me.

Then the spokesman wanted to know who else was in the house. Instead of telling him, I answered, "In spite of what you are doing to me, I do not believe you are evil men." Three times he asked me the same question, and each time I calmly answered with the same statement, adding the third time, "Some great need caused you to do this." He answered, "Yes, a great need." There was no further questioning as to who else was in the house. (All this time he was holding the gun very firmly against my body.)

Then he said they were going to ransack the house. At that I declared to myself very fervently, "God's reflection is not, cannot be, covetous." I spoke to the men again and said, "There really isn't anything in this house that you want or need."

Quite suddenly the speaker for the trio said, "We're going to leave now." This was a complete change from what he had indicated they were going to do a moment before, and it really took me by surprise. He told me that the other two were going toward the main street and that he and I were going up the road. Because there is only one other house on our road, "up the road" meant, to me, dark woods and no lights. He added, in a very matter-of-fact manner, "I can't leave you here to call the police. I'm just going to have to kill you."

We went out the front door quickly. I was grateful that they did not know anyone else was in the house. He transferred the gun to my back. I was so relieved when they closed the door behind us. My family was safe.

The two men ran toward the main road, and the other man and I went down the driveway. I was determined not to go any farther than the driveway. I kept silently affirming that right where we were God was, because His reflection cannot be separated from its source. I had forgotten I still had my little Yorkshire terrier in my arms, he was so quiet. As we went down the driveway, with the gun digging into my back, the man reached over and touched the dog and remarked, "He is a nice little dog." "Yes," I said, "he came to us when he was in trouble, as you have." The words came out without any prior thought on my part.

When we got to the road he nudged me along with the gun, and I heard myself say, "I'm afraid to go up the road. It's so black." He answered, "Yes, somebody could hurt you up there." He paused for a minute, reached over and touched my shoulder, almost affectionately, and then turned and ran off in the direction the others had taken.

When I got back home, I told my family what had happened and then called the police, who later told me that it was my speaking quietly to the intruders and showing no fear that had saved my life. The police, however, could not understand why the men had not ransacked the house. I knew. It was recognizing God's presence that had quieted my fear and provided me with the protection and strength I needed. It was also the persistent acknowledgment of God's presence and power that had prevented the three men from stealing any more than the money and from harming me.

My little dog was very still during the entire experience. Yet normally he does not like to be held, and fidgets and barks to be let down. Among other proofs this was evidence to me that God's control was manifested throughout the experience.

The men were not caught by the police. About a week later, though, a young man came to the door, inquiring about a nonexistent address on our road. I sensed that this was the man who had held the gun on me. He seemed uncomfortable, made some small talk, and sort of lingered as though there were something he wanted to say but could not. Then he left.

Some time later, when I was telling a friend who is also our insurance broker about the experience, he asked how much money had been taken. I told him, and he said that our insurance policy would cover the full amount so there would be no loss to us. This proved true.

God's man can neither sin nor be sinned against. Not only does God, as Truth and Love, comfort and console us; as omnipotent, omnipresent Principle, He protects and heals us as well.

WILHELMINA HANCOCK
Atlanta, Georgia
Christian Science Sentinel May 5, 1986

My calmness noticeably surprised him.

On a lovely summer morning in 1987 I took a walk through our city park, which stretches out alongside a river. This particular morning I met no one else along the path. Then suddenly a voice behind me sounded, "Hi there;" an arm was flung around my throat, and I was whisked across the grass into a wooded area. Because our community is a safe one, generally free of violent incidents, my first reaction was that this had to be a joke, that this couldn't be happening to me. But quickly I realized the danger. Frantically, I tried to cling to bush branches but was pulled away.

A glimpse of the river ahead evoked in me a terrible fear. The attacker wore a rubber suit, and I felt his intention was to drown me. Knowing that human struggle would not prevail, I reached out to God. I questioned: Is God, Truth, strong enough to deliver me from a situation like this? The answer came immediately in a short sentence from *Science and Health,* "Truth is always the victor" (p. 380). This message gave me courage.

I had the presence of mind to recall a testimony I had read about a man who was confronted by a person with a gun who tried to rob him. Turning to God in prayer, the man was led to say, "You don't have to do this; it will only get you into jail again." Apparently, the person holding the gun had been in prison before, and when he saw someone actually showing concern for him, he broke down in tears and freed his intended victim. As I recognized the power of Truth, divine Love, in this experience, all fear left me.

Though I was still being pulled toward the water, I no longer sought to hold on to branches. I turned my head and addressed this individual with "You don't have to do this." Slower, and with greater emphasis, I repeated these same words. As I turned around I fell to the ground several feet away from the man. Assured of God's all-presence and confident that no harm would come to me, I remained in my position on the ground, feeling this was the safest thing to do.

The man stood there and seemed to be waiting for me to scramble back on my feet. My calmness noticeably surprised him. Suddenly he seemed struck by terror; then he turned and ran away as fast he could.

I thanked God for His loving protection. Truly I'd witnessed that, as *Science and Health* states, "Error is a coward before Truth" (p. 368). I returned to the path, and I recovered my purse with everything intact.

MARGARET SWETMAN
Kamloops, British Columbia, Canada
Christian Science Sentinel February 13, 1989

I was very grateful to be alive.

A few years ago I was held hostage by a gunman and raped. Some friends were vacationing in our home at the time, and when it became known to them that I was being held hostage, they called my husband at work. He in turn telephoned a Christian Science practitioner, who began praying on my behalf.

After my release I was very grateful to be alive and back with my family again. But soon I became depressed, ashamed, and so afraid that I felt I no longer wanted to live.

The practitioner talked at length with me, stressing that my true spiritual identity had never been victimized. He explained that in reality I could not have two identities; I could not be a suffering victim of crime on the one hand and a spiritual idea of God on the other. In truth my identity was spiritual—created, sustained, protected, and directed by God. Mary Baker Eddy writes in *Science and Health,* "Whatever indicates the fall of man or the opposite of God or God's absence, is the Adam-dream, which is neither Mind nor man, for it is not begotten of the Father" (p. 282).

Although I was comforted by these wonderful spiritual truths, I struggled with a feeling of being separated from God. I knew that in order to be rescued from the desperate condition I felt myself in, I had to be awakened from this Adam-dream that seemed so real. So every time a sense of remorse or fear would come to me, I would immediately turn to God and acknowledge His government, realizing that despair comes from "neither Mind nor man." I began to recognize the whole experience as a suggestion, tempting me to believe that my life was outside God's care.

I turned to God many times to clear my thinking of the material picture, affirming unreservedly and steadfastly the spiritual facts of my true nature as revealed in Christian Science. At times I thought it was bizarre to deny that the assault had actually happened. But as my husband, the practitioner, and I continued to pray, reaching out for a higher, more spiritual understanding of my real being, I began to discern that material sense could in no way present the true view of life.

I read everything I could from the Bible and *Science and Health* about God's tender love for man, and I applied what I read to my own case. Statements such as this one from these textbooks were especially meaningful, "If you wish to know the spiritual fact, you can discover it by reversing the material fable, be the fable *pro* or *con,*—be it in accord with your preconceptions or utterly contrary to them" (p. 129).

Because I felt at wit's end so many times, I felt it was imperative to turn to God for reassurance of my reason for being. I was certain that no other help could offer complete release. Christ Jesus' plea on the cross, "My God, my God, why hast thou forsaken me?" (Matthew 27:46), reminded me of the desolation I was struggling with. Yet I realized that although I may have felt abandoned, Jesus surely suffered much more than this when he was betrayed, condemned, and crucified. Still, he had gone on to resurrection and ascension. Psalm 22, which begins with the same words Jesus used on the cross, declares of God that, "he hath not despised nor abhorred the affliction of the afflicted; neither hath he hid his face from him; but when he cried unto him, he heard" (verse 24). These and many other words of comfort gave me a deepening conviction that, indeed, I was God's creation.

At the outset of this experience my husband had called the police, and we had followed the course of action required by them. Several weeks later it was necessary for me to view a group of suspects. My prevalent concern at that time was that I didn't want to make a mistake and accuse an innocent man. However, at the time of the attack, my glasses were taken from me and I was blindfolded, so I did not have a clear memory of what the man looked like. I was unable to identify him in the police lineup. While I have never heard of the gunman again and don't know what happened to him, I have forgiven him. I had learned that healing would come as forgiveness was present in my heart.

To the extent that I cherished precious spiritual truths, I once again saw beauty in my life. For about two years following the incident, there were still moments when fear would flood my consciousness. But many times I was buoyed when I recalled the inspiration that had come with the loving, steadfast prayer of the practitioner and the support of my husband. Eventually the release from that frightening period was so great that I was able to turn on those recurring evil thoughts like a lion, expressing quickness of dominion and stability of strength. The Bible tells us, "God hath not given us the spirit of fear; but of power, and of love, and of a sound mind" (II Timothy 1:7).

Through prayer and study of the Bible and *Science and Health* I have set aside the incident as no part of my true being. My relations with my husband and family have been as wonderful as I can imagine. I am deeply grateful to my husband and the practitioner for their divinely impelled strength and clear thinking.

I thank God for this healing, which has been a continual reminder of His ever-present care.

Name withheld at author's request

I am the writer's husband. I witnessed the above healing. I share my wife's deep gratitude for God's great love for His children.

Name withheld at author's request

I was with the writer around the time of the occurrence that she relates. Afterward I was in her home for a week, and I observed the healing effects of prayer. I have seen the burden of shame lift from her and her natural vitality return.

Our families get together twice each year for a week and a half. The joyful and close relationship of the testifier with her husband and two sons is in constant evidence.

Name withheld at author's request
Christian Science Sentinel November 19, 1984

She told me there was an emergency in the city.

Excerpted from a radio broadcast

BEA ROEGGE: Friends, we are here with Corinne Teeter from Fort Lauderdale, Florida. Welcome, Corinne. Tell us about the incident you related to me earlier.

CORINNE TEETER: I'm a Christian Science practitioner, and I devote my time to praying for people. One day the phone rang in my office, and it was a distraught young woman from City Hall. I didn't know the young lady, but she told me there was an emergency in the city, and that a truck had broken down on the railroad tracks near the big general hospital. It was a huge van truck and it was full of chemicals. The chemicals were in containers, very large, heavy containers, and they were beginning to leak. And the problem was that if the chemicals in one container mixed with the chemicals in another one of the containers, there would be an explosion and the whole end of the city would be flattened. And they had ordered the general hospital to be evacuated. It was that serious.

BEA: Well, let me ask you, first, why did she call you? How did she get your name?

CORINNE: I had never met her. But she called the Christian Science Reading Room, and the attendant gave her my name. She asked if there was anything I could do. So I assured her that God is "a very present help in trouble," as the Bible tells us (Psalms 46:1), and that I would immediately pray, and there would be a solution.

BEA: Wonderful that you could offer that firm remark.

CORINNE: Well, I was convinced of it. She hung up the phone, and I began to pray. That is, I prayed to realize the presence and power of God. And the first thing that came to mind was where the Bible tells us to have the mind that was in Christ Jesus (see Philippians 2:5). I understood that mind to be God, the one divine Mind, the source of all right ideas, the source of all intelligence. And so as I prayed in this manner, to feel the presence of God, I understood as never before His great love for His children. I knew that He is the only creator and that He loves us. I saw that He expresses intelligence in His idea, man, His child. Later I found out what happened.

BEA: Obviously, what they feared was avoided; there was no explosion.

CORINNE: There was no explosion. Suddenly a tall young man broke out of the crowd that had gathered. He jumped into the back of the truck and began to wrestle these huge containers around until he had separated them so that there could be no mixture. And he had done in just a few minutes what this huge emergency squad of the city had failed to do.

BEA: Interesting. Where did he come from?

CORINNE: No one knows particularly where he came from. But the city did give him a medal. There was a ceremony, and he received a medal for outstanding bravery because the situation had been that serious. And I always thought the woman in City Hall should have had a medal for reaching out to God, who's equal to any emergency.

Bea: Didn't you tell me there was another time when there was a community problem?

Corinne: Yes. One time a high-school principal called me. She said, "We've had a bomb alert, and we're evacuating the high school, and it's very essential that we find it. Will you help?" And she expected prayer to be helpful. Again I turned my thought to God, and I saw Him this time as the divine Principle of all being. The Bible calls Him creator, Lawgiver, the Rock. To me the word *Principle* epitomizes all of these terms. And so I saw the order that this wonderful Father causes in His universe. I also saw that this Principle is entirely Love. Several minutes later the bomb was found, and the perpetrators were caught. The school principal called and told me.

Bea: Well, you've certainly inspired us, Corinne, to realize that when there are emergencies, even if we're not called but hear about something on the news, we can pray and expect results.

Christian Science Sentinel November 14, 1994

I sensed an unusually urgent need to continue praying.

I usually start my day with prayer and study of the Bible Lesson from the *Christian Science Quarterly.* One day as I prayed, I sensed an unusually urgent need to continue praying for a longer period of time. There was a strong demand to see more clearly that all men are brothers.

I pondered Jesus' response when he was told that his mother and brethren were desiring to speak with him (see Matthew 12:46–50). Perhaps they were fearful that his preaching would put him in danger and they wanted him to return home where he would be safe. But, continuing in his mission to love, teach, and heal the people, he asked, "Who is my mother? and who are my brethren?" And he answered his own questions with this important lesson: "Whosoever shall do the will of my Father which is in heaven, the same is my brother, and sister, and mother."

I also looked up many references to *brotherhood* in *Science and Health.* Two in particular gave me much to think about: "It should be thoroughly understood that all men have one Mind, one God and Father, one Life, Truth, and Love. Mankind will become perfect in proportion as this fact becomes apparent, war will cease and the true brotherhood of man will be established" (p. 467) and "One infinite God, good, unifies men and nations; constitutes the brotherhood of man; ends wars; fulfils the Scripture, 'Love thy neighbor as thyself;' annihilates pagan and Christian idolatry,—whatever is wrong in social, civil, criminal, political, and religious codes; equalizes the sexes; annuls the curse on man, and leaves nothing that can sin, suffer, be punished or destroyed" (p. 340).

When I first began to pray, I felt uneasy. Something was wrong and I didn't know what. But as I continued to turn to the Bible and *Science and Health,* I was comforted. I felt at peace. I knew that one God, one Mind, was in control, that all men are brothers, that divine Love is all-powerful. That evening I saw clearly how these truths of God and man were proved true and how only God was working His purpose out, even during a time when terrorist activity had been directed toward my immediate family and friends.

A terrorist disguised as an American military officer had entered a NATO facility where my husband worked. The man had left a stolen car near the NATO building (next to my husband's office and car). A German officer had noticed something "unusual" in the exit of this person at the gate and, rather than shrug it off, had proceeded to investigate. The investigation led to the fact that there was an abandoned car on the base and it, in fact, was stolen. The car was searched, and a trunk full of explosives was discovered. The explosives had been set to go off, but the timer had failed!

All this terrorist activity and investigation took place while I was deep in prayer. The spiritual truths were more powerful than any destructive force. My gratitude to God for this protection and my love for all mankind grew during this experience. I never felt any hatred for that young man and his accomplices who attempted such destruction. (They were eventually caught by the authorities.)

As we pray for ourselves and for others, we can all be blessed by the working of God that is forever going on.

DOROTHY BAUER
Southlake, Texas
Christian Science Sentinel October 3, 1988

The ambassador requested that I come to Beirut.

When the media report a tragedy that has happened somewhere across the world, far from us, or even in a town nearby, we may yearn to help those involved, but we may also at times feel helpless. A few years ago Margaret Estes Powell, a Christian Scientist, found herself propelled from being an "ordinary person" into the midst of a world news event. And what she learned of the power of prayer and of forgiveness offers a concrete answer to that question "What can I do?" The following is based on a talk she gave to the North Pomfret Congregational Church in Pomfret, Vermont. The church was presenting a series of sermons on forgiveness, and because of her experience the minister invited her to speak.

It was an ordinary day for ordinary people in Pennsylvania, April 18, 1983. It was Monday morning. My husband, Dick, went off to the office, and our son went to his class. But shortly after he left he came back and said, "Mom, the American Embassy in Beirut has been bombed. I just heard it on the radio. You might want to listen to the news."

So I turned on the television, and I watched with horror as the news explained that the American Embassy had indeed been blown up, and the confusion and reports were still coming in. My cousin, who is like a sister, and her husband had been living in Beirut. Bill was with the Agency for International Development with the State Department, and Mary Lee was teaching at the American University in Beirut.

We all pray in situations like that, and I prayed too. I made some telephone calls to the State Department, and they let me know that I would be informed as new information came through. About noon the call came from the State Department that Bill had been killed and that my cousin, who is a Christian Scientist, was in shock and had been taken to the hospital. She was on the critical list and in surgery. I sank into a kitchen chair and prayed to know that God was in control.

I called a close friend, an experienced Christian Scientist, and asked her for help through prayer. I prayed for strength and wisdom to make the phone calls to Bill and Mary Lee's three children who were scattered in schools in the eastern and midwestern part of our country. My prayers were answered; I was able to make those calls and talk to the headmaster or the dean of students and be sure that someone would be with the children when they called me back. They were not easy calls. But I assured the children that we loved them and that they must come and be with us, and they did come to our home.

During that afternoon many, many phone calls came in from Bill and Mary Lee's friends in the Foreign Service, from their neighbors, and from our friends and neighbors. People, some of whom I had heard of, many of whom I had never met, were asking that familiar, helpless question "What can I do?"

One man who called was in tears, and through his sobs said to me, "Tell me what I can do." And I heard myself say to him, "Yes, there is something you can do." And he said, "Tell me, I will do anything." And I said, "You can practice forgiveness in your own experience. We have got to begin somewhere."

I could not believe that I said that to a perfect stranger, but I did. And it felt right. I decided that I would say that as a response to that question for the rest of the day, and I did.

Later that day the State Department called and told me that the ambassador had requested that I come to Beirut to be with Mary Lee and to bring her home. I was flabbergasted over this because I felt that my role was to be with the children. Nevertheless, I decided to go. I went with the official American delegation. I was the only civilian nonofficial to go, and we flew from Andrews Air Force Base in a military transport C-141, taking just under twenty hours to get to Beirut.

On the flight it was almost impossible to talk or hear through the roar of the engines (we were all issued earplugs); I found this was a wonderful opportunity to be alone with my thoughts, to feel close to God, to actively love what I knew was true of Him and His creation. I needed strength, His strength, for what lay ahead. And I needed to know it was "the sustaining infinite" that I was leaning on. Mary Baker Eddy writes in *Science and Health:* "To those leaning on the sustaining infinite, to-day is big with blessings" (p. vii). My prayers and those of my family, friends, and church were such a support! At no time during the entire experience did I feel fatigued; rather I was fresh and ready to go.

When we landed in Beirut, I could feel the fear in that city. The destruction was apparent, and the confusion was rampant. I was able to go immediately to the hospital and to be with my cousin. The doctors' fear that she would lose an eye had turned into rejoicing that she would not.

Our short stay in that hospital was extraordinary. The kindness, the generosity, the love expressed by the Lebanese I will never forget. Two experiences that happened while I was there stand out, and I would love to share them with you. I had to go to the temporary headquarters of the embassy for some official papers, and the two American Foreign Service people that had been assigned to me escorted me there. We went as far as we could by car, and then we had to walk over rubble and around broken buildings. Suddenly we were confronted with the remains of the American Embassy. I had hoped to avoid seeing it. I had seen pictures of it, and I had no wish to see it.

But there it was, stark, grotesque. My escort pointed out on the left where Bill had been in the cafeteria, giving an interview. They pointed out the place, up on the fourth floor where the green carpet was hanging, where Mary Lee had stood when the plate glass side of the building blew in on her. And they mentioned how the Lebanese driver had carried her four flights down, a man not as tall as I. For a moment I thought I would be overwhelmed by this spectacle, and instinctively I turned around.

I turned my back to it. Just across from it was a group of young Marines, and I walked toward them, not really knowing why, but I guess to thank them for being there. As I got to the first one, I could not speak. So I put my arms around him and I hugged him and I said, "I am so proud of you." And he said to me, "God bless you, ma'am." Then I took the next Marine in my arms, he could have been my son, and I spoke to him and he to me. I embraced every one of those young Marines, and they all took me into their arms so tenderly, and we spoke gently, and it was so natural, so genuine, so beautiful.

As I turned to rejoin my escorts I thought, "Here is Love, right here in the presence of this awful symbol is the living presence of God, divine Love. Strong and alive and beautiful and ready to be expressed. In Mrs. Eddy's words 'And Love is reflected in love.'" [This statement is part of the spiritual interpretation of the Lord's Prayer and refers to Christ Jesus' words "And forgive us our debts, as we forgive our debtors." *Science and Health,* p. 17.]

When we got back to the hospital, there was the usual assortment of guests and visitors. I think there were thirty to fifty people that came every day, from the foreign minister himself and Bill's associates to Mary Lee's university associates, her students, her neighbors, her friends. Those who had heard about it and wanted to express their sorrow came with chocolates, with flowers, with gifts. They came expressing their own loss and grief.

When the visiting hours were over and Mary Lee and I were alone, we prayed together as we did every night, and then we prepared to go to sleep. As I crawled into the little cot that a very kind Lebanese doctor had given me so I could sleep in her room, my thoughts revolved around the discussion and the conversations I had heard, and suddenly one leaped out: the rumor, the insistent rumor that the hospital was the next target.

I became riveted with fear. I felt the imminent destruction of that building. I also realized that I was lying down in front of plate glass doors. So I got up. I could not sleep; I could not think clearly.

I crouched in a corner of that little dark room, and my fear gave way to terror and terror to the icy edges of panic. I reached out and grabbed the first antidote for fear I could think of: "The Lord shall fight for you, and ye shall hold your peace" (Exodus 14:14). It's a favorite of mine and was a lifeline in this storm. I wanted to run. But I knew that I could not leave Mary Lee, that I would not leave her. And so I held on.

Although I thought of going down to the nurses' station and talking to the nurses, I realized with chagrin that for me, an American who was going back in a few days to a safe country and a loving family, to talk to them about my fears would be absurd.

And so I said my favorite psalm, the ninety-first Psalm. I clung to it, and I tried to realize and know the presence of God right there where we were, loving us and protecting us. And I prayed. I prayed for Mary Lee. Again and again I insisted on what *Science and Health* calls "the great fact." "Insist vehemently on the great fact which covers the whole ground, that God, Spirit, is all, and that there is none beside Him" (p. 421).

Gradually my thought changed from fear for myself to love for her and love for all the patients. They were protected by God's love. Then naturally my thought had to reach out to the city and the whole country. I prayed for that beautiful—once beautiful—city. Those brave, courageous people who live on and work on and try. And I prayed for the whole country, so torn apart, so fragmented, so many trying in their own way to seek peace.

I felt more and more sure of God's love, that it can know no bounds. After many hours I saw that this love had to include those I wouldn't have thought of including, the very ones who might be contemplating destruction. It took the whole long night to see that there is no exception to the spirituality of man, but I came to see that even they were actually spiritual. I knew that they were God's loved children. (They are. God loves every one of us, dearly loves.) I felt something go into place. I felt a kind of resolution. I felt peace. And it was dawn. That's why I love that hymn "Still, still with Thee when purple morning breaketh."

I felt a kind of joy. A quiet, quiet, gentle joy, and so I crawled back into the cot for a little rest before the day began. It was an extraordinary experience experienced by an ordinary person.

We came home. Mary Lee is well. She has normal vision in her eye. An answer to much prayer. She's a Foreign Service officer, stationed abroad. I will never forget, and I'm still moved, by the tender, deep, learning experience that I had in Beirut. And I'm grateful for it and grateful for the opportunity to share it with you today.

Christian Science Sentinel January 20, 1986

12

Critical illness healed

No matter how bad the prognosis or the diagnosis, God's power brings healing. The writers in this chapter share their experiences of God's help in painful and extreme situations.

Six medical specialists told me that my body no longer responded to treatment.

Originally written in Spanish

"O Lord my God, I cried unto thee, and thou hast healed me" (Psalms 30:2). From girlhood on I felt a sense of loneliness because my parents had passed on. As the years went by I accepted other things, such as lack, disease, and what I believed was God's abandonment of me. Six medical specialists, after fighting to save my health for a number of years, finally told me that they were sorry but my body no longer responded to any treatment. They said that I was afflicted with a number of organic complications, so that when they tried to cure one, another was aggravated. Among these ailments were varices and phlebitis (from which I had suffered for twenty-three years), two slipped disks, thyroid trouble, excess of uric acid, and chronic pharyngitis. In addition, I was on the verge of losing my sight.

I prayed constantly to God in my own way. But I was sure that those doctors who had studied so much really had the ability to decide about my life, so I accepted their opinions and advice unconditionally.

But when I felt most helpless, the time came to make a decision. I thought that since I was going to die soon, there was no reason to be too obedient to medical prohibitions. First, I decided to read—with the help of a magnifying glass—in order to test my mental retention, which I felt I had lost. What I had at hand was a copy of *Science and Health with Key to the Scriptures* by Mary Baker Eddy, which a friend had given me more than a year earlier. I began to leaf through the book unenthusiastically, and then I came across these words: "To those leaning on the sustaining infinite, to-day is big with blessings" (p. vii). This statement made no real impression on me, as I didn't feel I understood it, but even so I insisted on reading the sentence again and then going a bit further. From the little I was able to grasp, I thought that the author might be mistaken on various points, because it was difficult for me to understand that something as marvelous as God's law of goodness could exist. This aroused my lively curiosity to know more, and I spent several hours absorbed in reading, without paying much attention to the symptoms of illness I still felt. From that time, I stopped all use of medicine. I just forgot about myself. Then I had a night of restful sleep.

The next day it was as if thick, dark curtains had opened to let in the illumination of the light of Truth, which shone in my understanding. That perception of divine Love changed my thinking and, at the same time, my whole life. It brought me a joy I had never before experienced. I felt protected and happy.

As I began to study the Bible and *Science and Health*, an awareness that I am important because I am the well-loved daughter of God has grown daily. Since taking those first footsteps over nine years ago, I have been completely well.

I am very grateful to God, the All-in-all, for a most precious treasure: the desire to know and to obey His divine laws.

GUADALUPE NAVARRO DE GUERRERO
Cuernavaca, Morelos, Mexico
Christian Science Sentinel July 4, 1983

I was back at my teaching position only nine days after the first attack.

Our children were quite young when I suffered a severe heart attack. The support of my husband and the sincere prayer of a practitioner sustained me through the next week when several more attacks occurred. Finally I began to gain some strength through deep prayer and study. The gripping fear was what had to be put down, and this was accomplished as I saw more clearly that in reality God's child is indestructible and safe in the Father's love. "Fear never stopped being and its action. The blood, heart, lungs, brain, etc., have nothing to do with Life, God. Every function of the real man is governed by the divine Mind" (*Science and Health,* p. 151). I studied this passage over and over.

Little by little I gained strength. I was back at my teaching position only nine days after the first attack. And although I had little extra energy by the end of the workday, I managed to fulfill my obligations. Each evening at home I would study about God and his creation, and progressively every symptom accompanying the belief of a heart condition was met by Truth. All during this period a passage from *Science and Health* held deep meaning for me: "When the illusion of sickness or sin tempts you, cling steadfastly to God and His idea. Allow nothing but His likeness to abide in your thought. Let neither fear nor doubt overshadow your clear sense and calm trust, that the recognition of life harmonious—as Life eternally is—can destroy any painful sense of, or belief in, that which

Life is not" (p. 495). Gradually I came to see that an illusion really is nothing and I had nothing to fear!

At the end of two years I realized I was completely healed and that I had energy and endurance that I had never had as a very young woman. And more recently I passed a required physical examination for an insurance policy with the doctor commenting on my very strong heart!

MARY STANDEN TURAK
Germantown, Maryland
Christian Science Sentinel September 8, 1980

I was absolutely convinced—if I were truly listening, I would hear a heavenly message of painless harmony.

An early healing of a painful condition of sciatic rheumatism in my right leg has served through the years as a reference point in my further expectancy of good. I am a university professor of theater, and three days before the start of one fall semester I was in such continuous pain I could neither sleep, eat, nor walk. Full of fear, I knew I had only a few hours to gain my dominion before facing a year of demanding teaching and play production.

I called a Christian Science practitioner, who stood vigorously by me night and day until the condition yielded and I was healed. I shall always be grateful for his unswerving support, even in the early hours of morning when the discomfort sometimes seemed very great. During this time, I laid aside an enslaving cigarette habit, which in the circumstances seemed a significant step toward the freedom from enslaving matter I was seeking. I also resisted the suggestions of others to take a medical pain-killer, since my difficulty seemed so aggressively unremitting.

Most importantly I determined to read *Science and Health* until such time as I had gained my release. I began at the first word and read to the end. When the going got rough I called the practitioner. Always I got temporary relief, so I knew I was on the way. But having read to the last page, I still did not have my healing. So, I thought, "I can still read and pray. Let's go round again!" Once more I started with page one.

When in the opening chapter, titled "Prayer," I reached again the sentence, "The 'divine ear' is not an auditory nerve" (p. 7), I was struck powerfully with the realization that the mortal, human mind could tell God nothing at all about its pains and problems. The only true communication going on was from God to man, His perfect spiritual idea. All I had to do was listen—be still and listen. What I would inevitably hear, if I were truly listening, would be a heavenly message of painless harmony and unbroken health. I was absolutely convinced of this. This calm center of Christliness in the midst of the sense-storm proved to be the turning point. I gained my freedom at last. And on the eve of my classes!

Not only has the condition never returned, but the practical discovery for me of the simple biblical command, "Be still, and know that I am God" (Psalms 46:10), has stood me in good stead many times since.

JACK DE WAYNE CLAY
Dallas, Texas
Christian Science Sentinel March 19, 1977

I became determined to see the epilepsy healed.

During college, some friends gave me a copy of *Science and Health* and I began reading it. At first little of it made sense.

I had been subject to epileptic seizures since childhood, and recently the attacks had become worse. I was eager to be free of this affliction; so one day, while talking with one of the friends who had given me the book, I asked if God could heal disease. Her response was an immediate and convincing "yes!" This encouraged me to continue to read *Science and Health.*

I began to learn that God is all good and that man reflects Him. The clearer these ideas became to me, the more good I saw evidenced in my own life.

I had quit college, but now I was able to go back and finish my education. This opened the way to a fulfilling and happy career in education. The smoking habit was dropped with ease as I found security in a new sense of self-worth. A relationship full of friction and discontent soon developed into harmonious feelings of mutual appreciation and joy. Learning that man is an idea of God who can express and experience only good left no room for old ways of thinking, which had been destructive to the relationship.

These healings came soon after I began studying, and I became determined to see the epilepsy healed in the same way. There were months of prayer and study, with no evidence of healing, but I remained faithful to the truth I was learning and loving so much. With the prayer of a Christian Science practitioner, feelings of inability and reluctance to cope with day-to-day problems were dissolved. The more I learned of God as the source of all true thought and activity, the more I understood that my inheritance from Him included insight, decisiveness, and serenity enabling me to successfully meet every challenge.

Getting rid of the fear seemed impossible. But I gradually learned to know myself as spiritual and in reality perfect, and to accept God as the source of this perfection. "Be still, and know that I am God" (Psalms 46:10) was a thought constantly with me. I reasoned that if God is all-encompassing Love and the only cause, then fear of a power or cause apart from God has no basis. Gradually, fear was seen as an aggressive mental suggestion that God isn't All and therefore not always in control of His creation. I knew the healing would become evident as I refused to indulge in fearful thinking and accepted instead the truth of God and my relationship to Him.

A turning point came one afternoon when a convulsion began. Aloud I vehemently declared over and over that God is the only power and I had nothing to fear. Just at the point of losing consciousness, the convulsion abruptly halted. The symptoms ceased. It was like seeing the first ray of light at dawn.

There was a gradual and complete release from fear as I persisted in daily loving and living the truth. I found my freedom, and the healing has been permanent. In the story of Christ Jesus' healing of the epileptic boy (see Matthew 17:14–21), the disciples asked the Master why they had not been able to cure the child. Part of Jesus' reply was, "This kind goeth not out but by prayer and fasting." For me this has meant refusing to believe in a power apart from God and acknowledging that man exists now as God's perfect child.

I joyfully offer this testimony as proof of the constant operation of God's law of good, which truly governs the universe.

JUDY E. WELCH
Garland, Texas
Christian Science Sentinel April 23, 1979

I had been told it could take a year or more for a complete recovery.

About fifteen years ago I was in the hospital with what the doctors had diagnosed as infectious hepatitis. I had been told to expect a long and slow convalescence; they said it could take a year or more for a complete recovery. I had been placed in a special room in the hospital and had been told I would have to remain there for a few weeks.

This was very hard to bear, as it meant a separation from my family. I had a nine-month-old daughter and a three-year-old son at home. I called some close friends and asked if they would help with the children; they agreed.

After being in the hospital for about a week, spending many pain-filled hours and sleepless nights, I began to think about previous conversations I had with a good friend, who practices Christian Science. We'd had many pleasant talks about God, and I had been very interested in how physical healings occurred through this Science. My friend had answered my questions, and I had felt the calm confidence and trust she had.

Although I was still in the hospital, I was receiving no medication. It came to me that I could be healed spiritually. I didn't know how to go about it, however, so I called my friend and asked her if she thought I could be healed of this condition through prayer. She lovingly assured me that I could and advised me to get in touch with a Christian Science practitioner and to have the Bible and a copy of *Science and Health* brought to me.

I arranged to have these two books brought to me. I also looked in the telephone book for a nearby practitioner. A kind woman agreed to help me, and I began to study the Bible and *Science and Health.* For three days and nights I drank in the beautiful truths in these books. The psalms were very comforting and inspiring, especially the twenty-third Psalm. So were certain passages in *Science and Health,* such as the description of man given in the chapter "Recapitulation." This description includes the following passage: "Man is idea, the image, of Love; he is not physique. He is the compound idea of God, including all right ideas; the generic term for all that reflects God's image and likeness; the conscious identity of being as found in Science, in which man is the reflection of God, or Mind, and therefore is eternal; that which has no separate mind from God; that which has not a single quality underived from Deity; that which possesses no life, intelligence, nor creative power of his own, but reflects spiritually all that belongs to his Maker" (p. 475).

I began to feel stronger and more at peace, and I became confident that I would be healed. On the fourth day I checked myself out of the hospital. Through my new spiritual understanding I felt confident of God's allness, His all-power, and His tender care.

I went home to my family and continued to study the Bible and *Science and Health* joyfully and gratefully. One citation in *Science and Health* was very helpful to me as I took care of my daily responsibilities: "Whatever it is your duty to do, you can do without harm to yourself" (p. 385). I was completely healed. The morning after I got home I put the baby in her backpack and hiked to the top of a hill with energy and strength. That was over fifteen years ago, and I have never had a recurrence of the trouble.

Since then I have had healings of severe burns, flu, a sprained ankle, and interpersonal difficulties.

CAROLINE COX-SIMON
Blauvelt, New York
The Christian Science Journal April 1990

When I woke the next morning, all symptoms of pneumonia were gone.

Many years ago I suffered recurring bouts of pneumonia, as well as of many allergies, which caused intense abdominal pain. At the time, our two children were just toddlers.

Medical tests resulted in a drastic restriction of food intake; I was able to eat only baby food. The constantly recurring pneumonia kept me bedridden a good deal of the time. Antibiotics only made the body swell and produced hives. Depression stalked me. When treatment for neither the allergies nor the pneumonia was effective, I was told nothing more could be done.

A friend in our church visited me one day, saying she felt compelled to bring over a little book she had found very helpful. She said, "It's about God's love for all of us, how it never fails if we care enough to know Him better, and it can be the key to better health and happiness." It was *Science and Health with Key to the Scriptures* by Mary Baker Eddy.

I read eagerly and often for the next three months, when the children were napping, when I had difficulty sleeping, and early in the morning before the family was awake. Whenever the depression, fear, or pain threatened, reading this beloved book was my refuge. It gave me much hope, deep strength, and a feeling of the reality and utility of God's love for us.

There were parts of the book I didn't yet understand, but I understood enough that at the end of these first few months I was inspired to discard all the medications my doctors had given me and just rely on God's care. This was quite a big step for me, and my husband and I prayed together for guidance. This was also a very sobering decision, since the last time I had gone to the hospital with pneumonia, the doctors had advised that one more attack would probably claim my life; there were so many scars on the lungs.

Before very many days had passed, I woke one night with all the same symptoms of pneumonia. I did not feel well enough to get up and read the book. Then the thought came just to lie still and see what phrases and sentences would come to my thought. I remembered thankfully that I was God's perfect, spiritual child, subject only to His law of genuine good for man. I felt comforted. Then I remembered that there is not a single spot in all creation where God is not present and all-powerful. And with that I realized that the Mind that is God simply could not know about bad lungs. He is divine Love and knows only man's perfection.

Finally, I was able to call a Christian Science practitioner to support this spiritual understanding. When I woke the next morning, all symptoms of pneumonia were gone! The allergies were healed at once when in my study I realized God could not be our Father-Mother Love and at the same time make things in His universe that would harm His children.

The simplicity of Christ, Truth, was so inspiring. In Psalms we read, "He shall cover thee with his feathers, and under his wings shalt thou trust: his truth shall be thy shield and buckler" (91:4). Also, "O thou that hearest prayer, unto thee shall all flesh come" (65:2).

Norma L. Harbin
Laguna Hills, California
Christian Science Sentinel August 31, 1992

I had been a cancer patient for three years.

I had a deep longing to bring more good into my life. I also wanted to be free from a lifestyle that included social drinking and shallow relationships. A woman, a Christian Scientist, whom I worked with seemed different from others and deep down I realized that she knew something I wanted and needed to know. I had made a decision to try to be a better person. I was afraid that I wouldn't be able to break away from my former behavior and relationships and would be drawn back into the way of life that had been so unsatisfying; however, this desire for a better way of life proved to be a source of strength and led to healing.

Eventually I asked my friend about Christian Science and she gave me a copy of *Science and Health.* At a church service I attended I heard read from this book the author's account of what followed her discovery of the Science of Christian healing: "For three years after my discovery, I sought the solution of this problem of Mind-healing, searched the Scriptures and read little else, kept aloof from society, and devoted time and energies to discovering a positive rule. The search was sweet, calm, and buoyant with hope, not selfish nor depressing" (p. 109).

I knew I had found what I was looking for. I read *Science and Health* at every opportunity, day and night, and soaked up its spiritual truths like a blotter.

At that time I had been a cancer patient for three years, having been diagnosed as having cancer of the cervix in the third stage. I had been treated with daily doses of cobalt radiation for a month, followed by a temporary radium implant treatment that required hospitalization. When I began studying *Science and Health,* I was on a regime of frequent doctor's office visits for cryotherapy.

After a few months I began to understand that my life did not depend on physicality. I was learning that my identity was spiritual, not subject to the laws of matter. I read in *Science and Health,* "Only through radical reliance on Truth can scientific healing power be realized" (p. 167). So I decided to rely radically on Truth for my healing of cancer. I discontinued medical treatment and continued my study of *Science and Health,* with no fear of the consequences.

That was almost seventeen years ago. I have had no recurrence of the symptoms of cervical cancer. I had been told that my hormone-producing capability had been greatly diminished by the radiation, and that I would age rapidly if I discontinued taking the medication prescribed for me. This has not occurred, even though I stopped taking the medication at the same time I quit going to the doctor.

About six years ago I became self-employed and wanted to buy some insurance. Because of my previous medical record, the insurance company required me to undergo a physical examination. After the exam, the doctor said he could find nothing wrong with me and remarked that all the company's customers should be in as good shape as I was.

JUDITH JACKSON
Washington, District of Columbia
The Christian Science Journal July 1993

The surgeon told me I might never walk again.

Throughout my career as an Army officer, I had lower back strain. I suffered several days each month, on the average, and I would often spend a weekend in bed to rest my back. During our frequent household moves, I always had to be careful not to lift anything heavy or I would be out of action for a while. On one occasion, over ten years ago, I was hospitalized when I was temporarily paralyzed from the waist down because of a pinched nerve in my back.

I was happy when I reached the age of forty because the Army wouldn't require me to take physical fitness tests anymore. Then the regulations changed, and those over forty had to be tested too. I restarted my physical conditioning program. While exercising one day, I ran into a wall and injured my back; for the next three months, it got progressively worse.

Only a few months before this incident I had taken an interest in Christian Science. But I waited awhile before calling a Christian Science practitioner for prayerful help about this injury, thinking my back would heal "by itself." For a few days I thought I had been healed. But several days later the condition worsened sharply. I found myself in great pain, totally unable to walk or even to stand upright. I decided I would seek medical treatment.

I dismissed the practitioner and dragged myself out to the car, and my wife drove me to the local military hospital. There I met with an orthopedic surgeon who examined my back and had X-rays taken. Afterward he informed me that I had a degenerating spine which required surgery but that I was lucky because he was the most experienced back surgeon in his branch of the service. Nevertheless, he gave poor odds that I would be totally pleased with the surgery, and told me there was a chance I might even be worse following the operation. Most alarmingly, he stated that, without surgery, my spine would continue to degenerate and I might never walk again.

Reluctantly, I agreed to the surgery, desperate for relief from the pain and fearing the consequences if I refused. Then, while a staff person was filling out my hospital admission forms, my wife entered the emergency room to see how I was doing. She had been praying during my examination. After we'd talked a bit, my wife encouraged me to try scientific Christian healing again. I said I would. The surgeon reluctantly agreed to sign a release form for two weeks of total bed rest and gave me a prescription for pills to relieve the pain. He said that he expected to see me back in two weeks as he had never heard of a degenerating spine improving without surgery.

The pain, he said, would surely force my return. The prescription was never filled, and I never returned to the hospital.

With a wheelchair and crutches, I returned home. Then I called the Christian Science practitioner again and said, "I like what you tell me so much more than what the surgeon told me." The surgeon's prognosis about my physical condition had been totally negative, while the practitioner's statements concerning the present perfection of my being as God's loved child had given me hope. For the next few weeks, the practitioner prayed for me and spoke with me daily. She provided specific passages I could read from the Bible, and from *Science and Health.*

Although those weeks included physical pain, they also brought much spiritual joy as my forced confinement afforded me the opportunity to study seriously for the first time.

Of all that I read and studied during this period, I found that I could most easily understand Christ Jesus' parable of the tares and wheat. I considered spiritual truth to be the "good seed" and error, or misperceptions about God and man, to be the "tares" (see Matthew 13:24–30). From the parable of the sower, I equated spiritual-mindedness with the fertile soil and mortal mind, or the belief in a power apart from God, with the wayside, the stony places, and the thorns, where the seed of truth would never thrive (see Matthew 13:3–8, 18–23).

In desiring to witness the separation of the "tares" of mortal mind from the "wheat" of spiritual consciousness, I especially studied the following words, "Stand porter at the door of thought. Admitting only such conclusions as you wish realized in bodily results, you will control yourself harmoniously. When the condition is present which you say induces disease whether it be air, exercise, heredity, contagion, or accident, then perform your office as porter and shut out these unhealthy thoughts and fears. Exclude from mortal mind the offending errors; then the body cannot suffer from them" (*Science and Health,* p. 392). Remarkably, the third sentence of this quotation contains five erroneous conditions that referred directly to my situation at the time: disease, exercise, heredity, accident, and fear.

What "offending errors" had I allowed to enter the door of thought? What "tares" had mortal mind planted in my mental garden?

With love and patience, the practitioner helped me realize the following through study of the Bible and *Science and Health:*

—The belief in the deterioration of life because of the passage of time was a "tare." *Science and Health* says: "Life and its faculties are not measured by calendars" (p. 246).

—My attitude toward the Army's mandatory fitness test was another "tare." I had viewed the requirement as a "have to" test to prove my physical fitness to others rather than a "get to" opportunity to joyfully verify my fitness, my perfection as God's child, as already known to Him.

—The belief that I had inherited a bad back from my father was another "tare." The truth is that, as a child of God, I have only the inheritance of good.

—The belief that I could injure myself by means of an accident was yet another "tare." The truth is again found in *Science and Health:* "Accidents are unknown to God, or immortal Mind, and we must leave the mortal basis of belief and unite with the one Mind, in order to change the notion of chance to the proper sense of God's unerring direction and thus bring out harmony.

"Under divine Providence there can be no accidents, since there is no room for imperfection in perfection" (p. 424).

—Finally, fear of the so-called condition, fixed in thought by the X-rays' "photographic proof" and the surgeon's alarming prognosis, was the most persistent "tare" to be weeded out. Through Science I began to learn that I did not consist of well matter and sick matter, as the medical prognosis and X-rays might indicate. Instead, I was learning that in my real being I was a perfect child of God, totally spiritual, totally good.

My progress was slow, and once, when I stated that I lacked the faith to continue the practitioner said for me not to worry; she had enough faith for both of us. Indeed, she did!

In the end, Truth was the victor. After two weeks I could stand up and walk slowly; I returned to work part time. After four weeks I could walk normally although there was some lingering pain. And after six weeks there was no more pain at all. To this date, years later, I have never had another backache of any sort, and I have made two more household moves in which I lifted a lot of heavy boxes and furniture.

David F. Maune
Alexandria, Virginia
The Christian Science Journal August 1984

I could no longer accept the verdict of a lifetime of mental illness.

Some years ago I was subject to attacks of severe depression that included extreme mental highs and lows. During the high periods there was frenetic and irrational behavior followed by deep and incapacitating depressions. The depressions included self-destructive impulses. At that time I had a small child and was active in community organizations. When the attacks occurred, I was unable to function normally in any capacity for months.

The trouble was diagnosed as manic depression. To stabilize the condition, I took medication daily. I was told to avoid any undue stress or demanding situations. My husband and I had wanted to have a second child. The doctor stated that because of the nature of the illness and the strong side effects of the medication, a pregnancy would be too difficult and inadvisable.

A severe episode occurred followed by a lengthy period of hospitalization. One night after I was home again, during a most difficult crisis with loss of rational control, I turned in great need to these verses in Romans: "I am persuaded, that neither death, nor life, nor angels, nor principalities, nor powers, nor things present, nor things to come, nor height, nor depth, nor any other creature, shall be able to separate us from the love of God, which is in Christ Jesus our Lord" (8:38, 39). These wonderful, comforting truths of God's all-encompassing love were like a ray of light in the darkness. I began to feel calmed and comforted by the presence and power of divine Love.

I decided to turn to Christian Science. I could no longer remain in a mental prison or accept the verdict of a lifetime of mental illness. With the assurance of God's presence and power, I stopped all medication. And with each visit to a Christian Science practitioner, I felt the powerful spiritual truths of Science bringing peace and stability back to my life. The attacks became less frequent. If one started, it was stopped immediately through consistent prayer.

Daily I dedicated myself to the study of the laws of God. As I prayed, I felt sustained by the spiritual truths in the Bible and in *Science and Health.* Also, *The Christian Science Journal* and the *Christian Science Sentinel* were of immeasurable spiritual support.

This powerful verse from the Bible stayed with me: "God hath not given us the spirit of fear; but of power, and of love, and of a sound mind" (II Timothy 1:7). And in *Science and Health* I found this passage: "The great truth in the Science of being, that the real man was, is, and ever shall be perfect, is incontrovertible; for if man is the image, reflection, of God, he is neither inverted nor subverted, but upright and Godlike" (p. 200).

In light of such powerful healing truths, I was letting go of the terrorizing fear and yielding to the all-power and supreme control of divine Mind. I felt sustained and supported by divine law. I was realizing that in my true, spiritual nature I was God's perfect, beloved image and had never been separated from good. This recognition brought increasing peace.

Where periods of long incapacity, fear, and depression had been, the days were filled with capability, spiritual enlightenment, and joy. Each day was dedicated to understanding my real spiritual identity, the reflection of the one perfect Mind. I learned to trust and live this powerful truth from *Science and Health:* "All that really exists is the divine Mind and its idea, and in this Mind the entire being is found harmonious and eternal" (p. 151).

An important step in the healing was prayerfully challenging the belief that man has a mortal history of hereditary disease. Man is immortal, perfect, created by God; Spirit is the sole origin and source of all real being. I knew that God's image, the real image, could never be touched by the illusion of an inverted image called disease. God is the only Life of man.

I now know with great trust that God is always with us, even during what appears as the most difficult of human trials. I have gained complete freedom from the illness. With wonderful mental peace and stability, I am fully active with a lovely family, which includes our second child. A friend recently asked what I considered to be a lifelong achievement. I responded "Thank God, to have peace of mind."

MARTHA H. NIGGEMAN
Kentfield, California
Christian Science Sentinel January 22, 1990

I was declared totally disabled.

About 1959, I was having increasing difficulty breathing. I asked a medical doctor for a complete physical examination. After the examination and two chest X-rays, I heard this verdict: "You do not have lung cancer but you do have emphysema. There is no cure for it, and the history of the disease is that it will get steadily worse." It was suggested that I start taking three different kinds of drugs each day, and I carried a fourth for emergencies. This diagnosis was later confirmed by the medical staff of Social Security at the time of my retirement, for I was declared totally disabled by them.

Although I had lived in Wisconsin all my life, I could no longer bear to breathe the cold winter air. The last two winters I could not drive my own car when the weather was cold. My wife drove me to the office and picked me up at night. I retired in January of 1967, and we moved to Arizona, but returned to Wisconsin during the summer.

In June of 1968, I became very discouraged, for I was having more difficulty breathing, could do nothing physical, and was taking more and more of the emergency drugs. I was so breathless that my wife had to bathe me, and shaving with an electric razor was a great effort. Finally, both my daughter and wife suggested that as medical science could do nothing for me I should try Christian Science.

A practitioner was contacted, and on June 30 I discontinued all medication, and Christian Science treatment began. Although I was told by the practitioner to keep expecting instantaneous healing, it was not to be. I was given sections of *Science and Health* to read and reread, and many of Mary Baker Eddy's other writings, along with the explanation that because God made man in His image and likeness, I could not have or be subject to this illusion of emphysema. I was given to understand that as a son of God I was and had always been His perfect idea.

For two days there was no apparent change, but on the third day I sensed a decrease of fear and a feeling that I was making progress. During these first days of prayer and study, when moments of extreme breathing distress occurred, I would obtain rapid relief by thoughtfully repeating "the scientific statement of being" and its correlative Scripture from I John: "Behold, what manner of love the Father hath bestowed upon us, that we should be called the sons of God: therefore the world knoweth us not, because it knew him not. Beloved, now are we the sons of God, and it doth not yet appear what we shall be: but we know that, when he shall appear, we shall be like him; for we shall see him as he is. And every man that hath this hope in him purifieth himself, even as he is pure" (3:1–3).

The opening lines of the statement in *Science and Health* are "There is no life, truth, intelligence, nor substance in matter. All is infinite Mind and its infinite manifestation, for God is All-in-all" (p. 468). These I had learned while attending church with my wife.

By the end of ten days I was sleeping through the night and was more comfortable than I had been for quite some time. By the end of thirty days I was walking slowly up and down the highway, occasionally stopping for breath, and in two months was walking a full mile each day at a fair pace. Unconsciously I was gauging my progress by the distance I could walk.

By the end of September I was walking up and down the fire lanes and through the woods of our tree farm, something I had not been able to do for some time.

When we returned to our home in Green Valley, Arizona, that October, our neighbors who had known of my condition would hardly believe I was the same person. The following spring after returning to the tree farm in Wisconsin I found that some large trees which had blown down required cutting up and removing. For the first time in almost four years I got out my 27-pound chain saw and went to work. And although I am now sixty-eight years old, my physical activity has increased each year.

LEIGHTON HOUGH
Green Valley, Arizona
Christian Science Sentinel July 1, 1972

I was seeing much better.

Some time ago I discovered I could not see clearly at night nor recognize familiar faces across the street or the room; neither could I see movie screens and TV pictures clearly. I was also having difficulty seeing well enough to play golf and bowl. An appointment with an optometrist revealed the need for glasses. Further checks over the years resulted in stronger prescriptions.

About two years ago I began consciously rejoicing that my vision was spiritual. Daily I denied the suggestion that my sight was affected or controlled by material circumstances. A renewed interest in rereading *Science and Health* and other writings of Mary Baker Eddy led to great inspiration for me. I understood many "things of Spirit" with greater clarity.

Some time after this I realized that I was seeing much better. I removed my glasses one evening while driving after dark, and discovered that I saw much better without them. One by one, I found that all of the activities that had once required glasses I could now do without them, and with much more comfort to my eyes. Bright days had always bothered me and made me run for dark glasses; now I was able to see comfortably, with no need for them.

The final proof of this healing came last June, when my driver's license was up for renewal. I passed the vision test satisfactorily without the aid of glasses, something I had not been able to do for twenty-five years!

My rejoicing, however, is not primarily for the renewed eyesight, but for the renewed vision of Life as completely spiritual, never dependent on matter for any of its manifestation.

DE DAVIS
Laguna Hills, California
The Christian Science Journal April 1995

My healing came about as I challenged more and more misconceptions about what health truly is.

When I was a young woman I developed a difficulty with my back. It was acutely painful. I had trouble with the most ordinary activities—standing, sitting, and especially walking. It was eventually diagnosed as ankyloseyspondylitis. Heavy doses of anti-inflammatory medication were prescribed, and I was told to learn to live with the condition.

Well, I tried numerous special diets, chiropractors, exercises I did faithfully for years, physiotherapy, positive visualization, psychotherapy, manipulative medicine, and homeopathy. I read every book I could find on arthritis and on the psychogenesis of disease. Nothing helped much, or for long. I was unable to work, my marriage broke up, and I lost my home.

My second husband is a student of Christian Science. When I first heard of Christian Science I was not the slightest bit interested. We both went to our separate churches on Sunday. By then I was attending a mainstream Christian church that had healing services, and I felt very loved and happy there. My physical troubles had not diminished, however, and I lived a most restricted life.

The crunch came for me when I was four months pregnant and experiencing even more difficulties with my back. My husband and I had prayed about the decision to have a child and felt deeply that it was right for us. I knew God is good, and I came to feel that if I wasn't experiencing that good, perhaps I had to change my thinking about how Biblical promises come to fruition in our lives. I decided to turn to Christian Science.

When I got home from the hospital with our new baby, a wonderful happy girl, I did not know how I would manage. I worked with a Christian Science practitioner during that period and am most grateful for her prayerful help. Day by day I prayed to know that I was always being given the strength I needed and that in a spiritual sense my real "backbone," you might say, was Principle, divine and immortal.

The turning point came one evening when I realized that if prayer could change and overcome the physical evidence, then the evidence was not the indisputable reality it seemed to be; and I could and should dispute it. I learned to identify myself wholly as God's idea, spiritual and not physical.

My healing came about as I challenged more and more misconceptions about what health truly is and what I truly am as God's likeness. I denied the physical evidence and affirmed the fact that I could not be separated from God's love. I held to this verse from Romans: "Neither . . . height, nor depth, nor any other creature, shall be able to separate us from the love of God."

Science and Health by Mary Baker Eddy states, "To those leaning on the sustaining infinite, to-day is big with blessings" (p. vii). I learned to really lean on the bedrock of Truth, to put all my weight on God's ever-presence instead of focus on my own discomfort. As I did so, and only as I did so, reality emerged. The healing was complete about a year after the birth of our daughter.

After nine years during which the most I could walk was a block, I can hike for miles now.

God's promises are real. It took Christian Science to show me how to unlock them from the Bible. I did not want to study Science at first and often feared it would never work for me, but I am thankful for all the support my husband gave me and for the healings I saw him experience, which gave me the impetus to keep on studying. He was always confident I would be healed.

I have been blessed immeasurably as, step by step, I continue to venture further into a trust in and understanding of God as the harmonious and ever-present law of good in our lives.

ZOË LANDALE

I am the husband Zoë mentions in her testimony. On our first date I took Zoë to the museum in her wheelchair. The freedom she gained came through Christianly scientific prayer and a firm reliance on Truth.

GARNET BRUCE COBURN
Delta, British Columbia, Canada
Christian Science Sentinel November 13, 1989

13

Healing the effects of accidents

Many people have experienced firsthand how God's law leaves nothing to chance. God gives "His angels charge over thee, to keep thee in all thy ways" (Psalms 91:11).

My husband found our son at the bottom of the swimming pool.

Five days after our second child was born, my husband found our two-and-a-half-year-old son at the bottom of our swimming pool. My husband dived in and retrieved him. I called for an emergency service, but by the time they arrived, our son was breathing again. However, the child was unconscious and he was taken to a hospital and put in intensive care.

The next fifteen hours were ones of constant challenge and of spiritual growth. The Christian Science practitioner who had prayed with us during the birth of our baby was called. Her first words, "Divine Love fills all space," were exactly what I needed to hear. They reminded me of the truth that God's children (including our son) could never be separated from divine Love. Nothing can interfere with Love's ever-present, all-powerful care of its child.

When I was at the hospital with our unconscious son, I spoke to him of how his Father-Mother God, divine Love, loves and cares for him. I remembered that normally at that time in the evening his daddy and I would have been tucking him into his own bed. We would have sung with him several of his favorite hymns as well as shared together a prayer for little children in *Miscellaneous Writings* by Mary Baker Eddy (p. 400). In a deliberate effort to maintain our normal bedtime routine, I sang and spoke to him. When I finished, I said goodnight just as I would have if he had been at home and assured him I would see him in the morning.

I returned home to feed the new baby. My husband stayed with our son during the night and continued singing hymns to him. My husband loves the hymns and often plays them on our piano.

At home I continued to pray. Before the baby was born, the practitioner had encouraged me to read and sing the hymns. Now inspiring thoughts came from these. How grateful I was for the promise in one of the hymns with words by Mrs. Eddy: "O Life divine, that owns each waiting hour." I stopped waiting for a telephone call to tell me that the child had regained consciousness. Instead I looked for evidence of continuous, uninterrupted life within my understanding of God as eternal Life. A lesson I learned that night was that in truth one's joy is God-given and so is constant and never in danger.

Twice my husband phoned during the night to report that the child had a high fever. These words from the hymn helped me, "O gentle presence, peace and joy and power." My fear was replaced with the certainty of God's gentle, powerful presence, and my husband soon reported the child's fever healed.

At first our son was not expected to live. He was kept under observation, and the prognosis was that should he regain consciousness there would be brain damage. The practitioner referred us to some statements in *Science and Health with Key to the Scriptures* by Mary Baker Eddy including one on page 215 that says, "Whatever is governed by God, is never for an instant deprived of the light and might of intelligence and Life." We sought to understand deeply the meaning of these words for the child, for ourselves, and for everyone. We prayed to realize that the child's intelligence is a perfect gift derived from God, "with whom is no variableness, neither shadow of turning" (James 1:17).

Mere words cannot express our gratitude for the dedicated practitioner who prayed all night and answered our anxious calls with words of healing assurance. She told us later that as she prayed in the early morning hours, she remembered the child's favorite hymn, which begins, "Be Thou, O God, exalted high." She realized that our son had already acknowledged, in his childlike way, that God is exalted, and thus she understood that he was safe. Indeed he was! In the morning he woke at his normal time, completely well.

A neurologist present when he woke commented that doctors know little to do in a case such as our son's and asked us thoughtfully if we knew that someone "up there" had cared for our son. Yes, we did!

Another doctor said that the child's recovery was a miracle, that the only way to explain it was that God had healed him. This doctor had lovingly brought his wife to comfort us soon after the child was taken to the hospital. Later she told us she would never forget the spiritual atmosphere she felt when we greeted her. It had comforted her.

Our son is now attending high school. His program includes all available honor classes. We consider this further proof of the completeness of his healing. We thank God for His all-encompassing love of all His dear children.

Nancy Winburn Tinsman
San Antonio, Texas
Christian Science Sentinel October 24, 1988

My fellow workers took me to a hospital at once.

Originally written in Portuguese

I had been in a condition of invalidism for more than four years due to a disease of the spinal column called tuberculosis of the bones. I suffered much pain from this disease when I attempted to stand. This forced me to remain in bed almost all the time. After exhausting all medical means, including going to another city where those means were considered more efficient, I still found nothing to ease the suffering. I tried varied doctrines, including hypnotism, without obtaining improvement.

One day when I was in this condition of despair, a friend came to my home accompanied by a Christian Science couple who told me about God's healing power. They left some things with me to read, which I studied. In a short while, with the aid of prayer from a Christian Scientist, I was in condition to return to work again and have been at it during the eighteen years since. New horizons opened for me, and the consciousness of life in God strengthened me more and more. Since then I have had many proofs of the unreality of the testimony of the physical senses, thanks to the wonderful understanding that Mary Baker Eddy gives us of God and spiritual man in *Science and Health.*

On one occasion, when I was handling a jar of nitric acid, the liquid accidentally splashed in my eyes. I was again able to make use of this scientific system of Christ-healing.

At first I was overcome by discouraging thoughts, including the fear that I was blind. However, this thought came to me: "God is present, and in the kingdom of God accidents do not occur." This truth calmed me, and I felt no more fear whatsoever.

To comply with the work laws, my fellow workers took me to a hospital at once. Upon concluding their examination the doctors held out no hope at all for my sight, stating that both eyeballs were burned. Thanks to divine Love, I did not let myself be impressed by such affirmations of mortal mind. I was upheld and inspired by the right thought of the true man. Powerful statements from *Science and Health* of man's spiritual being came constantly to my mind, as did the meaning of sight as an indestructible faculty created by God, which nothing could change. I asked a friend to help me through prayer.

At the hospital, although I was experiencing severe pain, I refused analgesics of any kind, because I knew that by accepting the pain as real I would have to accept as real everything else that the testimony of the senses was presenting. The affirmation of the absolute truths about God and man overcame the intense pain after several hours of fervent prayer, and the victory was definite.

When I left the hospital and went to present myself at the firm where I worked, there were still black spots on my face, and the director, who had accompanied me, said, "You are very lucky not to have remained blind, but those spots on your face won't disappear," to which I responded that they certainly would disappear.

When I had recovered, my family told me that the doctors had predicted that I would hardly be able to see again, and that if I did see the sight would be very weak, and, in addition, I would have to undergo plastic surgery in order to correct the effects of the accident. Thanks to trust in God, all the medical prognostications were repudiated, and my vision is impaired in no way and I bear no sign of that experience.

DELMAR MARQUES
Porto Alegre, R. G. Sul, Brazil
The Christian Science Journal May 1971

I was told I should go home to die peacefully.

In 1968 I was a cattle and grain rancher in Idaho. One day that fall I was using a very concentrated insecticide (a normal practice on ranches in the western United States at that time of year), when I spilled the entire gallon can of the mixture on my clothes. I was very busy and did not change for several hours. A few weeks later, I began bleeding internally.

I was pressured by close relatives to have medical treatment. I soon came to believe that this situation was different from others I had faced and healed in the past through Christian Science alone, and that the answer was to be found in material medicine. I agreed to have medical treatment and, before long, I was receiving daily blood transfusions.

After three months of treatment at two prominent medical facilities, I was told that I had contracted a type of leukemia and should go home to die peacefully.

At this point I was actually relieved to be dismissed by the medical faculty. I stopped all medical treatment, went home, and immediately called a Christian Science practitioner. Deep down I knew that material medicine could not really cure me; only God could. But I needed to trust God fully and better understand His true nature and my own, as His reflection.

This statement in *Science and Health,* recommended by the practitioner, provided a basis for my prayer and study: "The starting-point of divine Science is that God, Spirit, is All-in-all, and that there is no other might nor Mind,—that God is Love, and therefore He is divine Principle" (p. 275).

During the weeks that followed, whenever I was tempted to become discouraged, I turned to these verses in Proverbs: "Trust in the Lord with all thine heart; and lean not unto thine own understanding. In all thy ways acknowledge him, and he shall direct thy paths" (3:5, 6).

I realized that because I had believed the problem was materially caused, I had been tricked into accepting the notion that the problem itself was physical and could be materially resolved. Now I made a determined effort to stay with the right "starting-point," by recognizing, accepting, and understanding that all cause and effect belong to God. Not only could I avail myself of this correct interpretation of cause and effect; I could demonstrate my true nature as the spiritual offspring, or effect, of God.

The healing was complete in about six months. Soon after it, I was very active again in my agricultural work, and three years later I joined the Peace Corps as a volunteer. At that time I was required to undergo a medical examination, during which I had to tell the doctor about the leukemia. This led to a more thorough examination, and the ultimate finding which confirmed that I was perfectly healthy.

GEORGE JAMES HELLYER
Atascadero, California
Christian Science Sentinel October 6, 1986

It was not venom I must deal with but a mental concept.

Recently I went on tour with a band through Central America. During our off time we often had the chance to do other activities, which allowed us to take advantage of the area.

One day early in the tour, some of us were snorkeling off the Atlantic coast of Panama, when I was stung by a Portuguese man-of-war. A split second later one of my friends was stung by the same one. Some people in the group who had lived in the area for some time began to warn us about the danger of these stings, and started describing various symptoms that might appear.

My friend and I both made our way slowly back to shore. The excruciating pain made it hard for me to think, yet I held to the very simple, profound idea that God alone is power. The pain was spreading, and I knew I must use what I had learned to prove that the law of God includes perfect health.

Once on shore, I walked off alone, and prayed first to destroy my own fear, and then my concern about the fears of those around me. Right at the moment, when it seemed that some venom could harm me, an idea from *Science and Health* brought me comfort—that regardless of the disease, if you silence the fear, and understand the spiritual reason why you have freedom from any hurt, the illness is destroyed. This showed me that it was not venom I must deal with but a mental concept. It was a belief that there could be any power other than God.

I continued to pray. The thoughts started to come naturally. I thought about how the only true nature could be God's nature, which includes only harmony. Therefore there could be no possibility of encountering a power conflicting with God. Just as good fruit yields only good seed, the power of God, omnipotent good, must mean only good for man. I knew too that man cannot be susceptible to any attack, since God, whom man reflects, is incapable of being a victim.

An incident from the Bible had particular relevance and helped me to get rid of the fear. The ultra-dedicated preacher of Christianity, Paul, was bitten by a poisonous snake; he shook it off into a fire and didn't give it another thought. Paul just knew his freedom from harm (see Acts 28:1–6). He wasn't about to be distracted by some snake from his mission of preaching what Jesus taught. Taking this to heart, I knew my mission was to learn from Paul's actions and do my best to be an example of God's perfect man. In addition to this account, the twenty-third and ninety-first Psalms gave me a wonderful sense of peace and protection.

Lines from a poem by Mary Baker Eddy (*Miscellaneous Writings*, pp. 396–397) gave me great comfort also:

> And o'er earth's troubled, angry sea
>   I see Christ walk,
> And come to me, and tenderly,
>   Divinely talk.

It was this "tender talk" which came to me and showed me that the sea cannot truly include any anger.

My fearful thoughts evaporated in the light of this prayer. The pain lessened, and within minutes was virtually gone. I then returned to the rest of the group. The friend who had also been stung was on a stretcher, having intravenous aid from paramedics who were attending him. They had called a helicopter to come and fly him to a hospital. I then realized I had to understand all men as immune from evil, not just myself.

I walked off again, quietly declaring the truth about man and his relationship to God. I knew that regardless of religion, race, or any other human classification, God envelops each of His children in love. In regard to both of us, I declared that right where a poisonous substance had appeared to do harm, there was only God, Spirit, whose specific love for each individual included all good and nothing harmful. The understanding of this was and is an antidote to any harm.

I was relieved when I returned fifteen minutes later to find that he was recovering. The helicopter was later called off in midflight, and my friend was driven to a hospital to rest for the night.

For me, this incident set the tone for the rest of the tour. It gave me a heightened sense of how God's healing power can be proved any day! It had taken trust and a little courage to rely only on an understanding of God for my health during the trip, and not on immunization that was so highly recommended. The reward for having made this stand for divine Truth before the trip has been invaluable to me.

The remainder of our stay was terrific, and numerous times band members commented to me about a calmness they thought I brought to the trip. I knew that it was God who brought this calmness, and it was a journey filled with healing that I'll not forget.

BLAKE ELLIOTT WINDAL
Los Angeles, California
Christian Science Sentinel July 25, 1994

I became more confident that I wouldn't die.

One Thursday in the spring of 1991, when I was working in our woods, I carelessly reached down into a mountain laurel bush to clear away some of the weeds that were choking it. I felt a sharp prick on my hand and looked down to see a coiled copperhead snake. I was frightened and jumped back. The two men who were working with me were terribly afraid. We went back to the house as fast as we could.

Trembling with fear, I called a Christian Science practitioner to pray for me. I got my Bible and *Science and Health* and tried to pray to calm myself. When a neighbor stopped by, the men told her what had happened. She came right into the house, declaring that I should have a doctor look at the hand. I was so frightened, I agreed to let her drive me to a nearby doctor's office.

Our neighbor is very religious—in our area people would say, "She really loves the Lord." She was very quiet during the drive down the mountain, and I was able to get my own thoughts in order and to pray.

When the doctor saw my hand, he strongly recommended that I enter a hospital for several days to have an antitoxin treatment. Otherwise, he said, I might experience permanent nerve damage, lose my thumb, or in the worst possible case lose my life. As I sat there, I rejected the idea of going into the hospital. I felt an atmosphere of uncertainty and fear in the doctor's office. I have always experienced spiritual healing and at that point I decided to rely wholly on God through prayer.

Then a nurse told me an anecdote about a drowning man who refused various forms of rescue, not recognizing them as sent from God; he finally drowned. Her story prompted me to think that God's law is applicable even if one were drowning in the middle of the ocean. I knew then that depending on God's law for healing was the way of safety and solution for me, and I became more confident that I wouldn't die.

When we left the office, I asked my friend to take me home. There I thanked her for her help and said goodbye.

I remembered this Bible verse, which welcomed me home: "In returning and rest shall ye be saved; in quietness and in confidence shall be your strength" (Isaiah 30:15). This verse also completely changed my thinking about how to deal with emergencies. I called the practitioner again, less fearful, and able to listen to the truth. He said he thought that this was an important watershed experience for me, spiritually. He talked to me about the power of divine Love, God, who includes all creation in His care. He pointed out that the snake had been trying to protect itself and suggested I deepen my understanding of man's safety as a child of God.

As I prayed and studied, I began to see much more clearly that God's goodness doesn't have an opposite. The truth is that the nature of God—His perfection and harmony—is reflected by man, and that no evil power can interrupt this reflection. We can trust God's goodness to bless us, guide us, and protect us without fail. I didn't tell the children what had happened when they got home.

My husband was able to return from Philadelphia, where he had been on business, that same night. He took very good care of me all the next day as I continued to pray. There never was any pain, and by that afternoon the swelling began to subside. My youngest sister was graduating from law school and getting married that weekend. I was able to attend the rehearsal dinner Saturday night, and the wedding on Sunday. No one noticed anything amiss with me at all. Sunday morning I met another neighbor in a hotel elevator. He was amazed to see me and asked about the snakebite. I held up both my hands, and he could see no difference. They were both perfect.

The lessons I learned during this experience have continued to increase my spiritual understanding, enrich my life, and bless my family and me.

SUSAN B. BRADLEY
Lookout Mountain, Georgia
Christian Science Sentinel October 26, 1992

My dad told me God's goodness couldn't stop.

While I was in Florida I went to Sea World. My dad and I were going to a show when my dad slipped in some water and fell down. I was on his shoulders, so I fell down too. I hurt my knees and my head. I cried and my dad carried me. I knew he was praying and I was too. My dad told me God's goodness couldn't stop.

I knew that God, who is Spirit, is always perfect. That means that I am perfect too. God made me perfect. Christ Jesus helped us see that man is perfect. *Science and Health* says that man is spiritual and not material.

My dad and I went to see the stingray tank. I patted and fed the stingrays. They mostly wanted me to pat and feed them, and that made me really, really happy. By then I felt perfectly fine. I could tell that God was there and He loved me.

Erin Swinney
Natick, Massachusetts
Christian Science Sentinel January 9, 1995

My hand was severely burned.

I had borrowed an electric heating element to start the coals in our barbecue pit, and since we decided to go for a boat ride on the lake, I thought it wise to remove the element before we started. I lodged it on top of the barbecue, but the weight of the handle caused it to fall. Quickly I grabbed the hot iron, and my hand stuck fast to it and was severely burned.

When I freed my hand, I did not mention to the family what had occurred. As lightheartedly as I could, I called to them to go ahead on the boat ride because I had something that I must take care of (and so indeed I did!).

The pain was excruciating and the palm of my hand was badly burned, but I held my hands together tightly and walked slowly up the hill, pondering "the scientific statement of being" (*Science and Health*, p. 468). I then sat down quietly on the grass to pray and to demonstrate God's healing power to the best of my ability. The ninety-first Psalm came naturally to me—my favorite since childhood. I also remembered statements from *Science and Health* about the spiritual and perfect nature of man.

Within twenty minutes the pain left and I returned to the house to wash the dishes with no discomfort whatsoever. Charred skin on my palm came off quite painlessly within a few days, and the burn healed completely. This was one of my first spiritual healings, and through it I learned that God is always present to help us in times of trouble.

Renée Dain
Unionville, Indiana
The Christian Science Journal May 1994

My husband was involved in a serious car accident.

In the fall of 1979 my husband was involved in a serious car accident. This event was to lift both of us to a new level of spiritual understanding, for which I give thanks continually.

He was driving home one night, when he came upon an icy spot on the curve of a road and lost control of our Jeep. He was thrown approximately fifty feet, and lay unconscious until the police found him later that night.

When the police called me at 3 a.m., telling me to meet them at the hospital, I responded immediately. First, I called a Christian Science practitioner to begin praying for us. Then I gathered up my son and took him to a friend's house to stay the night. When I reached the hospital, I was met by the attending physician, who candidly told me, "If your husband lives through the night, he will be a vegetable for the rest of his life." This was quite a shock to me. I immediately called the practitioner back. The love and sincere faith in God he expressed strengthened me, and I felt the peace of God with us.

There were many dire predictions in the following days about my husband's condition. Each time, I prayed to understand the absolute statements of spiritual truth the practitioner shared with me. This verse from Isaiah was ever in my thoughts: "Fear thou not; for I am with thee: be not dismayed; for I am thy God: I will strengthen thee; yea, I will help thee; yea, I will uphold thee with the right hand of my righteousness" (41:10). This was a time to draw on all of the truths about God and man I had learned in my life.

After two weeks of constant prayer and nightly vigils, there seemed to be little, if any, progress. My husband was in a coma, paralyzed on his left side. And the prognoses continued to be dire. The doctors suggested an operation that would remove part of the brain to alleviate pressure and keep him alive. To me that was no solution. Even though their motive was to save, I could not accept anything less than a perfect healing.

I resolved not to act on any decision until I knew my direction was coming from God alone. That was the pivotal point for me. I realized that I had been holding to the truths of spiritual man, but that I was still waiting for "something" to happen. Here was a subtle misunderstanding that had to be healed. I had to look to God alone for healing, understanding that His goodness was already a permanent fact and not something that was going to come at a future time.

I reached out to God with all my heart and soul. I prayed simply, "Perfect Father, there is nothing that You can't do. Please lift this burden. I will do only what You tell me to do. Please show me the way." Knowing that God is the only power and that nothing can separate man from this power, I resolved to hold firmly to the perfection of the man that God created—even when I couldn't see it with my eyes.

In the morning when I woke, I held firmly to my resolution to listen only for Love's inspirations. For the first time I felt safe, for I had begun to *know* that God was in control, and only good could be the result. As I sat on the side of my bed that morning, I waited for God's ideas to guide me through this day. What came to me was a surprise: I felt prompted to polish my husband's shoes. This seemed strange, but I kept my resolve to follow Mary Baker Eddy's counsel in *Science and Health,* "Hold thought steadfastly to the enduring, the good, and the true, and you will bring these into your experience proportionably to their occupancy of your thoughts" (p. 261). The next thought that came was to gather his clothes, and this I did promptly. Placing these items in the car, I went to the hospital to see my husband, listening earnestly for the next directive.

When I arrived at the hospital I sat quietly in the car praying for guidance, "Father, should I take these things in?" The thought came, "It never hurts to be prepared." With that, I gathered them together and took them up to the intensive care unit where my husband lay. I felt I was living with the statement "Thus founded upon the rock of Christ, when storm and tempest beat against this sure foundation, you, safely sheltered in the strong tower of hope, faith, and Love, are God's nestlings; and He will hide you in His feathers till the storm has passed. Into His haven of Soul there enters no element of earth to cast out angels, to silence the right intuition which guides you safely home" (*Miscellaneous Writings* by Mary Baker Eddy, p. 152).

The practitioner came and prayed with me, and together we listened for Love's intuitions. At the very end of the day, the doctor came to me and announced that they were moving my husband out of the intensive care unit and placing him in his own room. I was so grateful for this sign of progress.

Up to this time my husband had not been able to talk at all, but I felt I needed to know what he would like me to do. I asked him this, telling him where he was and what had happened.

I am not sure he understood everything, but when he uttered the word *home* I knew he was aware.

I waited patiently for one week, but then felt impelled by Love to move him to our home. When I told the doctor I was taking him home to care for him, he was adamant that this was a mistake because of the severity of his condition. But, with the help of a Christian Science visiting nurse, we did bring my husband home.

As we cared for my husband, I felt tremendous anticipation of good. There was no outlining of how healing should come, nor was there fearful doting. I simply observed that there was a growing awareness of the perfection of God's man within our home. My husband's healing progressed rapidly, and he began to be able to walk and talk.

One day we were out walking, and he looked at me with a strange expression on his face and asked where our Jeep was. I gently told him that it had been totaled, that God had lifted us all out of that problem, and that he was on the path of healing. After that day his mental awareness increased markedly. The practitioner prayed with us daily and frequently visited our home. My husband started reading again and studying passages that the practitioner shared with him. Within one week we were out Christmas shopping and able to attend church again. A family member heard of the healing and proclaimed, "It's a miracle." Within two months of the accident, my husband was driving again; within three months he was back at work fulltime, performing his duties as a computer programmer.

At the doctors' request we went for a medical visit so that they could see the healing progress for themselves, and know that Christian Science doesn't ignore problems but rather heals them. When the doctor learned that my husband had driven himself to the doctor's office, he exclaimed, "You don't need me!"

This healing—a lesson in knowing God's love—has been a beacon to us, and an inspiration to the family members who witnessed it. Our family saw firsthand that there is nothing God cannot do! I learned through heartfelt prayer that faith and willingness to follow Him unquestioningly were the keys to this healing.

Linda M. Newgent

I am the husband mentioned. I am happy to verify that the healing has been complete and permanent. The injury was severe enough that medical science offered little hope for survival, and no hope for recovery. The healing was entirely the result of Christian Science treatment.

Though I have no memory of the accident or of my stay in the hospital, I have seen the official records; this is a documented event. My first memory is from a time shortly after I came home from the hospital. I felt as if I were waking from a long, deep sleep. There was significant mental confusion and spatial memory loss, and my entire left side was paralyzed.

After I had been home for several weeks, I had taken to walking around the block each day for exercise and fresh air.

I limped quite badly because one side of my body was still severely impaired. I was walking one day when the thought came clearly to me, "God did not intend for me to walk this way." As I accepted that spiritual fact, I could feel my stride lengthen to a smooth, normal gait, and I soon regained full use of the affected arm. I also remember the whole period of recovery as being filled with intense, radiant joy.

Philip L. Newgent
St. Louis, Missouri
Christian Science Sentinel December 20, 1993

I was hit and tumbled in the air.

On April 25, 1993, my whole family worshiped with me in our branch church at Imo River-Obigbo, Nigeria. The account of Jesus healing the centurion's servant was read during the service (see Luke 7:2–10). The correlative passages from *Science and Health* brought me much encouragement, and when I returned from the service I went to my office to study more, especially this statement: "Man, being immortal, has a perfect indestructible life" (*Science and Health,* p. 209). I saw this statement as one of the absolute truths of man's being.

As I was leaving my office a message rang in my thought saying, "Be conscious." I went back and used my concordance to *Science and Health* to find a statement on page 14: "Become conscious for a single moment that Life and intelligence are purely spiritual,—neither in nor of matter,—and the body will then utter no complaints." While thinking deeper, I remembered another truth: "Consciousness constructs a better body when faith in matter has been conquered" (*ibid.,* p. 425).

I left my office for home, happier for this communion. About 8 p.m., I decided to go and thank a friend who had dropped my son off at his school some few days before. I took my torchlight to walk a distance of about three poles off. Just a pole off my house, on the major road, I saw a Land Rover loaded with iron rods in the back, moving at a very high speed in the opposite direction. I continued walking along the edge of the tarred road.

As the Land Rover was passing me at that high speed, I was hit, and I tumbled in the air and landed on my two legs on the ground, still standing. (What had hit me were some of the rods that were extending out from the side of the Land Rover.) My torchlight fell from my hand and dropped on the road, and I picked it up. It was wonderful that my shirt was not even torn, nor was I injured by the impact in any way. "Under divine Providence there can be no accidents, since there is no room for imperfection in perfection" (*ibid.,* p. 424).

People who saw the incident pursued the driver of the vehicle to mob him for having hit someone without stopping. But I ran to them, pleading for them to leave him alone—that God had demonstrated His presence to us all, and that Moses actually saw a burning bush that was not consumed.

The most glorious aspect of this incident was that, at the time the Land Rover was passing me I had been walking alongside a parked trailer; by the time I landed on my feet I found myself behind the trailer. Even though I had been thrown backward that great distance, I saw that "metaphysics is above physics, and matter does not enter into metaphysical premises or conclusions" (*ibid.*, p. 269).

JOSEPH OZIOMA NWOSU
Obigbo, Rivers State, Nigeria
Christian Science Sentinel December 5, 1994

I asked the crew to pray, each in his own way.

On a Christmas morning during World War II, a convoy of eight ships was traveling through mountainous seas. Our ship, on her maiden voyage, was a large ten-thousand-ton freighter with a crew of seventy-seven Americans.

We had traveled across the submarine-infested Atlantic Ocean without incident and were within twenty-five miles of a safe haven. However, to reach safety we had to go through the dangerous waters of the Ellen Troddy Passage of the Hebrides, islands off the western coast of Scotland.

A magnetic mine had been set in the channel and was triggered to blow up the fourth ship in the convoy to pass over it. This fourth ship was my command. The explosion lifted the bow of the ship out of the water, tearing away the whole lower forward section. It was a terrifying moment. I humbly turned to God in prayer. I knew God, all-knowing, intelligent divine Mind, was totally responsible for our lives. With regard to the vessel and crew, according to the law of the sea the people aboard must come first. I acknowledged as my guide the Christ, Truth, that speaks to human consciousness in the still small voice. With this confidence I felt directed to drive the ship into the rocks in order to keep it safely above water and rescue the crew.

Grateful, I knew that man as God's image is safe, fully protected, always in the tender care of our Father-Mother God. It was clear to me that in divine Truth there are no accidents.

The ship came to rest on the rocks. We were in black darkness. Gale-force winds were driving heavy seas over the stern, covering the ship as it smashed up and down against the rocks. It appeared certain that a lifeboat would be destroyed in such a gale. In the pitch darkness and violent storm there seemed to be no hope.

The crew and I assembled on the ship's bridge and boat deck. As I prayed, I recalled the Bible account of Paul's shipwreck (see Acts 27). Even though there was destruction of the ship, Paul and those early seafarers were saved, each one. Recalling that Bible rescue, I felt an inner peace that was like a vision of light in the darkness, and assurance of safety. It was the radiancy of the ever-present Christ telling me we were safe. Truly, God was working out His purpose of safety.

The human picture had not changed. With her bow on the rocks and her stern in deep water, the ship was slowly starting to break up, with the full crew still aboard. Under the stress of the circumstances, the crew threatened to disobey orders and to launch the lifeboats. Their fear caused them to be angry. Reassured with the Christ, Truth, I knew no material elements could withstand God's omnipotence. With this spiritual conviction, I asked the crew to pray, each in his own way. This quieted the men. Divine Love had put the right words in my mouth.

Soon after, we saw a light on the lee side of the island. The British Navy had sent a ship to help us. They sent us a rope to rig a breeches buoy that is used in rescue work for ships in deep trouble. It was a slow, weary process but one by one the crew was sent safely ashore.

Six or seven men are normally needed aboardship to haul the breeches buoy back to the ship from the shore. On the third day of the wreck, all but three men had been saved. After much pounding by the waves, the ship's back was broken. We were expecting her to fall into the deep water at any moment.

Despite our weariness the three of us remaining were able to retrieve the breeches buoy. An ancient law of the sea is that the captain remain until last to leave the ship. After much persistent arguing based upon brotherly love, the two remaining officers were sent safely ashore. As captain, I was alone. With rejoicing I knew that God's promises are always kept. There was never a doubt about getting safely ashore.

The problem of the moment was how to get the breeches buoy close enough to the ship's side for me to get into it. This would take some doing. With God's help I knew it could be done. Praying for the direction of all-knowing Mind, I hauled the breeches buoy with block and tackle to within about ten feet of the ship's side. To human sense I was completely exhausted after three days without sleep, plus all the physical exertion and anxiety of getting the crew ashore safely.

"Dear Father, save me, I can of myself do no more. Please show me the way," I prayed. Then I remembered the first verse of the poem "Satisfied" by Mary Baker Eddy (*Poems*, p. 79),

> It matters not what be thy lot,
> So Love doth guide;
> For storm or shine, pure peace is thine,
> Whate'er betide.

At that very instant I realized I was looking at the antiaircraft gun—an enormously heavy monster, mounted on the bow. The gun could turn in azimuth without electrical power, by mechanical gears. Here was the answer. I secured a heavy rope to the very end of the gun, trained it toward where the breeches buoy was waiting. Making the rope secure to a line from the buoy, I then trained the gun to the opposite side of the ship, bringing the breeches buoy right alongside the ship.

The rest was easy. Everything fell into place. I got into the buoy, thanking God for all His love, for the truth, for His beloved Christ, for man's spiritual indivisible relationship to Him. Next, I cut the gun's rope and slid down into the waves. Then our British friends hauled me ashore.

When I reached the shore I collapsed, and awakened later in the cottage of a kindly Scottish shepherd. As with Paul's shipwreck experience, I too was fed and cared for until

I was strong again. God's dear love saved every one of the seventy-seven-man crew. Some of the men were months recovering but everyone was saved. Saved by God's omnipresent love, eternal truth.

Robert Mac Alvanah
Lighthouse Point, Florida
The Christian Science Journal December 1976

14

Addiction, compulsive behavior, and spiritual rehabilitation

Although addiction and compulsive behavior may seem to have a strong hold, God's love and strength enable everyone to live freely. As these testimonies reveal, the law of spiritual rehabilitation is always present.

I had tried every way I knew to break the cigarette habit.

I had tried on numerous occasions to stop a habit of consuming between two and three packs of cigarettes a day, knowing even in a physical sense that it was limiting and degrading. I had tried every way I knew to break the habit, including the substitution of candies or gum, and had used various patent medicines. I had even read books on "methods" for breaking the habit. I'd tried "tapering off," and sudden, complete cessation. All these availed nothing. I seemed to be hopelessly addicted. At one time I had been able, through exerting sheer human willpower, to stop for six months, but it was a terrible experience because I never lost the desire to smoke and had not been able to put it out of my thought, finally succumbing to temptation, taking "just one" cigarette, so that in a matter of a day or so I was indulging at a greater rate than ever before.

The answer to my problem came after I began concentrated study of the Bible Lesson outlined in the *Christian Science Quarterly*. Through continued study and prayer, I realized that substitution was, for me, the basis of the healing. Not substituting candy, gum, or some other habit for smoking, but changing the entire basis of my thinking, substituting spiritual aims, goals, and expressions for material ones.

First, I started from the premise that "there is no power apart from God" (*Science and Health* by Mary Baker Eddy, p. 228); therefore I *could* be healed by turning to God, Spirit, for help.

Secondly, I realized that I had been acknowledging a "power apart from God" in thinking that smoking could hold me to addiction.

Thus I knew that if I could gain the absolute conviction, based upon reason and understanding and not just faith, that God *is* the only power, *is* omnipotent, then nothing, not even smoking, could possess power over me.

At this time I discovered the sentence in *Science and Health* "Right motives give pinions to thought, and strength and freedom to speech and action" (p. 454). This, plus the statements on page 228: "The enslavement of man is not legitimate. It will cease when man enters into his heritage of freedom, his God-given dominion over the material senses," seemed to me to be a key to unlock and open the door to freedom. I knew my motives were right in seeking freedom from this habit in order that I might increase my service to God and mankind.

I then started to recall and examine my motives in starting to smoke as a teenager. In thinking back, I remembered that our high school had set aside a room for students who wished to smoke during the lunch hour. I had wanted to be accepted by those who frequented that room, and before I realized it I was trapped by the habit. To be released from the trap it was clear that I had to see what it was that made one truly accepted and truly popular, and to whom.

With more study it became apparent that we are not attracted to others because of physical characteristics or actions, except in a very temporary or fleeting sense, but because of the good qualities they express, such as forthrightness, honesty, enthusiasm, compassion for others, gratitude, and so forth. In other words, qualities which are Christlike, lasting, and spiritual attract us rather than those which are material.

As I daily strove to express more of these qualities and to see and appreciate them in those around me, I could see that these Christlike attributes were God's power expressed in my experience and that nothing could oppose them. I found I lost my desire to smoke, and I have been free of this habit for more than ten years.

WILLIAM M. MACKENZIE
Indianapolis, Indiana
Christian Science Sentinel April 20, 1968

She told me that I could be healed of the drinking.

For several years I drank to have a good time, to be with the "in" crowd. But, as time went on, I could not stop with one or two drinks. I had to get drunk. My wife could no longer trust me with so simple a task as going to the grocery store; she never knew when I would come back. I was drinking in the morning before work, at lunchtime I would have a few, and at night I would get so drunk that sometimes, the next morning, I could not remember what I did the night before.

My wife begged me to stop drinking. I would promise her that I would, knowing that I did not mean it. Finally she threatened to take our only child and leave me, but even this had no effect upon me. I told her that drinking was the only enjoyment I got out of life, the fellows I drank with were the only friends I had, and if I stopped drinking, my friends would desert me.

About this time my wife became interested in Christian Science and tried to get me to go to church, but I was never sober enough. Whiskey had such a hold on me that nothing else meant anything to me, not even my family. My wife began to pray for me, and she asked a Christian Science practitioner for prayerful help regarding our home situation.

One night I came home very drunk, but my head was clear enough to understand what my wife was saying to me. She was calm, expressed no anger, and did not raise her voice. She told me that I could be healed of the drinking habit and that she wanted to read to me. I sat down to listen. She read from *Science and Health with Key to the Scriptures* by Mary Baker Eddy for about an hour. I will always remember what she read to me: "There is no enjoyment in getting drunk, in becoming a fool or an object of loathing; but there is a very sharp remembrance of it, a suffering inconceivably terrible to man's self-respect" (pp. 406–407).

These words also affected me deeply: "Resist evil—error of every sort—and it will flee from you. Error is opposed to Life. We can, and ultimately shall, so rise as to avail ourselves in every direction of the supremacy of Truth over error, Life over death, and good over evil, and this growth will go on until we arrive at the fullness of God's idea, and no more fear that we shall be sick and die. Inharmony of any kind involves weakness and suffering,—a loss of control over the body.

"The depraved appetite for alcoholic drinks, tobacco, tea, coffee, opium, is destroyed only by Mind's mastery of the body. This normal control is gained through divine strength and understanding" (p. 406).

I realized that the prayerful work my wife was doing for me had some effect. One day at work the thought came to me to stop smoking. I gave my cigarettes up at once and never again desired to smoke.

I was still apprehensive, though, for I had a feeling that if I stopped drinking all at once my heart might stop beating. My wife then read from *Science and Health:* "We should relieve our minds from the depressing thought that we have transgressed a material law and must of necessity pay the penalty. Let us reassure ourselves with the law of Love" (p. 384).

I can't describe the feeling which came over me. I felt contrite, yet I had a wonderful feeling that love surrounded me. It was like coming out of the dark into the light. I went to bed, and the next morning I awoke feeling so good that I did not take a drink. I went to work, and that evening I disposed of the whiskey I always kept in the car. This healing took place sixteen years ago, and I have not had the desire for alcoholic drink since.

JOSEPH C. HELMICK

When I reached the point where I could see the man made in God's image and likeness instead of the demoralized mortal, I was able to reach out with love and my husband's healing followed. One other aspect of this healing was the way the past, with all its heartbreaks, resentments, and disappointments, was completely wiped out of our thinking as though it had never been, and we were both free to go forward and establish a happy home built on an understanding of God as Truth and Love.

IRENE F. HELMICK
Hampton, Virginia
The Christian Science Journal September 1969

I had the right to be free of addiction.

While employed in film production and traveling worldwide, I developed a serious problem with alcohol, eventually drinking to excess three or four times a week. At first it had little effect on my business and personal life because I drank so secretly that no one was aware of my addiction.

I could stop drinking for a month or two through human willpower, but I always returned to the habit. I became more and more depressed; my business suffered, and most of my social life and friendships were unfulfilling. I felt I could not discuss this problem with any one, as I was ashamed of the control alcohol seemed to have over me.

One afternoon while in a Christian Science Reading Room I came across a passage from a letter that Mary Baker Eddy wrote to a student. It said: "You are *growing.* The Father has sealed you, and the opening of these seals must not surprise you. The character of Christ is wrought out in our lives by just such processes. The tares and wheat appear to grow together until the harvest; then the tares are *first* gathered, that is, you have seasons of seeing your errors—and afterwards by reason of this very seeing, the tares are burned, the error is destroyed. Then you see Truth plainly and the wheat is 'gathered into barns,' it becomes permanent in the understanding" (quoted in *We Knew Mary Baker Eddy,* p. 90).

I was determined to burn the tares and gather the wheat, so to speak. I decided to turn as wholeheartedly as I could to the study of God's healing law to resolve my business, drinking, and personal problems.

Everyday I pondered this statement from *Science and Health,* "Let the slave of wrong desire learn the lessons of Christian Science, and he will get the better of that desire, and ascend a degree in the scale of health, happiness, and existence" (p. 407). I began to see my true self was not that of a human struggling to be free of addictive, destructive practices; but in reality, my spiritual birthright provided me with a joyous freedom from lack or limitation of any kind. I had the right to be free of addiction to alcohol, lack of work, and depression. They were not of God and could not be part of me, as God's loving and loved child.

One day, after several weeks of seeing myself in this light, I looked at a display of alcoholic beverages in a supermarket and realized I was not battling with myself, as I had in the past, over whether I should purchase a bottle. At first I couldn't believe it! I had absolutely no interest in drinking. The healing had occurred so calmly and effortlessly that for days afterward I wondered if I was really healed or if the desire would return. Then I remembered this statement from *Science and Health:* "The drunkard thinks he enjoys drunkenness, and you cannot make the inebriate leave his besottedness, until his physical sense of pleasure yields to a higher sense. Then he turns from his cups, as the startled dreamer who wakens from an incubus incurred through the pains of distorted sense" (p. 322). I realized I had been awakened to the spiritual truth of my being, and the "tares [were] burned, the error [was] destroyed."

This healing has given me much-needed inspiration to apply these healing truths to all areas of my life. It has also made me more compassionate toward people who are involved in working out similar problems. Daily I think about and strive to emulate this thoughtful statement from *Science and Health* (p. 248): "We must form perfect models in thought and look at them continually, or we shall never carve them out in grand and noble lives. Let unselfishness, goodness, mercy, justice, health, holiness, love—the kingdom of heaven—reign within us, and sin, disease, and death will diminish until they finally disappear."

John Holmstrom
Hollywood, California
The Christian Science Journal March 1988

I had never realized I could refuse this behavior.

It was the conversation with a friend concerning her struggle with alcoholism that alerted me to pray about man's true nature as the spiritual child of God. This prayerful metaphysical work led to the healing of a difficulty I had been having.

One idea that helped me a lot as I began this focused prayer was from *Science and Health,* "God controls man, and

God is the only Spirit. Any other control or attraction of so-called spirit is a mortal belief, which ought to be known by its fruit,—the repetition of evil" (p. 73). I looked up many helpful references to *order* and *control* in the writings of Mary Baker Eddy.

As a result of this prayerful study, I became very aware of a habit I had long felt I might never be free of. For years I had been waking up in the middle of the night and "raiding" the refrigerator. This insomnia and compulsive eating left me tired the next day and embarrassed by my own lack of control. Often I felt like a victim. I tried various human alternatives such as eating more during the day, reading at night, and not keeping tempting goodies in the house.

In an effort to pray about alcoholism, however, I wanted to prove that what I was knowing was really true—for me, too. I called a practitioner of Christian Science for help through prayer. Of all the constructive ideas shared with me, the one that stuck like glue was that man is not compulsive, that he is impelled by divine Life itself to do right. I had never realized I could refuse this behavior that seemed so much a part of me. A passage in the Bible was brought to my attention. In Deuteronomy we read, "I call heaven and earth to record this day against you, that I have set before you life and death, blessing and cursing: therefore choose life, that both thou and thy seed may live" (30:19).

After praying with these thoughts that day, I had hope that the problem had been solved. That night I went to sleep with this thought on my mind, that I move "at the impulse of Thy [God's] love," which is a line from a hymn in the *Christian Science Hymnal*. I knew I was in truth spiritual, not a struggling mortal that unpleasant traits could cling to. I also knew that I was governed by God and not temptation. Although I did wake up that night, I did not open the refrigerator. All fear of this habit, and the habit itself, left me.

It has been over a year now, and the insomnia too has been completely healed, although I had this condition for twenty-two years prior to this healing. The truth is I can hardly believe it was ever a problem for me because I now always experience only a restful, full night's sleep without interruption. I feel that I followed this directive in *Science and Health* (p. 442): "Christian Scientists, be a law to yourselves that mental malpractice cannot harm you either when asleep or when awake."

JANEY ALEXANDER HEIDENBERG
New York, New York
Christian Science Sentinel September 28, 1987

I was completely healed of my dependence on drugs.

I lived in an orange tepee built on a platform high above the ground in a huge redwood tree. I was addicted to heroin and supported my habit by burglarizing houses. This way of life wasn't new to me. I had been addicted either to alcohol or drugs for years.

In April, 1971, I was arrested on a charge of burglary, and sentenced to a California rehabilitation center for heroin addicts. This is where Christian Science found me. While browsing through the institution's library, I ran across Mary Baker Eddy's book, *Unity of Good.* I was attracted by the title. As I read, some wonderful things began to happen.

Can you imagine a mental light show? How else can I describe the brilliant flashes of spiritual insight and understanding that flooded my consciousness with truth! Suddenly I began to understand a little of the true nature of God and man—God's allness, man's total unity and coexistence with his Father-Mother God—the unity of good! This realization brought destruction to the dark imprisoning thoughts that had held me for so many years—thoughts of deep alienation, complete separation from all good. I'd always felt I was alone and somehow didn't fit in at all. Now I began to see very clearly that my true being is spiritual, complete, fulfilled, and that I am a loved and accepted part of all that really exists. The peace and satisfaction

I couldn't get through the material senses I found to be the natural state of true existence within myself, here and now!

Almost two thousand years ago Jesus expressed this very thought when he said, "The kingdom of God is within you" (Luke 17:21). I had been searching for this kingdom in directions leading nowhere—in alcohol, marijuana, reds, whites, speed, LSD, and heroin. With this change of thought, I was completely healed of my dependence on drugs that had ruled my life for nearly fourteen years. But this healing was only the outward manifestation of the tremendous spiritual awakening that took place. It is this awakening that I am most grateful for.

The Apostle Paul, whose thought went through a great transformation, gave this counsel in his letter to the Ephesians: "That ye put off . . . the old man, which is corrupt according to the deceitful lusts; and be renewed in the spirit of your mind; and that ye put on the new man, which after God is created in righteousness and true holiness" (4:22–24).

Speaking in wonder of this spiritual rebirth, Mary Baker Eddy comments, "What a faith-lighted thought is this! that mortals can lay off the 'old man,' until man is found to be the image of the infinite good that we name God, and the fulness of the stature of man in Christ appears" (*Miscellaneous Writings*, p. 15).

Jon Kilpatrick
Riverside, California
Christian Science Sentinel June 2, 1973

I asked God to free me from this dependence.

Originally written in Spanish

From a very young age I resisted many of the attitudes prevalent in society; I especially couldn't accept human suffering as a necessity. This impelled me to investigate different psychological and religious paths. When I was a student in high school, my friends and I had used amphetamines in the belief that they improved intellectual output. I became dependent on marijuana over a period of twenty years, until I began to question why I was using it. I decided that it increased my intelligence, making me more lucid and connecting me more with my inner self.

When I became dissatisfied with that justification, I asked God to free me from this dependence. At that time I became acquainted with Christian Science and began to study the Lord's Prayer, with its spiritual interpretation from *Science and Health* (pp. 16–17). The part of the prayer "Hallowed be Thy name" and the interpretation *"Adorable One"* was illuminating. It helped me to see that I should put only God before me, since He is the Adorable One. I found "the scientific statement of being" and read the words "There is no life, truth, intelligence, nor substance in matter" (*ibid.*, p. 468). I thought about this concept daily. As a result, I didn't feel the urge to smoke for several months. I didn't even think about it.

Then one day when I was visiting some friends, they wanted to share a smoke with me. I was afraid. I thought, "Thy will be done, and not mine." At that moment I felt a great confidence. When a marijuana joint was passed to me, I said very calmly, "Thank you, I don't smoke."

I returned home feeling a wonderful freedom and indescribable joy that no drug could give me. I knew I had been healed.

ADA MARIA M. BARRIONUEVO
Rio Negro, Argentina
Christian Science Sentinel October 24, 1994

Within a very short time the gambling habit had completely dropped away.

I found myself searching for a better understanding of God and also needing to search my own thought. This search for God led to my becoming acquainted with Christian Science. As I made a dedicated study of Mary Baker Eddy's writings, I was led to search my own thought to see who I was, why I was here, and what I was doing. This was a beautiful search, and out of it came many blessings. In *Miscellaneous Writings,* in an article titled "The Way," Mary Baker Eddy writes of three stages of mental growth (pp. 355–359). The first one of these is self-knowledge; the second, humility; the third, love. During this period of search, one of the great treasures that became mine was the ability to break the gambling habit.

This habit had started many years before and in a very small way with the thought of enjoying myself. As time progressed, the stakes kept getting bigger until the time came that I no longer had control over the habit. At that time I was working for another person and was able to feed this addiction by taking advantage of every situation that came my way. Many times I created situations that I should not have and knew to be extremely dishonest. In other words, it was downright thievery.

Later, as I became a businessman, somewhat successful, I was able to further indulge this habit. However, the time came when I found myself heavily in debt, and yet the appetite of the addiction was increasing. Many evenings I had gotten up from the gaming table and written a check for several thousand dollars. On one particular evening I wrote an extremely large check and then made up my mind never to gamble again. But I was finding it impossible to break such an addiction through self-will.

When the day arrived that I began to see the futility of all this, I turned to a greater will than my own. I found myself endeavoring to carry out God's will. The three stages of growth described in "The Way" gave me much food for thought, and surely that first stage of self-knowledge, which called for self-examination, began to awaken me. The thought came, "Why do I gamble?" With that came the answer that it was because I had no sense of peace. As my dedicated study of God's law progressed, a lovely sense of inner peace began to come into my experience, one that heretofore had been unknown. I found then, as a natural result, that stages two and three, humility and love, were being lived in my daily activities, whether I was dealing with myself or another. Within a very short time I found that this gambling habit had completely dropped away from me. After this, the ideas began to come as to how I was to take care of all of the debts that had been created by gambling.

As I look back on this experience today, my heart is full of gratitude.

BEN B. TAYLOR
Tempe, Arizona
Christian Science Sentinel June 5, 1971

None of the immoral activity had ever been part of my true being.

I began dating a young man when I was a freshman in high school. We dated regularly for four years, and during that time we became sexually active. I had always thought that premarital sex was wrong. Still, I was very attracted to my boyfriend, and it all seemed so exciting, romantic, and pleasurable that I did not want to stop. All during our relationship I was afraid of the possibility of becoming pregnant. At one point while I was still in high school, I mistakenly thought I was pregnant and felt miserable and afraid. Later, during my first year of college, I found myself involved and sexually active with another man in addition to the one I have just mentioned. Gradually I grew to feel very guilty and ashamed, yet I felt I still wanted and needed sexual activity.

I began studying the Bible along with *Science and Health,* searching for an answer. I quickly learned the first step I had to take toward gaining freedom. Christ Jesus told the woman caught in the act of adultery to "go, and sin no more" (John 8:11).

And *Science and Health* states: "The way to escape the misery of sin is to cease sinning. There is no other way" (p. 327). I realized I had to stop, but I did not know how.

In *Science and Health* I read "Every supposed pleasure in sin will furnish more than its equivalent of pain, until belief in material life and sin is destroyed" (p. 6). I knew from my experience that this was true. I always had more problems caused by my sinning than the pleasure I had while sinning. Then I asked myself, "If this kind of pleasure causes so much pain and misery, is it really pleasure?"

This question is answered in *Science and Health,* "The pains of sense quickly inform us that the pleasures of sense are mortal and that joy is spiritual" (page 265). And, on page 404: "This conviction, that there is no real pleasure in sin, is one of the most important points in the theology of Christian Science. Arouse the sinner to this new and true view of sin, show him that sin confers no pleasure, and this knowledge strengthens his moral courage and increases his ability to master evil and to love good."

Recognizing "that there is no real pleasure in sin" was the first big step on the road to my healing. It gave me enough courage to stop my sexual activity. It did not, however, quiet my sexual desire or the fear that I might yield to such temptation again.

What is comforting to know is that no matter what we are struggling with, our answers and freedom can be found through a better understanding of God and man, a spiritual understanding that heals. I found the answer to my problem in Jesus' Sermon on the Mount, where he says that "whosoever looketh on a woman to lust after her hath committed adultery with her already in his heart" (Matthew 5:28). I realized then that in order to obey the Ten Commandments, which meant living in obedience to God, I must not look on any man with any thought of having sex with him, for this too would be immoral.

This realization helped a great deal, but there were more obstacles to overcome. I sometimes became angry because I could not seem to be completely free of the discontent and fear.

I kept remembering how long I had been involved in immoral activity. Also, as I thought about these things, I began to blame my grandfather, who used to abuse me sexually when I was young.

I could not seem to get past this point, and I struggled mentally a great deal. By this time I was engaged to a different young man with whom I had been good friends. He knew of my struggles and tried to help me. We married, but the beginning was a little rocky. I knew for the sake of our marriage that I must overcome the fear of sinning again.

One day I went to visit a Christian Science practitioner and told her of my troubles. She assured me that none of the immoral activity had ever been part of my true being as a perfect, spiritual child of God. She reminded me that I could never have been truly outside of God's government and care, which do not include sin of any kind. We prayed together about this, and then I went home feeling much freer. After that, as a result of prayer and study, I gradually overcame all my fear.

It has been a number of years since I was involved in immoral activity. I have a wonderful and warm relationship with my husband. I am also free of the fear of being unfaithful to him—a freedom that I am very grateful for.

Since this healing, peace, purity, and happiness are among my newfound joys. For this I am most grateful. I pray that others struggling as I did will realize that they, too, can be healed if they trust in God and spiritually understand Him.

Name withheld at author's request
Christian Science Sentinel January 23, 1989

As I learned that my true identity is not material but spiritual, I saw that I was spiritually satisfied.

During my teenage years I believed that I was homosexual and practiced homosexual activities. Progressively, my whole life became affected. School, career, and social interactions all suffered because of what I now consider immoral and unethical behavior. I felt handcuffed, embarrassed, and dependent on momentary pleasures of the body. For eleven years I struggled along, feeling desperately alone with the problem and having no one to turn to.

I knew a little about Christian Science, mainly through reading *The Christian Science Monitor.* One day, out of a great need for help, I picked up a telephone directory to find the nearest Christian Science Reading Room. Through contact with the Reading Room I learned the telephone number of a Christian Science practitioner.

The practitioner, who was most kind, agreed to pray for me. She gave me some passages to read from *Science and Health.* This passage was very encouraging to me: "Mankind will improve through Science and Christianity. The necessity for uplifting the race is father to the fact that Mind can do it; for Mind can impart purity instead of impurity, strength instead of weakness, and health instead of disease. Truth is an alterative in the entire system, and can make it 'every whit whole'" (p. 371).

I reasoned that spirituality is the basis of morality; spirituality lifts us out of sensuality, enabling us to discern reality.

The practitioner helped me awake to the fact that I am now, always have been, and always will be God's pure and perfect spiritual child. The basis for this view is found in the Bible in Genesis: "God created man in his own image, in the image of God created he him; . . . And God saw every thing that he had made, and, behold, it was very good" (1:27, 31).

As I learned that my true identity is not material but spiritual, I saw that I was spiritually satisfied by divine Love. This realization began to free me from the misconception that I was a physical puppet governed and controlled by false appetites and pleasures.

The practitioner and I worked together over a period of time, and the amount of love and care shown to me was remarkable. Gradually the validity of this passage from *Science and Health* became evident in my life: "Let the slave of wrong desire learn the lessons of Christian Science, and he will get the better of that desire, and ascend a degree in the scale of health, happiness, and existence" (p. 407).

That is just what happened. One day I simply felt free! It was a wonderful feeling. I had lost all desire for homosexual relationships. I was free. I rejoiced and thanked God for releasing me from the grip that had seemed to hold me physically, emotionally, and mentally.

Shortly after my healing I was introduced to a young woman who later became my wife. We continue to be very happily married, and I have found it difficult to write this testimony, simply because I am so free. My heart reached out to God in prayer and my prayer was answered.

Name withheld at author's request
Christian Science Sentinel May 28, 1990

I decided to call the VD clinic.

Throughout my adolescence and young manhood, I was a confirmed "girl watcher" with a strong physical attraction to the opposite sex. I blamed my feelings of frustration on a lack of opportunity to physically satisfy sensual desires. Nevertheless, I managed to maintain the appearance of a reasonably well-adjusted male.

Later I met and married a lovely young woman. We had many similar interests and both shared a love for God and Christian Science. To all outward appearances we were a happy couple. But it was soon obvious that we didn't have identical levels of desire for the physical aspect of marriage. I prayed to refine and spiritualize my concepts of manhood and marriage, and I gained brief glimpses of my spiritual wholeness.

Nevertheless, I continued to rationalize that I had a right to a more active sex life, that it was a normal and natural need. Occasional business trips provided opportunities for physical relationships with anonymity.

When I honestly faced up to what I was doing, I knew it was wrong. I realized that I was harming my marriage by breaking the seventh commandment, "Thou shalt not commit adultery" (Exodus 20:14). The remorse I frequently felt and the shame I knew that exposure of my activities would bring were clues enough for me to recognize the counterfeit nature and deceit of such actions. I knew there was a higher, purer road, and I prayed to be able to follow it.

Physical and mental suffering forced me to seek a genuinely satisfying solution. And all this was worth the blessing that followed. One day I noticed strange physical symptoms. These were so alarming that I felt I needed the prayer of a Christian Science practitioner. When the practitioner agreed to help me, I knew that in spite of the physical discomfort, I was willing to accept the opportunity to grow spiritually, which every problem, as understood in divine Science, provides. I didn't suspect what would be uncovered through our prayers. I hadn't yet made the connection between the physical problem and my extramarital activity.

The practitioner explained that we can certainly be grateful that we can understandingly turn with confidence to God, Mind, for the uncovering of error. Then the activity of the Christ in human consciousness makes plain the spiritual ideas necessary to heal every discordant situation. Employing these ideas in our prayers—by affirming and claiming man's spiritual, pure, and perfect relationship to his Father—enables us to successfully deny and replace the false, material belief, whatever its nature.

The scientific concept of anatomy meant recognizing my inviolate relationship to God as His loved son. It required turning thought away from the physical symptoms. Mrs. Eddy states: "Anatomy, when conceived of spiritually, is mental self-knowledge, and consists in the dissection of thoughts to discover their quality, quantity, and origin" (*Science and Health,* p. 462). Then she asks, "Are thoughts divine or human?" To answer this question honestly in his prayers, the practitioner had to replace the false beliefs of fear and physical and mental distress with an awareness of the divine attributes of freedom, purity, and dominion. Then he realized with conviction that these spiritual qualities constituted a recognition of my true selfhood as the child of God.

Although I felt more spiritually uplifted, the physical symptoms appeared to worsen. I was very uncomfortable. Then one evening, alone with my thoughts, it occurred to me I might have a venereal disease. I decided to call the VD clinic at a local hospital and ask them to describe the symptoms of gonorrhea. The nurse listed in order the symptoms I'd been having.

I hung up the phone and sat paralyzed. Overcome with shame and anxiety, I felt I didn't deserve healing and therefore shouldn't be healed. I couldn't remember reading of a spiritual healing of VD.

I decided to call the clinic again and ask some more questions. At the end of the conversation the nurse finally said, "Well, I can tell you one thing, it won't go away by itself."

At this point an overwhelming wave of abhorrence, self-condemnation, and guilt swept over me again. But I knew there was no choice but to be completely honest with the practitioner. I gained support from Mary Baker Eddy's statement: "We never need to despair of an honest heart; but there is little hope for those who come only spasmodically face to face with their wickedness and then seek to hide it" (*Science and Health*, p. 8).

I determined to challenge the self-condemnation and guilt and other arguments as they came to thought. I must reject them on spiritual grounds, acknowledging God as the only creator and cause—my Father, who loves me as His son.

I faced squarely the nurse's comments: "It won't go away unless we treat it medically. You just come over here to our clinic, and we won't ask any questions. You'll retain your anonymity, and we won't even charge you. In one quick treatment you'll be clean and the world will be better off because you won't infect anyone."

That sounded like a simple way out of my dilemma, and I was tempted to take it. But I knew that if I took this route (it wasn't required by law), I wouldn't be accomplishing the important goal of every scientific healing—spiritual regeneration. Mrs. Eddy says in *Science and Health,* "Material methods are temporary, and are not adapted to elevate mankind" (p. 318). So it wasn't just a change in the physical condition that I was seeking, as painful as the situation seemed to be. I had a spiritual need.

Another suggestion I had to master was the argument that Christian Science doesn't apply to immorality. I immediately realized this wasn't true. I recalled that Christ Jesus wasn't dismayed by immorality, nor did he condemn the individual. He said to the adulterous woman, "go, and sin no more" (John 8:11).

These firm assertions helped me regain my composure, and I realized this healing could help me take a great step forward in expressing a higher, purer concept of true manhood.

This was a vital realization for me, and I was glad that when I reached the practitioner he listened quietly and without any condemnation reminded me of these words in *Miscellaneous Writings:* "Christian Science never healed a patient without proving with mathematical certainty that error, when found out, is two-thirds destroyed, and the remaining third kills itself. . . . The wisdom of a serpent is to hide itself. The wisdom of God, as revealed in Christian Science, brings the serpent out of its hole, handles it, and takes away its sting" (p. 210). Then he made the point that when the sin is destroyed, the penalty ceases.

That was an important point to understand, because the physical healing followed shortly after our conversation.

The venereal disease was healed quickly. However, I knew that I must continue to gain a deeper insight into the nature of spiritual man, my selfhood made in the likeness of God. This was the regeneration I was seeking, my spiritual need.

I recall that throughout this experience I had a desire for spiritual regeneration. The practitioner said that this point is so important and rewarding in seeking healing. When regeneration is truly the goal of our prayers, we're helped in finding answers to our problems more quickly. It disciplines thought and keeps us engaged in proving spiritual facts instead of busily trying merely to change material conditions.

To just abstain from this, or refrain from that, is not necessarily a full healing. In the ensuing months I began to see that the longer I clung to the deceptive allurements of the bodily senses, the more I was impeding my spiritual growth. This was a dead-end path, while allowing myself to be governed by divine Spirit would lead to an ever clearer glimpse of man's innate dominion over beliefs of the flesh.

As the alternatives came into sharper focus, the choice was no longer difficult. I was eager to relinquish the past and go forward, to have further proof of my spiritual completeness.

I now have a new perspective. Claiming my dominion over sensual indulgence has given me a higher respect for myself as God's son. It has unfolded a deeper and purer sense of love for my wife. What a joy to see the sensual depravity and bondage of the past yield to the wholesome satisfaction and freedom of the present!

The healing of venereal disease was impressive, but the deeper, more significant healing was transformation of character—something that continues to bring much joy and fulfillment.

Name withheld at author's request
The Christian Science Journal April 1981

Section IV

Christian healing throughout life

These writers, who have relied on God throughout their lives, tell how daily prayer benefits them and enables them to help others. The law of spiritual healing guides all the details of a prayer-filled life.

15

Prayerful living

The strong currents of God's goodness and love flow continuously in a life lived in prayer.

I just wanted the strength to care for my mother-in-law.

My husband's family was of a different religion than mine, but this caused no friction. He was loving and considerate, and went faithfully to church with the children and me. When my mother-in-law became sick and needed hospitalization I asked her if she would like to know how prayer could help her. She smiled but didn't ask for help.

Because my father-in-law was retired, my husband became concerned about the mounting hospital bill and felt he should pay it. I agreed, although this meant we had to borrow the money on our house, and to put our mortgage back to the beginning balance. The time came when a doctor reported Mother had only a short time to live, and suggested we put her in a nursing home or care for her at home. My father-in-law gathered his six children together to tell them what the doctor had said, and to ask them what they wished to do. No one wanted to put her in a nursing home, but no one offered to take her into their own home, until my husband said he would like to do it.

I remember calling a Christian Science practitioner and talking to her about this situation, for I really didn't know whether I could do this. I don't remember anything specific about the conversation, but I do remember how deeply I realized I couldn't think any resentful thoughts as to why others hadn't offered to help; I needed to stick to what we felt was right, and do it with love. I'll have to say at this point I hadn't thought about healing, I just wanted the strength to care for my mother-in-law.

In the beginning this care was like that for a small infant. But it wasn't long before she was up using the bathroom and eating at the table. As I look back on it, I don't ever remember thinking about her dying. But I do remember how thoroughly she enjoyed my reading to her from the Bible Lesson and the *Christian Science Sentinel* every evening.

One afternoon as my father-in-law was attending to Mother, I heard her moaning. Being aware that the problem seemed to be an internal blockage, I stopped right where I was to realize for myself that it was impossible for God, divine Mind, to be inactive; God is always active, and nothing can block the activity of Mind. In a very short time they came to me and, with overwhelming joy, reported that the blockage had given way.

Five weeks from the day that she had come to our house, Mother went home healed. I know this to be true, for shortly afterward Dad took her to the doctor. He found no evidence of the life-threatening condition.

This healing continued to bless everyone. It wasn't long, a year or so, before Dad was able to repay us the money for the hospital bill. With that, and other resources that showed up, we were able to put together enough to pay off the entire mortgage. To me this was proof that "the rich in spirit help the poor in one grand brotherhood, all having the same Principle, or Father; and blessed is that man who seeth his brother's need and supplieth it, seeking his own in another's good" (*Science and Health with Key to the Scriptures* by Mary Baker Eddy,

p. 518). We found we weren't denied anything, but rather were supplied more than sufficiently.

I am so grateful for the help of the practitioner, for this entire experience, and for the awakening to the fact that, when we keep our thought free from the clutter of mortal beliefs through spiritual understanding, divine Mind does the rest. I give thanks also for all the many other healings in our family over the years. I have found that trusting God is the most reliable source of help and healing.

LUCILLE JEWEL TEMPLETON
Shawnee, Kansas
Christian Science Sentinel March 7, 1994

I was asked if I would like to let God take care of me.

I can never express enough gratitude for a children's Bible storybook given to our family before I was born. As soon as I could read, I delighted in the simple lessons from the Bible stories of the unquestionable power and loving care that God provides for all His children. I enjoyed reading this book aloud to my younger sister, then to my own children and grandchildren. I believe the great-grandchildren are benefiting now from the same little book, although it has become so worn that it is difficult to read!

When I began school, a local doctor diagnosed me as having diabetes in the last stages. A specialist in this field confirmed the diagnosis, telling my parents that I could not possibly live more than two or three weeks. After the two men left, I remember my parents' discussing what steps to take. My parents had seen the healing effects of prayer. I was asked if I wanted to take the medicine prescribed, or if I would like to let God take care of me. I felt confident in His love for me.

A Christian Science practitioner prayed with us. At the request of the doctors, my mother took me to be tested each week. The first week the doctors couldn't understand why the symptoms had not become worse; at the end of the second week they were simply astounded at my progress; and a week later they dismissed me as completely free of all symptoms. The healing was permanent.

At one time in my early teens, I would waken in the night with my heart pounding rapidly. My parents never knew of these times, because it didn't occur to me to say anything to them. I simply turned to God and prayed with the words of "the scientific statement of being" from *Science and Health* until I felt normal action, and then went to sleep trusting God wholeheartedly. In this way the difficulty ceased.

When one of our sons was in the service overseas, he wrote me that he needed all the spiritual help he could get. He neglected to say specifically what his problem was, so I asked God what I needed to know. The concept of *justice* came to me, and I prayed accordingly, knowing that God is a just God and that His divine law could not be overturned. I prayed to know that this truth included all mankind, and continued praying along these lines for a day or so until I felt completely at ease about the situation.

I later learned that our son had been called in for a court-martial hearing, having been accused of an offense of which he was not guilty. He told me that the testimony being presented had seemed to be so watertight that he didn't see how he could possibly escape a guilty verdict. However, in the last hour a witness appeared who could give needed evidence of his innocence, and he had been completely exonerated of all charges.

One time a member of our household who was under medical care seemed to resent all my efforts to care for him. After one particularly exasperating time with him, I went into my room to study the Bible and *Science and Health*. First I prayed, "Father, I know I can't pray specifically for this man without his consent, but what can I do for harmony in our home?" The angel message came, "No, you can't provide spiritual treatment for him, but neither can you withhold the truth from him" (in other words, God is already on the scene and cannot be denied). I'd hardly begun my study when he walked into the room fully dressed, saying, "I feel like I could go to work right now!" He decided first to get a doctor's report. He said the doctor told him he was the healthiest man of his age that he had ever examined. The doctor said one thing puzzled him, however, and showed him X-rays revealing a small sign of scar tissue on one of the lungs, indicating he must have had tuberculosis in that lung a long time ago but that the condition was now healed. The patient had received regular medical checkups throughout the years with no such evidence of tuberculosis. In telling me this, and pondering the doctor's remarks, he suddenly turned and looked at me, and said with a big smile that he thought something had been going on—that he felt he had just been healed through prayer.

Our family has had so many beautiful proofs of a loving and caring Father-Mother God that I could write for hours!

Louise Kyes Grover
Fortuna, California
Christian Science Sentinel January 31, 1994

I was the oldest female to run and finish that marathon.

I've always liked to run; it has made me feel so free. When I was in high school, we lived five miles away from my school, and sometimes I would run to school in the morning and back home again at night.

When I was seventy-three years old, I read about an uphill race in New Hampshire. I prayed to know if it would be right for me to run the race. Indications were that it would be. So I filled out the form, and ran. And I won first place in the "over fifty" age-group. Then in the spring of 1988 I ran in the Boston

Marathon in Massachusetts. Afterward I found out I was the oldest female to run and finish that marathon. "Let us lay aside every weight, and the sin which doth so easily beset us, and let us run with patience the race that is set before us" (Hebrews 12:1).

When I run races, I always know that God is with me, and of course He is, because He fills all space.

Before I ever went to school, my aunt, who herself had been healed of a terminal disease through prayer, began to pray for my well-being. I never had the many diseases a child was expected to have.

When giving birth to each of my three children, I knew I was the exact reflection of a perfect God, and that my little ones had always had, and would always have, their lives in God. These births were all easy and painless.

God has always cared for me throughout my own life. "My mouth shall speak the praise of the Lord: and let all flesh bless his holy name for ever and ever" (Psalms 145:21).

MARGARET MERRY SAWYER
Waterford, Maine
Christian Science Sentinel May 1, 1995

I'm here to keep my promise to God.

Some years ago, while I was serving as a night librarian in a Christian Science Reading Room, a man came in just before closing time and made a startling statement. He announced, "I'm here to keep my promise to God." He then shared the following story. His mother had worked in the home of a Christian Scientist, and one day she was given a *Christian Science Sentinel.* Even though she couldn't read, she took it home with her and put in on the coffee table in their living room. But as far as she knew, no one read it all the time it was in the house, even though her son—the man I was now speaking to—could read.

Some years later, this same son got into a fight with the police and was shot seven times. At the hospital, as he was being wheeled into the operating room, he heard a surgeon say, "This man has lost too much blood. He won't come out alive." My friend (I call him my friend now, because we became good friends) said a picture came into his thoughts of the words *Christian Science* which he had seen on the cover of the *Sentinel.* And then he said he made a promise to God that if he came out of that situation alive, he would look into Christian Science. "What is this Christian Science?" he asked.

I spent an hour explaining to him what it is, showed him the Bible Lesson, and lent him a Bible and a copy of *Science and Health.* I told him if he had any further questions, to please call back. Well, he came back the next night, and we had another wonderful hour of discussing this truth. Then he told me he was to be taken to court in a few days to be sentenced. I offered to go with him. I felt I wanted to continue communicating with him. He was given a seven-year sentence in the state penitentiary. From that time on, I wrote him weekly. He asked wonderful questions, and we had a thoughtful exchange with our letter writing. I've never met anyone, before or since, who took in this truth so voraciously.

About a year later, I was going through the city where the state penitentiary is and thought this would be a good time to see my friend. When I arrived, he came up to a window where we could talk. I had never seen a face as beautiful as his. One of the seven bullets had gone up through his face and had made a very ugly scar, which I had noticed the first night he visited the Reading Room. As I looked at that face now, it was like the face of the Apostle Stephen—"the face of an angel," the Bible described it in Acts (6:15). In that one year, the material picture of a face scarred by bullet wounds had vanished. It was replaced by a face as beautiful as anyone could want to look at.

We had a good visit, and then I told my friend that I wanted him to prepare to get out on early release, because I knew with good behavior the sentence could be cut in half. I suggested that he go to the prison library and get some books to study. I asked if he had a preference as to what occupation he'd like to follow when released from prison, and he said, "I've always wanted to be a bookkeeper." Soon after he did go to the library, but there were no bookkeeping manuals available. He wrote to me a couple of weeks later, explaining the problem. I wrote back assuring him that, as spiritual ideas of God, we already include whatever we need. "Let's pray to know that you'll have what you need. If you need a boat in the middle of the ocean, or water in the desert, it can appear." I pointed out that there are Bible stories that illustrate how our needs can be met.

In his next letter, he wrote that when he went back to his prison cell one Friday afternoon, the door wouldn't open. Since the locksmith was gone for the weekend, they put him in another cell until Monday morning. He said that as he went into the cell and sat down, he saw a complete set of bookkeeping manuals. A bookkeeper had previously been in that cell, and had been released that very day, leaving his books behind. How wonderful it was that, right in the middle of that prison, my friend had what he needed.

After three and one half years he was released because of good behavior. I contacted an employer in the city in which my friend resides, and he soon was employed. After his first payday he wrote, "I want to give you my first check." I said, "No, I really don't want any money from you. The only way you can repay me is to strive to be the man you've truly always been, the expression of God, good." And he did. He is a model citizen in his community.

RUSSELL LUERSSEN
Ballwin, Missouri
Christian Science Sentinel November 27, 1995

An invitation to learn more

We hope that wherever you live and whatever you do, you have found a sense of hope and peace in the pages of this book. The healings recounted in it flow out of a God-centered approach to life which can bless anyone who turns to it. And why? Because it is based on law. Just as the law of gravity operates equally in Paris, New York, and Sydney, and the law has always been in effect, so it is with God's law of love—His law of healing. Referring to Sir Isaac Newton's discovery of this law of gravity, Mary Baker Eddy, who discovered Christian Science—the universal law of God as applied to humanity—wrote:

"My immediate recovery from the effects of an injury caused by an accident, an injury that neither medicine nor surgery could reach, was the falling apple that led me to the discovery how to be well myself, and how to make others so" (*Retrospection and Introspection,* p. 24).

After being healed, Mrs. Eddy devoted three years of her life to the understanding of this discovery. Her subsequent publishing of just one book—*Science and Health with Key to the Scriptures*—made the knowledge of this law available to the world. The healing accounts which you have just read demonstrate that this law of God is as effective now to bring health, happiness, and security to mankind, as it was when Jesus trod the hills of Galilee, in the first century, or when Mary Baker Eddy was healed in 1866.

If you would like to know more about the healing that God's law can bring to your own life, you can find a copy of *Science and Health* in bookstores, in libraries, and in Christian Science Reading Rooms (usually listed in telephone directories) throughout the world.

Today, there is increasing recognition of the power of prayer in healing spiritually any troublesome condition—on the basis of law. *Science and Health with Key to the Scriptures* establishes the primacy of prayer as the most effective religious health-care system ever presented to mankind.

About the author of *Science and Health with Key to the Scriptures:* Mary Baker Eddy

The Discoverer and Founder of Christian Science is recognized outside her church as one of the most remarkable religious figures of modern times. The daughter of staunch New England Calvinist parents, Mary Baker Eddy protested against the idea that suffering and pain are God's will. She knew intuitively that God's will was only good, and she turned to the Bible for answers. The insights she gained from her Bible study replaced hopelessness with hope and fear with love. She explained the spiritual laws she discovered through her study in her book *Science and Health with Key to the Scriptures.*

Mrs. Eddy dedicated her life to finding permanent solutions to the world's struggles. And it is to all humanity that she offered her book.

In 1892 she established The First Church of Christ, Scientist, in its present form. In 1894 she designated the Bible and *Science and Health* as its textbooks and pastor.

It was intended that her book would reach beyond denominational boundaries, and to date more than nine million copies have been sold.

Publications mentioned

Bible. King James Version. The Holy Bible containing the Old and New Testaments, Authorized Version.

New English Bible, The. New York: Oxford University Press, 1961.

Phillips, J. B. *The New Testament in Modern English.* New York: Macmillan Publishing Company, 1972.

Century of Christian Science Healing, A. Boston: The Christian Science Publishing Society, 1966.

Christian Science Hymnal. Boston: The Christian Science Publishing Society, 1932.

Eddy, Mary Baker. *Science and Health with Key to the Scriptures.* Boston: The First Church of Christ, Scientist, 1906.

Manual of The Mother Church. Boston: The First Church of Christ, Scientist, 1925.

Miscellaneous Writings (1896) and other works in Prose Works Other than *Science and Health.* Included are *No and Yes* (1887) and *Unity of Good* (1891). Boston: The First Church of Christ Scientist, 1895.

Poems. Boston: The First Church of Christ, Scientist, 1910.

Tomlinson, Irving C. *Twelve Years with Mary Baker Eddy.* Boston: The Christian Science Publishing Society, 1973, 1996.

We Knew Mary Baker Eddy. Boston: The Christian Science Publishing Society, 1979.

Helpful information

Bible Lesson: [See: *Christian Science Quarterly*]

Branch churches: Branch Churches of Christ, Scientist, are governed locally by their members and hold Sunday worship services and Wednesday testimony meetings. They share Christian Science with their communities through these and other activities, such as Christian Science Reading Rooms, lectures, and Sunday Schools. There is no ordained clergy. [See: The First Church of Christ, Scientist]

Christian Science: Mary Baker Eddy asks and answers this question in her book *Rudimental Divine Science:*

"How would you define Christian Science?

"As the law of God, the law of good, interpreting and demonstrating the divine Principle and rule of universal harmony." (1:1–4)

Spiritual healing in Christian Science is not to be confused with human mind cure, mere positive thinking, Scientology, or New Age thinking. [See: Christian Science treatment]

Christian Science college organization: An organization of students, faculty, or graduates of a college or university offering Christian healing to that campus.

Christian Science Journal, The: A monthly publication of The First Church of Christ, Scientist. It contains reports of healing, inspirational articles, editorials, features, poems, and important church news. Each issue also includes a worldwide directory of Christian Science churches and their services, Christian Science organizations at colleges and universities, practitioners, teachers, nurses, and Committees on Publication.

Christian Science Monitor, The: An international daily newspaper founded in 1908 by Mary Baker Eddy. The *Monitor* has won six Pulitzer Prizes and innumerable other awards from such organizations as Sigma Delta Chi, the Overseas Press Club, the American Society of Newspaper Editors, the National Press Photographer's Association, and the National

Association of Black Journalists. An article published by the Gannett Foundation Media Center at Columbia University cited the *Monitor* as one of the top six newspapers in the United States and top twenty in the world, for its "solid quality and intellectual perspective." The *Monitor* is published in print, and its radio edition is broadcast worldwide on shortwave, and in the United States on public broadcast stations.

Christian Science nurse: An experienced Christian Scientist who has a demonstrable knowledge of Christian Science and is able to give nonmedical physical care. A nurse may work either in private homes or in Christian Science nursing facilities. He or she does not administer drugs or therapy. The physical care is given in performance of services incidental to the practice of the religious tenets of the church.

Christian Science practitioner: Every Christian Scientist practices his or her religion, including spiritual healing. However, a public practitioner is an experienced Christian Scientist who devotes his or her full time to the healing practice of Christian Science. Christian Science practitioners are self-employed, paid by patients on a fee basis, and usually advertise in *The Christian Science Journal* as a practitioner. There are about 2,500 *Journal*-listed practitioners throughout the world.

In the United States, their fees are recognized by the Internal Revenue Service as a deductible medical expense.

Christian Science Publishing Society, The: The Publishing Society is a trust established by Mary Baker Eddy for the publication of the *Christian Science Quarterly, The Christian Science Journal,* the *Christian Science Sentinel, The Herald of Christian Science,* and other periodicals, such as *The Christian Science Monitor,* and general publications including approximately 300 titles of books, pamphlets, leaflets, cassettes, videos, and other items.

Christian Science Quarterly: A quarterly magazine containing the weekly Bible Lessons, with citations selected from the Bible and correlative passages from *Science and Health with Key to the Scriptures* by Mary Baker Eddy. These Bible

Lessons comprise the sermon in the Sunday worship service in Christian Science churches, as well as providing an outline for individual study the preceding week.

Twenty-six Lesson-Sermon subjects, chosen by Mary Baker Eddy, are covered twice a year on a rotating basis. New citations for these Bible Lessons are selected for each subject by a Lesson Committee and published in the *Christian Science Quarterly.*

The *Quarterly* is published in fifteen languages. The Bible Lessons are also produced in audio and video editions for radio and television, or home use.

Christian Science Reading Room: A bookstore, usually including a place to read or study, where the writings of Mary Baker Eddy, the Bible and Bible reference books, and other literature published or sold by The Christian Science Publishing Society may be purchased. Librarians, who are local Christian Scientists in charge of Reading Rooms, are available to answer questions.

Christian Science Sentinel: A weekly magazine focusing on contemporary issues and spiritual solutions, with features, poems, editorials, and reports of healing. The magazine illustrates the practical relevance of an understanding of God in finding answers to individual and societal problems. It also includes Christian Science lecture schedules. A radio edition of the *Sentinel* is broadcast weekly on shortwave and by various radio stations around the United States and overseas.

Christian Science Students Association: [See: Teacher of Christian Science]

Christian Science Sunday School: In The Mother Church and branch churches, classes are held on Sundays for pupils up to age 20. Children are taught from the Bible and *Science and Health.* The instruction shows the relevancy to daily life of Biblical teachings such as the Ten Commandments, the Lord's Prayer, and the Sermon on the Mount. These lessons help young people learn how to heal and how to deal with the moral and social questions that confront them. Sunday Schools, like church services, are for the public.

Christian Science treatment: The systematic application of the Bible's underlying spiritual truth to the healing of disease, sin, and other discords. Christian Science treatment consists entirely of prayer based on a growing understanding of God and of man's relation to Him. [See: Christian Science practitioner]

Class instruction in Christian Science: [See: Teacher of Christian Science]

Committee on Publication: An individual appointed to correct misconceptions about Christian Science with the public, the media, educational institutions, other churches, and public officials. There are more than 160 of these one-person committees, working in every state in the United States and in many countries around the world. A Manager of these individual Committees on Publication has offices at the world headquarters in Boston, Massachusetts.

Eddy, Mary Baker (1821–1910): [See: About the Author of *Science and Health with Key to the Scriptures*, p. 345]

First Church of Christ, Scientist, The: Also referred to as The Mother Church, has administrative offices in Boston, Massachusetts, activities worldwide, and a web site at http://www.tfccs.com. Approximately 2,400 branch churches of The Mother Church are located throughout the world.

Herald of Christian Science, The: Monthly and quarterly magazines and audio cassettes featuring spiritual solutions to global and regional issues, poems, editorials, and international directories of practitioners, teachers, nurses, and Committees on Publication. Published monthly in German, French, Spanish, and Portuguese, and quarterly in several other languages. A radio edition of the *Herald* is broadcast in several languages on shortwave.

Lesson-Sermon: [See: *Christian Science Quarterly*]

Mother Church, The: [See: The First Church of Christ, Scientist]

Readers: Two Readers, who are elected lay members of the congregation, conduct the Sunday and Wednesday worship services of Branch Churches of Christ, Scientist.

The First Reader reads mainly from *Science and Health* on Sundays [See: *Christian Science Quarterly*] and equally from the Bible and *Science and Health* on Wednesdays.

The Second Reader reads selections from the Bible at the Sunday services.

Science and Health with Key to the Scriptures: Mary Baker Eddy's primary work, first published in 1875. *Science and Health,* the textbook of Christian Science, is published in English, 16 other languages, and English Braille and in audio cassette, compact disk, and computerized formats. More than nine million copies have been sold, and it remains a best-seller each year.

In 1992, the Women's National Book Association (WNBA) named *Science and Health* as one of 75 books by women "whose words have changed the world." Mrs. Eddy also wrote and published 12 other books on Christian Science in English, which have been translated into several languages.

In 1895, Mrs. Eddy ordained the King James Version of the Bible and her book, *Science and Health with Key to the Scriptures,* as the pastor of all Churches of Christ, Scientist.

Sunday service: The Sunday service in The Mother Church and all branch churches includes congregational singing, silent and audible prayer, a Scriptural selection, the reading of a Lesson-Sermon consisting of passages from the Bible and *Science and Health* [See: *Christian Science Quarterly*], and a benediction. All Christian Science services are for the public; Sunday services from The Mother Church are broadcast each week by shortwave.

Teacher of Christian Science: A Christian Science teacher, one who has earned a certificate from the Board of Education of The Mother Church, is qualified to teach primary classes in Christian Science. Teachers may hold one class each year of no more than 30 pupils. There are about 250 active teachers in countries around the world.

The pupils of each teacher form an association that meets each year for continuing education by the teacher or, in his or her absence, another experienced Christian Scientist.

Wednesday testimony meetings: Each Christian Science church holds a Wednesday testimony meeting, which is conducted by the First Reader [See: Readers]. The Reader chooses a subject, prepares readings from the Bible and *Science and Health,* and selects the hymns. The meeting also includes spontaneous sharing by those attending of testimonies of healing (like those in this book), experiences of God's directing, healing, and protecting power. No collection is taken. As at the Sunday service, the public is always welcome.

A list of healings

Section I – *Finding a path to spiritual healing*

1 *God heals anything!* 3

2 *Spiritual healing and two books that lead the way* 25

Section II – *Healing and guidance in every stage of life*

5 *Hereditary conditions healed* 79

6 *Pregnancy and birth* 101

7 *Children and prayer* 113

9 *Jobs, pay, and work hazards* **181**

10 *Relationships and getting along* **207**

14 *Addiction, compulsive behavior, and spiritual rehabilitation* 311

Section IV – *Christian healing throughout life*

15 *Prayerful living* 335

Op

L
sp
inv

Last we
named "cro
continuing
bill. Lawn
and pande
Becaus
ernment
to write
policy go
nor redu
hobble a
tives in
spendin
On t
er jets
distric
Me
menta
dren.
child
boge
the
F
rec
not

the
co
bu
b
l

EP9608020